You Do Not Travel in China at the Full Moon

You Do Not Travel in China at the Full Moon:

Agnes Moncrieff's letters from China 1930–1945

Edited by Barbara Francis

VICTORIA UNIVERSITY PRESS

TE WHARE WĀNANGA O TE ŪPOKO O TE IKA A MĀUI
VICTORIA
UNIVERSITY OF WELLINGTON

VICTORIA UNIVERSITY PRESS
Victoria University of Wellington
PO Box 600 Wellington
vup.victoria.ac.nz

First published 2017

ISBN 978-1-77656-088-2

A catalogue record for this book is available from the National Library of New Zealand.

Printed in China by 1010 Printing International

For my friend Nessie.
Your hopes of writing a book one day are now realised.

Contents

	List of Illustrations	7
	List of Maps	11
	Acknowledgements	12
	Introduction	17
1.	A Different Course, 1898–1929	19
2.	First Term: Peiping, 28 February 1930–July 1934	25
3.	Home, Travels and Return to China, 1934–1937	53
4.	Hankow, September–December 1937	70
5.	Hankow and the Godown, January–March 1938	91
6.	After the Godown, April–July 1938	119
7.	Travels, July–October 1938	143
8.	Back in Shanghai, October–December 1938	169
9.	Sojourn in Hong Kong, January–February 1939	177
10.	Return to Shanghai, March–May 1939	185
11.	More Travels, May–August 1939	193
12.	Final Time in Shanghai, September 1939–July 1940	205
13.	The Burma Road, 1940–1941	219
14.	Third Term: Chengtu, December 1941–October 1945	247
15.	After China, November 1946–June 1988	263
	Notes and References	266
	Bibliography	275
	Index of Names	278
	Index of Places	288
	General Index	291

List of Illustrations

Nessie in 1958 16

The Moncrieff family of Carterton, c. 1915 20

Student Association of Victoria University College Executive, 1921 20

YWCA residence, 17 Hsiao Po Koh Shih, 1930 24

Interior of the YWCA residence, 1930 24

The Peiping student hostel, 1931 27

Nessie's corner of study at the hostel, 1931 27

The hostel Christmas party, 1931 30

The gate house and wisteria vine outside the hostel, 1931 30

View overlooking the boys' school, 1931 35

Children playing at the YWCA playground, Peiping, 1932 40

A Student Christian Movement committee meeting, 1933 44

Nessie pulling a colleague in a ricsha, 1931 48

Nessie and her bicycle, 1932 48

Nessie ready for adventure, 1933 49

'Lunch on the wall', 1931 52

Visa for Nessie's return to China, 1936 56

Pearl Pollock and Nessie with their Chinese teachers, 1931 62

Nessie, colleagues and the 'chair men', 1931 66

Colleagues at the third national convention of the YWCA of China, 1933 75

Medical supplies at the Hankow International Red Cross godown, 1937 83
Drums of liquid at the godown, 1937 83
The Skinner family of Dunedin, 1933 94
Nessie working at the International Red Cross godown, 1938 100
Chinese quilts and medicines at the International Red Cross godown, 1938 100
Dr Robert Grey operating in Chengchow, April 1938 118
Visa for travel in China, 1938 118
YWCA spring staff meeting, 1938 147
Four New Zealand friends in Shanghai, 1939 175
Nessie with Danny in Peiping, 1933 183
Sampans at Weihaiwei, August 1939 206
Visa issued in Wellington for return to China, 1941 230
Visa issued in Rangoon for entry into China, 1941 242
Nessie, Jesse and their boarders, 1943 256
Visa for departure from China and India, 1945 256
Stamps showing Nessie's path home, 1945 and 1946 262
Nessie's arrival stamp in New Zealand, 1946 262

List of Maps

Both maps are supplied by Geographx, Wellington.

China and the surrounding area, c. 1937 14–15

Wuchang, Hankow and Hanyang, c. 1937 69

Acknowledgements

So many people have helped and supported me over the past ten years as I've attempted to unravel the life of my friend Nessie when she was in China, and then present her story for others to appreciate.

Foremost is my long-time friend Christine Elder (née Harvie), who sixty years ago introduced me to her mother's great friend Nessie Moncrieff.

Receiving from the New Horizons for Women Trust the 2009 Peg Hutchison Research Award of the New Zealand Federation of Graduate Women, Wellington branch, certainly gave me new horizons, which resulted a year later in the YWCA of Greater Wellington publishing my book *Our Secretary in China: The Story of Agnes Moncrieff.*

Right from the beginning I have been overwhelmed by the help I have received from many quarters, but I am especially grateful to the staff of the manuscript room at the Alexander Turnbull Library who had to deal with a raw novice with no idea how their processes worked. Also my thanks to Pauline Keating, who, when senior lecturer in history at Victoria University of Wellington, encouraged me to persist with my project, and to Désirée Patterson, who was so impressed with Nessie's story she took on the convoluted task of formatting my very lengthy manuscript.

My grateful appreciation goes to my daughter Rose and son Ken who, when young, received messages signed 'Auntie Nessie', and shared my vision of seeing her recognised, as did Nessie's nieces and nephew along with Eva Skinner's granddaughters. Also to my friends who for so many years have put up with Nessie being my chief topic of conversation and encouraged me to continue on this journey.

My most sincere thanks must go to Fergus Barrowman of Victoria University Press, who recognised what a fascinating story Nessie's is and persevered with the novice to produce this polished publication, with input from Chris Elder, whose expert knowledge of China and advice was crucial to selecting the most appropriate of the letters. And to my editor Holly Hunter, whose empathy with Nessie and me has enabled *You Do Not Travel in China at the Full Moon* to show so clearly what my friend experienced. For Nessie to have her correspondence published by her alma mater, Victoria University of Wellington, would have thrilled her.

Among the tributes paid to Nessie in 1988 was, 'Many in the YWCA regarded Nessie as a living legend. Although she is no longer with us physically her spirit will endure and her life will serve as an example for generations to come.' You have all helped me ensure that this happens. Thank you.

0
300
600 miles
0
500
1,000 kilometres
Hwang Ho
Sian
(Xi'an)
CHINA
Ichang
(Yichang)
Chengtu
(Chengdu)
Ya-an
Chungking
(Chongqing)
Yang Tze
INDIA
Kweiyang
(Guiyang)
Burma Road
Yunnanfu
(Kunming)
Kweilin
(Guilin)
Xi Jiang
Lashio
Mekong
BURMA
(Myanmar)
Hanoi
FRENCH
INDOCHINA
(Vietnam, Cambodia, Laos)
Hainan
SIAM
(Thailand)
Rangoon
(Yangon)

Peking
(Beijing)
Tientsin
(Tianjin)
Chefoo
(Yantai)
KOREA
Tsinan
(Jinan)
JAPAN
Nanking
(Nanjing)
Shanghai
Wuchang/Hankow/Hanyang
Kiukiang
(Juijiang)
Yochow
(Yueyang)
Changsha
Hengyang
Canton
(Guangzhou)
Hong Kong
Formosa
(Taiwan)

Nessie in 1958. Photo Barbara Francis.

Introduction

Agnes Moncrieff first came into my life in 1956, when I was an eighteen-year-old student at Wellington Teachers' Training College and a member of the New Zealand Student Christian Movement (NZSCM) of which she was vice-chairman. Nessie, as everyone called her, made an immediate impact on me as an inspiring woman with a great personality. Since 1951 she had been a geography teacher at the Correspondence School and a committee member for the national executive of the Young Women's Christian Association (YWCA) of New Zealand. In 1957, 38 years after joining the YWCA in 1919, Nessie – then their Public Affairs chairperson – was appointed to New Zealand's Council for Equal Pay and Opportunity, and subsequently to the committee on Women and Employment, which went on to establish the National Advisory Council on the Employment of Women. She was also a member of the Federation of University Women and represented Wellington at their first conference in Dunedin in 1923.

Three years after meeting Nessie, when I was a travelling secretary for the NZSCM, I boarded with her in her Brooklyn home. It was only then that I discovered she was actually Agnes Moncrieff and had spent 1930–1945 in China with the YWCA. Saturday morning coffee in her rooms, which were full of mementoes from China, and encouraging her to talk about her days there, was always a great highlight. She had recently become a member of the newly established Wellington branch of the New Zealand–China Friendship Society and in the previous year, 1958, had been a delegate to the inaugural national conference.

Although there was an age gap of forty years between us, we became good friends and kept in correspondence when I moved to Christchurch, as well as met up when family and I holidayed in Wellington or when Nessie came south to stay with her friends the Skinners, in Dunedin. Her letters to me were such a delight that I kept them. The final one, written a few months before she died, ended with, *Much love to you all. Wish I could have a good old yarn, Nessie.* As I never called my friend Agnes, and she always ended correspondence to family and friends with Nessie, I've used that name when referring to her in this text.

All the time she was in China, regularly sending reports to the YWCA of New Zealand, Nessie corresponded with her mother in Carterton and a good friend, Eva Skinner, in Dunedin. In her late seventies, Nessie sorted through the vast collection of the letters to her mother, and those to Eva which had been returned to her on Eva's death. There were also carbon copies of reports to the YWCAs of both China and New Zealand. From her fourteen years in China Nessie chose to keep only 210 letters, 98 of which have been selected for this volume. After her death in 1988 at the age of ninety, the collection was given by her executor to the Alexander Turnbull Library, Wellington, New Zealand, where as MS-Papers-7492 they form the major part of the Moncrieff, Agnes Meikle, 1898–1988 Collection.

Almost twenty years after Nessie's final letter to me I learned of the Agnes Moncrieff Collection in the Alexander Turnbull Library and have spent the past nine years unravelling an amazing yarn. Although my friend often spoke of her time in China, it was usually in a light-hearted way. As I read her correspondence I was frequently moved by what she had experienced, the work she had done and the very high regard in which she was held by the YWCA of China. As well as descriptions of her life in China from 1930–1945, much of it in the midst of the Second Sino-Japanese War, there are also interesting observations on the current scene and how the YWCA of China coped.

I realised these letters needed to be known by others, so initially I set out to share what I had discovered with those who had known her in an unpublished document, *Our Friend Nessie.* Later, with the encouragement and support of the YWCA of Greater Wellington, *Our Secretary in China* was published in 2010. Now I believe this fascinating life in China needs to be more widely shared.

As there were three main recipients of Nessie's correspondence, she frequently wrote three versions of an incident. Only the letter or report which best describes it is used here.

Agnes Moncrieff had close links with Victoria University of Wellington, which she entered in 1917 to begin an Arts degree, graduating with an MA in 1921. She was also very involved in student life. It is altogether appropriate that on the centenary of her enrolment at Victoria it should be the press of her alma mater that honours her achievements by publishing these letters.

Barbara Francis
Wellington
January 2017

1
A Different Course
12 May 1898–13 January 1930

'You do not travel in China at the full moon if you can help it. There are always air raids.' These are the words of Agnes Moncrieff of Wellington, New Zealand, writing home to her mother in Carterton from Hankow, China, on 26 April 1938. Since 1930 she had been working with the YWCA of China as a foreign secretary, with her salary paid by the YWCA of New Zealand.

Agnes Meikle Moncrieff, known to many as Nessie Moncrieff, was born in Carterton in 1898. At age fourteen she won an Education Board Scholarship to Wellington Girls' College, where she threw herself with great gusto into college life, as shown by the numerous mentions of her in the college magazines of 1913–1917[1] and even later in alumni notes. Pride of place at the college now is their Head Prefects' Honours Board. There are only two names there twice, and one of them is Agnes Moncrieff for 1915 and 1916. In 1916 she was proxime accessit to dux.

From Wellington Girls' College Nessie went on to Victoria University College, graduating in 1921 with an MA in Latin and French. Again she was involved in student life, especially the Student Christian Movement (SCM) and the College's student association, where in her final year she was women's vice-president – then the highest office a woman could hold in the association. In 1921 she trained as a secondary teacher at Wellington Teachers' Training College.

In 1922, instead of taking up a teaching career, Nessie embarked on a different course. She had been chosen by the NZSCM to be their national delegate to the 11th World Student Christian Federation (WSCF) Conference, to be held during April at Tsinghua University, Peking, China. In January of that year she took up an appointment with the NZSCM as a travelling secretary working with women students in universities and secondary schools. At the end of February, at age twenty-three, Nessie left for China.

The WSCF was formed in 1895 in Sweden, at a gathering of student leaders from ten European and North American SCMs. Its 1922 Peking conference, with the theme 'Under Heaven One Family', was the second to be held in Asia. The first had been held in Japan in 1907.

Top: The Moncrieff family of Carterton, c. 1915. Back row, from left: Doyle, Nessie, Catherine. Front row, from left: Janet, Catherine Agnes (mother), Jean, James (father), Dora. Moncrieff family collection

Bottom: Student Association of Victoria University College Executive, 1921. Nessie sits front row, second from right. J C Beaglehole Room VUWSA5017.

Nessie was the only New Zealand delegate, and after the conference she was chosen to be member of a team which visited different Chinese universities to report on the work done at the conference, a trip which she later described as 'the famous luggage car tour in China 1922'.[2]

In 1941, when home on furlough after her second term of service, Nessie spoke of her first impressions in an interview published in the *New Zealand Listener*: 'I fell in love with China. I was so impressed by the eagerness and enthusiasm and general aliveness of the young men and women of China.'

The unnamed interviewer commented on Nessie's impressive height and calm dignity and the impression she gave of being in full control of her own destiny.[3]

Almost forty-five years later, when interviewed by Chris Elder and Michael Green, Nessie commented about that time:

> China fascinated me, it absolutely fascinated me. We had a huge conference at Tsinghua University and I really wanted very much to get back. But I didn't want to go as a missionary. I knew I'd be absolutely no good in some out of the way place, tucked away by myself.[4]

An alternative to missionary work presented itself in 1927, when the YWCA of New Zealand invited Nessie to take up an administrative position it supported within the YWCA of China.

The YWCA had been founded in Britain in 1855 by Mary Kinnaird and Emma Robarts. They were concerned about the welfare of young women who had moved to live and work in London as the Industrial Revolution gained momentum and the Crimean War needed nurses. Hostel-type housing with 'a warm Christian atmosphere was provided in an endeavour to see young women's mental health and physical needs were met to enable them to cope with the pressures of work.'[5] The initiative of Kinnaird and Robarts quickly spread, and by 1898 seventeen countries had YWCAs, and the first World YWCA conference was held.

As a result of Christian women in Shanghai appealing to the World YWCA in 1900 for workers who would come to China 'on behalf of the one hundred millions of women who sit in darkness and the shadow of death',[6] trained YWCA secretaries from countries in which the association was already strong went to China, where they were known as foreign (later international) secretaries, with their salaries paid by their home countries. They were not office workers, but executive leaders – well educated, broad-minded and capable.

By 1923 twelve of China's leading cities had YWCAs and there were foreign secretaries from many countries, including Australia. The support these women gave to the YWCA of China enabled the first Chinese national secretary, Ting Shu-ching, to be appointed in 1926 (the previous two national secretaries had both been American foreign secretaries).

At the end of 1926 Eleanor MacNeil, the Australian secretary, resigned after eleven years of service, having been financially supported by both the Australian and New Zealand YWCAs. The YWCA of New Zealand, now autonomous from Australia, felt the time was right for it to have and support its own secretary in China. Hence the approach to Agnes Moncrieff.

As this was the first time New Zealand had appointed an overseas representative there were some teething problems to overcome. Since the majority of the foreign secretaries were from the YWCA of America (in 1923 there were forty-seven), their association was approached. In 1927 the incoming general secretary of the YWCA of New Zealand, Ethel Law, wrote to Sarah Lyon, head of the American YWCA overseas secretaries department, recommending Nessie:

> She is just the personality we should wish to see represent us in China – frank and sincere, a thinker – willing to view things from the Chinese standpoint . . . She has many friends because she gives friendship unstintingly . . . She will be a real gift to China.[7]

Fortuitously, Eleanor MacNeil came to New Zealand and was able to advise. She recommended that as foreign secretaries needed to be specialists in some branch of knowledge in order to stand behind the developing Chinese secretaries, the New Zealand secretary should specialise first in methods of girls' work so as to gain entry into the government schools of China that the YWCA considered most strategic. Before leaving New Zealand, she should acquire technical knowledge of club work and be given experience in building up work in a large city.

Following on from these recommendations, the New Zealand association drew up a training schedule for Nessie to gain relevant experience in New Zealand's local associations, along with factory visits and health department projects. To assist with this a document entitled 'The Aim of This Course of Training' was circulated, which recommended that:

> Our China Secretary be given opportunity of sitting at all types of meetings – Board, staff, leaders, etc. and is not to work on more than four nights in any week . . . Associations will understand that in setting out these directions the National Executive is aiming at achieving for our China Secretary the maximum of knowledge and experience of the Association with a careful regard for Miss Moncrieff's physical well-being. She must on no account be allowed to go to China tired or overworked.[8]

On completion of the training programme, the YWCA national committee drew up a contract for the China secretary. Her first term of service was to be of four years followed by a one-year furlough, or one and a half years if she wanted to take any special course of study, after which 'we hope to send Miss Moncrieff back for a second period of five years.'[9] The contract included a stipulation that monthly reports must be furnished to the New Zealand YWCA World Fellowship committee. Nessie was to receive an annual salary of £300 and be paid an outfit allowance of £40, with extra if bedding was necessary. Her salary was to be converted to Mexican silver dollars, which were widely adopted as the standard unit of currency in China at that time. (In 1927 £300 equalled 2,750 Mexican dollars.) For the fifteen years Nessie's salary was paid by the YWCA of New Zealand, whose members undertook to raise the money for 'our Secretary in China', which was how she was known. At least twice, when China's inflation far exceeded the salary, there were special financial appeals for her and they were quickly achieved. Several years after returning to New Zealand she was amused at a colleague remarking, 'Do you mean to say *you're* the person we put our pennies in the tin for?'[10]

Top: YWCA residence, 17 Hsiao Po Koh Shih, Peiping, 1930. ATL PA1-o-1191PA1-o-1191-05-2

Bottom: Interior of the YWCA residence, 1930. ATL PA1-o-1191 -01-3

2

First Term: Peiping

28 February 1930–July 1934

From her secondary school days, Nessie kept a 'birthday book' in which she recorded important dates of her family and friends. Beside 13 January she noted, 'Left home 1930.' Home was then 21 Victoria Street, Carterton, New Zealand. Nessie was thirty-one and had left home for China.

Forty-five years or so later, when sorting through her correspondence from China, Nessie chose not to keep any personal letters from her first term. She did, however, keep fifteen reports and letters to the YWCA of New Zealand, many of them carbon copies. Several are round-robin letters intended for wider circulation. Most use the Peiping YWCA address of 29 Li Lu Hutung, Hai Sau P'ai Lou, Peiping, China.

For most of her time in Peiping (the name assigned to Beijing when the Provisional Government of the Republic of China shifted the capital to Nanjing), Nessie lived in the YWCA's residence at 17 Hsiao Po Ko Shih along with other YWCA foreign secretaries and overseas women teachers, nurses and workers who were not missionaries. After a first year devoted to language study, Nessie was put in charge of a newly opened YWCA students' hostel.

Later letters in Nessie's correspondence hint at problems she encountered, and when interviewed by Chris Elder and Michael Green in 1985, she said:

> We put seventy girls in there to live. And they were a wild crowd. They were away from home and away from authority and for the first time in their lives the world was theirs. . . . It was very, very hard to staff because with girls of that kind anybody in charge is losing face all the time and of course as you know Chinese must not lose face. But I had one or two very good people [on the staff].[1]

It would have been the Peiping hostel's Christmas party which Nessie wrote about in a letter dated 13 January 1932 to the YWCA of New Zealand Girl Citizens:[2]

Dear Girl Citizens,

I think you all would have enjoyed our Christmas party this year. Only three of the students I am living with had ever been to one before but some of the others had heard of them and were eager to have one. The students elected a small committee to arrange the programme and decorations and we had long discussions as to whether we should have special feast food for supper just before the party. The main problem was the expense. We had no funds in the Association for providing a Christmas dinner and the girls were not all willing to pay extra money for it. In the end the cook prepared one extra dish, the committee decorated the dining room with paper streamers and we had to be content with that.

One good thing about our Hostel is that we have ever so many rooms big enough for a party. The girls' study was cleared and a stage made out of Chinese wooden beds (that's one advantage of having to use wooden beds.) The decorations were very simple, mostly paper and our stage curtains were the window curtains from one of the club rooms. We borrowed the Christmas tree that had been used over in the East City Hostel and had Chinese lanterns and big red paper bells. The whole effect was very pretty.

Each girl in the hostel was allowed to invite one friend and everyone was expected to bring a five cent present to put on the Christmas tree. The girls decided too to give everyone an opportunity of giving something to the flood relief – money or old clothing or bedding or whatever they could spare. We wanted to help the non-Christian girls to understand that the real spirit of Christmas is a spirit of giving and sharing and that without that Christmas is not really Christmas at all. As a result we had 48 garments and various other things such as hats and warm gloves to send down to the Association in Wuchang,[3] for distribution among the women and children who are their special care.

The programme began with seven items, but the main thing was a pageant which Miss Shao had helped the girls prepare. During the pageant a group behind the stage sang Christmas carols to illustrate the scenes. Our stage was a little too small and the girls rather too crowded, but they did it very well and everyone was impressed with Mary.

When the pageant was over we cleared all the seats away and played the maddest games. You couldn't hear yourself think for the noise. At the end the five cent presents were given out. Every parcel was numbered and every girl was given a number and they had to fish for them over the top of a screen. Some of the things were very funny and the party broke up with a good deal of laughter.

A group of girls had been practising carols for three weeks with a view to getting up early on Christmas morning and singing them. The group that finally did get up consisted of two girls and three secretaries. It had snowed heavily two

Top: 'The Student Hostel from the West. My study windows are to the left of the chimney.' 1931. ATL PA1-o-1191-18-1

Bottom: 'S.W. corner of study'. 1931. ATL PA1-o-1191-20-2

> days before and everything was beautifully white. We got up at 5.30 and sang all the way downstairs and out into the snow. We went over to the London Mission houses, woke up the gate keeper and sang under Mrs. T. Z. Koo's windows till she opened one and wished us a Merry Christmas. Then it was the turn of the London Mission people. They had heard our first carol and got up to make us coffee. It was the best coffee I have ever tasted I think. We munched biscuits and talked for a while and then with a chorus of 'Merry Christmas' we sang our way back to the Hostel.
>
> On New Year's Eve we had a Watch Night Service. I did not expect many of the girls to come because they are not Christian, but we put up notices about it and announced it at meal times so everybody knew about it. One of the London Missionaries led it in Chinese and we sang in English. During a period of meditation the twelve strokes were sounded on a lovely old Temple gong. I have to admit that they were a little late but that didn't matter. The next evening the girls had a riotous party and more turned up to it than to the service. . . .
>
> Yours affectionately,
> Nessie Moncrieff

A shared letter dated 24 October 1932 gives an insight into the work of the YWCA of China and life for Chinese children at this time:

> You would have been interested to see on a day last June fifty ragged, uncared for children squatting in the shade of a tree with their eyes fixed on a teacher whose only equipment was a blackboard hung from the tree. It was their first chance to learn to read and write and they came promptly at eight each morning and watched the teacher form each character on the board before they themselves traced it in the dust. Later they were promoted to pencils and paper and their self-respect increased enormously. By the end of the summer there were only twelve pupils. They could calculate accurately, read and write a considerable number of characters and were considerably neater and cleaner in their personal appearance. The remainder of the fifty had had to drop out as chances of earning a little money were offered. Their parents could not afford to keep them even in a free school. Some found a chance to sell newspapers; some were hired to carry heavy banner poles in funeral processions and spent long hot days struggling under their too heavy burdens along the dusty roads to remote burial grounds. Others pushed heavy rubbish carts from door to door along the little alleys, and others spent their time – an indistinguishable medley of urchins and dogs – on evil smelling piles of newly deposited rubbish, scratching for small scraps of dirty paper or an occasional half burnt coal ball that could be sold for a copper or two.
>
> This free summer school was organised by the Peiping Y.W.C.A. For many

years a free half-day school has been held in the Association owned property in Ma Ta Jen Hutung (Horse Big Man Alley). In fact the Association was the first organisation to start such schools in Peiping. Now the property is rented as a Girls' Middle School which by Government regulation is required to have a free school attached, and our school is no longer needed in the neighbourhood. The summer school was an experiment carried out in the children's playground – a piece of land against the east wall of the city, bought by the National Y.W.C.A. of U.S.A. and originally intended to be the site of a residence for American Association secretaries. Owing to national changes the number of American secretaries decreased suddenly and the residence was never required. It became dilapidated and squatters took possession of it.

Towards the end of 1930 an enquiry came from the China National [YWCA] as to whether the land could be used as a children's playground by the Peiping Association. The result was that, not without a great deal of effort, the squatters were evicted and their shanties torn down, the walls patched up, swings, seesaws and chutes erected, a caretaker installed and a games director appointed for half-time work. Dirty little scamps swarmed all over the playground from dawn till dark and incidentally learned songs, games, stories and the rudiments of personal hygiene.

The Association has always been fully aware of the possibilities of the playground as a social service centre, but the financial problem has proved an insurmountable obstacle in the way of development. Apart from the caretaker's one roomed dwelling there is no building on the property and efforts to find a suitable building nearby have met with no success. The Bureau of Social Services promised free rental if we could find a temple or other public building that could be adapted for use as a free school, but there is nothing available. Meantime the conviction has been growing in the minds of the Board members that any piece of social service undertaken by the Association should be developed round the playground as a centre. Therefore a building would have to be erected.

China has as yet no Truby King[4] and the problem of finding a Chinese substitute for humanised milk and Plunket emulsion is a baffling one. In a country where milk is a luxury which can be afforded by very few and where the cost of one tin of patent food would keep a whole family alive for a month it was very difficult to find a substitute that was within the reach of a poor family. However, a very useful preparation from bean-curd – bean milk – has stood the test of a long period of experimentation and is highly recommended by the doctors. Several baby welfare centres exist in which this milk substitute is prepared and dispensed at a very low cost for the feeding of very young babies.

The Y.W.C.A. has made investigations in the neighbourhood of the

Top: Peiping hostel Christmas party, 1931. 'Stage made out of Chinese wooden beds, Chinese lanterns and big red paper bells.' Skinner family collection

Bottom: 'Our gate house & wisteria vine.' December 1931. ATL PA1-o-1191-22-4

playground and has found the establishment of a bean milk station would be of great assistance to many poor mothers. But the problem of a building presents itself. A three-chien building (a chien is a division of a Chinese house, not necessarily partitioned into a separate room) would house a free school, a bean milk station and the necessary office. Chinese houses cost $200 a chien to build and the Association would have to suspend all its secretaries for several months to meet the bill. However, a very practical Social Services Committee discovered that by using carefully selected old materials and having a mud instead of a tiled roof which is expensive each chien could be built for about $100. An energetic Jumble Committee that last year made over $700 in five months decided that this year's Jumble Sale proceeds should go towards a Playground Building Fund.

Now another problem has reared its head. Last summer's downpours were hard on old walls and the walls enclosing the playground are collapsing and must be renewed. Even the ropes and bolts from our swings are stolen if our protecting mud walls are down. The East wall alone would cost $500 for a durable wall and the Board at its next meeting will have to consider the estimates. It will take more than this to bring the Peiping Board of Directors to a standstill and I hope before too long to be sending you a picture of our 'free school' and bean milk station.

All good wishes,

Agnes M. Moncrieff

This next letter, dated 7 March 1933, was addressed to the YWCA of New Zealand national general secretary, and commented on both the current political situation and the work of the YWCA of China:

Dear Miss Stevenson,

You will probably have seen in the New Zealand papers that Jehol has fallen to the Japanese. It has been a terrible blow to the Chinese people as reports say that it was due to political intrigue rather than to military success. Tang Yu-Lin was military governor of Jehol with his headquarters at Chengte, the provincial capital. These military governors are the curse of China. They own the armies and levy taxes on the people in their province at will. Consequently the people of the province frequently hate them and will do anything to get rid of them. This was so in Jehol and the handful of Japanese soldiers, about 120, who took the city were led over the mountain passes from the east by disgruntled peasants who hated the oppression of Tang Yu-Lin. Tang fled at their approach. Reports are rather confused, but the truth seems to be that the army had no supplies and had to retreat. The reason for the lack of supplies was that Tang had commandeered two hundred military trucks to convey his personal belongings from Chengte to a place of safety inside the Wall. You can imagine how bitterly the Chinese who care for their country feel over such a betrayal. It is quite in line with many things that happen here. Tang was not successful in getting away with his belongings. They were held up by Chang Hsueh-liang's gendarmes and had to be abandoned. No one seems to know where Tang himself is.

It is terribly hard to write about China at present. Apart from the educated minority there seems to be very little real patriotism or national spirit. Peasant farmers don't mind as long as they are allowed to farm their lands in peace, and often they cannot do that because their small holdings are fought over and the few things they have are looted by one army or another. The military officials are a corrupt group – greedy for money and power and thinking only of their own skins in time of trouble. Until they are wiped out as a class there is small hope for China. The only way to get rid of them would be an organised revolt on the part of the country people; and the very patience of the Chinese is a hindrance. Also the Chinese do not organise well. They have not had much desire to in the past nor much experience and there is a general mistrust of each other which makes any form of co-operation very difficult.

Last week the National Y.M.C.A. sent two groups up to Jehol and Shanhaikuan respectively to investigate conditions there and to find out what the Y.M.C.A. could do to help in the situation. Dr. Nan, National Student Secretary, came to lunch with us the day after he got back from the Jehol end and told us of a good many things that had come under his personal observation. He spoke of the exasperation of the peasant farmers. Tang's soldiers have not been paid for nine months and consequently are taking food wherever they can find it. There is enough food in the province for the armies, but naturally the farmers do not want to feed the troops for nothing. Some were trying to sell their grain outside the province, others were burying it, but the soldiers easily discovered the hiding places and dug it up. The farmers were in many cases armed and had got to the stage where they were shooting the soldiers on sight. They are uneducated of course and know little of the cause of the fighting and have no sympathy with the soldiers who come from the lowest economic and social groups and can often be bought by anyone who will promise them food and clothing.

Another thing Dr. Nan mentioned was the lack of co-operation among the military leaders who have troops in Jehol. Japan's success would have been impossible, at least for a long time, if all the Chinese forces in Jehol had been united; but they are not government troops. They belong to their own general and mistrust of each other on the part of the generals prevents any form of co-operation. This has been more than apparent to everyone in the last few days.

War in China is hardest of all on the country people. On Saturday evening, as I was leaving the C of E Mission about 9.30, I stood in the Cathedral gateway and waited for a long line of carts to pass up the road. These carts were piled high with gear and on top of each were several soldiers each heavily armed. Others walked alongside. There were far more donkeys and mules than were needed to draw the carts. There was something sinister about that procession as it passed along the dirt road in absolute silence, except for the bumping of the wheels in the ruts. I knew that the carts and animals and gear had been looted from farmers outside the city and many a family must be facing despair and starvation as a result. They get no compensation and are shot if they resist.

On Saturday morning there was not a ricsha in sight as I set out for the West City. In the three and a half miles over to the Student Centre I usually meet hundreds, but that morning I saw perhaps five or six. For two days the ricsha boys were afraid to come out because word had gone forth at every police station – and there are hundreds in the city– to press into service ricshas and pullers to pull rice and grain to Mi Yun Hsien which is about half way between Peiping and Kupeikou – the pass into Jehol. In spite of the fact that the ricsha boys were in hiding about three thousand were secured and given a little money for the work, but their ricshas would be wrecks as likely as not after such a bad pull over bad roads and they would get no pay for the return trip.

China is not a united nation yet. Her officials are in no way representative of the people. They are a self-perpetuating group with a few mere parasites who live on the people. Meanwhile there is a gradually increasing group who care very deeply what happens to their country and feel humiliated by the disgraceful greed and intrigue of the military leaders. One has a tremendous respect for them because they are endeavouring to deal constructively with the problems of their country against tremendous odds and are steadily training their children in decent ideals and standards of honour and justice in an environment which makes graft and face-saving and corruption the natural thing. In this nation building the Y.W.C.A. plays no small part. It is the one national organisation for Chinese women. In each city where there is an Association it is the centre of community life for women. All Chinese women's organisations look to it for assistance and its standards of honesty and integrity are acknowledged everywhere. Through it women are learning to co-operate and to organise. In its organisation and activities it provides a real training in leadership and gives women of every group an opportunity to express themselves in constructive social service. It is undoubtedly making a great contribution to the life of China.

Personally I am conscious again and again of the privilege it is to work with this group and I am inspired by their courage and persistence and good cheer with which they meet their nation's problems. You can imagine the hopelessness and heartbreak of many of them these last few days. They have worked unceasingly preparing thousands of comfort kits and padded garments to increase the morale and add to the comfort of the forces in Jehol. The defence of Chinese territory against Japanese invasion has been a matter of deep conviction with them. They have been prepared for any sacrifice to keep their country from enemy occupation and they have been abominably let down.

The groups of students who are willing to make sacrifices for the high ideals they have for China need our sympathy and encouragement too. I stood with a group of students on Sunday afternoon in a two minute silence in recognition of their national calamity on the loss of Jehol. They were a social service group who are putting their hand to all kinds of work to help build up their country. Some were due to leave Jehol next day on tours of the villages explaining the reasons for fighting and trying to rouse a spirit of resistance to Japan among the villagers and farmers. It has been a matter of deep conviction with them. It is no wonder they feel discouraged and helpless when the military power remains in the hands of men like Tang Yu-lin. Helping people of such calibre to face hopefully the task of building their country and keeping their ideals high in such times as these is a job that is tremendously worthwhile.

I do not feel that war between China and Japan, whatever the outcome, can bring any permanent solution to their problems. They are neighbours and there will continue to be conflicts and disagreements until they learn how to be friendly neighbours; but I sympathise with the Chinese in their conviction that national honour demands a stout resistance to the shameless annexations of territory that is going on north of the Great Wall and I feel for them in the deep distress that the loss of Jehol has occasioned.

Yours sincerely,
Agnes M. Moncrieff

A month later, on 4 April 1933, another letter to the New Zealand national general secretary provided an update on the political scene and work the YWCA was doing for the Chinese soldiers:

Dear Miss Stevenson,

Things move forward at such a rate here it is hard to keep up with them. I often think I will wait till something that is imminent has actually come to pass before I write, but there is never a time when there isn't something just about to happen.

For a week or more the fighting has not been so severe up at the Wall and the Chinese have been holding their positions and preventing the Japanese from seizing the passes. No one is certain just what is happening as the Japanese equipment is so superior that they could easily oust the Chinese if they really

'View looking N.W. Boys' school building is exactly like ours so now you know what a barracks we are. The row of three houses are the London Mission residences. The T.Z. Koos live in the far end.' 1931.
Skinner family collection.

wanted to. They may be waiting for further reinforcements, or the financial situation in Japan may be restricting their movements. Some think that Chiang Kai-shek is trying to negotiate a settlement. Rumours of such negotiations are increasing, but it is impossible to say whether there is any truth in them. It would certainly be a very unpopular move with the students. It is said too Feng Yu-Hsiang is still a factor in the situation. He is up at the front with his soldiers. The man who commands the soldiers is the man with political power in this country and that is one reason why the armies of China are never united into national forces.

There are several thousand wounded soldiers in temporary hospitals in Peiping. These are organised by the Red Cross Society and the Red Swastika Society.[5] Some of the cases are very serious, but the most serious cases never come as far as this. They are looked after nearer the fighting lines. There is a base hospital at Ta'un Hua, just inside the wall. Vera Liu, the girl with whom I work, is a Ta'un Hua girl. Her father and mother are in the south staying with their son, but it was a sad day for Vera when she heard that her home town had been bombed. She does not yet know of course, whether her home is still standing.

The big imperial temple in front of our student centre used to house the Kindergarten Normal School in which we had our most promising student club has been taken over by the Swastika Society as a hospital for a thousand seriously wounded soldiers. While the buildings were being prepared some of them were used as a refugee camp for two hundred of the many men, women and children who have been driven off their holdings in Jehol and Heilungkiang by Japan's occupation and by bandits. Most of these people originally came from Honan and Shantung and were among the thousands who migrated north in the past few decades. The Swastika Society is bent on returning them to their original homes in Honan and Shantung, but the refugees are most reluctant to go because they have no home and no people left there now and would be as entirely without resources there as they are here. It is a great problem because most people's attention is taken up with caring for the wounded soldiers and the refugees are not getting much thought or care.

I went over to the Temple camp not long ago and though conditions were passable there was much distress that could have been avoided with a little more organisation. These refugees were later moved out into a big covered market in the south of the city. There conditions are very much worse. The camp was very dirty, crowded and unsuitable. The group on the ground floor were peasant families without money, without possessions and without hope. They are in rags and are sick and weary after their long trek to Peiping. They are herded together with no privacy for either births or deaths and no care apart from the somewhat dilapidated roof overhead and the dry millet cakes every day.

All good wishes to the National Committee and Staff,

Yours sincerely,

Agnes Moncrieff

Shared letter of 9 May 1933:

Correspondence, even of this general and impersonal variety, becomes more and more hopeless as the years go on. It would be such a help if I could broadcast to New Zealand once a week. . . .

The International Labour Day, May 1st, is observed in China and it was good to have the girls in our student hostel take up the suggestion that they should do the work and let the servants off for the day. They couldn't manage the kitchen work because they had to attend classes as usual, but they all were up at 5.a.m. cleaning their own rooms, corridors, offices and club rooms. They also swept the yard and paths, kept the gate and answered the telephone. The rooms were all cleaned by 8.a.m. and my part in the day's work was to help two of the students judge the rooms. They were models of cleanliness and tidiness and it was very difficult to judge them fairly. However we selected a first a second and two thirds and I took photos which turned out rather well. The girls on the gate and telephone took duty in two hour shifts. I got the shock of my life when I was challenged from the gate house on my arrival.

In the evening the servants and the girls combined for a party. The boys [male servants] provided part of the evening's fun and the students the other part with a short talk about working conditions in China. The whole thing was a grand success and I couldn't help thinking of the impossible tangle we were in this time last year. The spirit of the Hostel has certainly changed. Most of these girls are very co-operative. The chief impression of the day's work was the fact that they had never realised how hard the work of the boys was. Both Vera Liu and I are very pleased with the outcome of this project.

Last weekend Miss Danuser and I took a long-promised week-end off and went out to Chieh T'ai Ssu, one of the more remote and most peaceful temples in the western hills. It is a very famous temple, perhaps the most famous north of the Yang Tzu, because nearly all the priests in North China are ordained there. We went out on a little side railway line which ends in a coal-mining valley about fifteen miles west of Peiping. There we hired donkeys for our bedding, food baskets and camp stretchers and walked about eight miles skirting the foot hills and then climbing a very steep, stone-flagged pilgrim path to the temple. The most distinctive thing about the temple is the grand ordination terrace that extends right across the full width of the temple enclosure, and is so high up that only the roof of the main temple building obstructs the view right out across the plain. Along the terrace are planted lovely old cypress trees at fantastic angles and beautiful white bark pines. We pulled our camp beds out on to the terrace and slept with the moon shining through the leaves of the trees. It was so absolutely peaceful and war was for a short time most refreshingly out of the picture. I woke in the morning to the sound of the priests chanting their morning service. Incense was hanging heavy in the air and the east flushed with a deep orange. It was certainly a rare experience and an unforgettable one.

The next day we did seventeen miles, partly on foot and partly on donkey, calling in to another famous and very beautiful temple Tan Che Ssu on the way back to the railhead. Summer descended on us with a rush as it does in this part of the world and we were very weary at the end of the day. I am still somewhat stiff but I do not know whether it is from the walking or the donkey riding. Both were stiffening processes. I didn't know which was to be more pitied – the donkey or myself.

War still hangs over us in the North and no one seems to know where it will end. An aeroplane flew over the city about 5.30 this morning and the boom of a gun showed that it was Japanese. This is the first visit we have had. Everyone hoped that the dispute with Russia over the C.E.R. railway would occupy Japan's attention for a while, but they are certainly getting busy again just north of us, both inside and outside the Wall.

Nessie Moncrieff

Shared letter of 25 May 1933:

Practically all my work has been brought to a standstill by the present Sino-Japanese situation. There are twelve girls left in the Student Hostel. All the Girls' Middle Schools except two or three Mission schools have closed, one University Women's College has removed bodily to Suchow and several thousand University students including most of those with whom we have contact, have left the city. During the last few months all the most valuable of the Museum's treasures have been moved down to Nanking by special trains, and in the last two weeks the Universities have packed their valuable books and records and sent them away.

In the last five or six days we have talked, and thought about very little apart from the Japanese drive on Peiping and its possible complications. The waves of panic that sweep over the city as alarming rumours spread are impossible to control. They sweep on until they break and then we wait exhausted for the next.

At the moment we are waiting, as proceedings for a truce are going on; but there are rumours this morning that proceedings are not going very smoothly and also rumours that there is likely to be trouble between the northern and southern forces which have fallen back upon Peiping. All the soldiers at present in the city are from the south and the northern soldiers are not allowed in because their discipline is not so good. They feel that they belong here and are getting annoyed the southern soldiers are given preference. By night there will probably be accounts of pitched battles between the two and rumours that the city is in imminent danger of being looted and burned.

The constant need to pacify people who are genuinely terrified by such rumours is the thing I find most wearing. I am inclined to get thoroughly out of patience because such unlikely rumours are given any credence at all, and yet I have to remind myself that the Chinese have suffered so horribly in the past at the hands of retreating and disgruntled soldiers, that the panic is quite understandable. And to be perfectly honest I have to admit that I have had several moments of extreme unease myself, not to mention one of sheer panic.

In the last few days thousands of people have left the city with trains packed to the doors. People have climbed in through the carriage windows and not only has there been no standing room inside, but people have been packed on the carriage platforms, on the buffers and on top of the cars. The railway department must be making a fortune. The streets were thronged for several days with cars and ricshas piled with people and their belongings making their way to the stations. There are also hundreds of people coming into the city from the country. They are mostly coming in from the east because the Japanese soldiers have been advancing on Tungchow. Many of them come in on their farm carts, perched on top of bundles of clothing and sacks of grain. Yesterday's paper reported a cessation of fighting; but people are still too terrified to remain in the country if they can possibly find a means of coming into the city.

Japanese bombing planes flying over the city are almost a daily occurrence. They sometimes fly so low that the bombs can be seen distinctly with the naked eye. The fact that Peiping has so far not been bombed is no proof that the next planes will not drop one or two. Twice when I have been on my way over to the West City they have flown right over my head. It is not pleasant, and I could not help feeling uneasy lest a bomb should drop down by mistake! Yesterday showers of leaflets came down upon the city from one plane, but I have not heard what the advice was this time.

Last Saturday I was supervising Ginling College[6] entrance exams when eleven planes came over with an awful noise bang in the middle of the mathematics paper. The exams were being held in the Chin Shih Middle School which is a private school in which the discipline is not proverbially good. All the Chin Shih girls rushed out screaming and yelling. The other examination students cast some agonised glances in my direction but I was having a busy time registering a

'Taken at the Y.W.C.A. playground, Peiping.' 1932. Skinner family collection

close up of complete unconcern so they all went on with their work. I wouldn't have blamed them in the least if they had got excited and behind my apparent unconcern I was hectically wondering what on earth I should do if a bomb came down. The first few visitations were greeted with splutterings from the anti-aircraft stations on the city walls; but I am glad to say that that day there was no firing from the Chinese guns.

Retreating soldiers have been falling back on the city for some time and until two or three days ago there were thousands of them in the city demanding billets which the residents were too scared to refuse. However on Monday night they were all marched out to a point south of the city, much to everyone's relief. Any change of control in the city would have given them a grand opportunity for looting. The chief of police in Peiping is awfully good on his job and the police force here is probably the best in China. It was at his request, I believe, that the soldiers were removed. Those who live near the route the soldiers took as they left could not sleep all night for the tramping and shouting. Every village between Peiping and the hills is full of soldiers, but the majority are said to be south of the city. They are a serious menace to the country people because if food supplies fail they will be ruthless in their demands. Apart from the looting it is a bad time for the farmers to be away from their farms. The season is a particularly good one, but if there is no one left to tend the crops there may be a serious shortage of food later on.

There have been rumours of a truce for some days now, but very little is known of the terms except that a report from Tokyo said that the Chinese suggestions were absurd and not to be considered. It will be equally difficult for the Chinese to consider the Japanese terms because they are bound to be exorbitant. The Chinese are already very bitter and there is a section of the population that refuses to consider terms at all. It will be a brave Chinese who sets his seal to a truce agreement or treaty. Members of the blood and thunder society or of some other group will be quickly on his track and he is quite likely to be murdered as a traitor. Of course, the longer the truce is put off, the more territory Japan will grab and there's apparently no power in heaven or earth to stay her hand.

I begin to understand the bitterness of the Chinese attitude to the unequal treaties forced upon her in the past by Great Britain. Perhaps one reason why Britain does not care to interfere on China's behalf now is because the condemnation of Japan's method would be a condemnation of her own method of 1840 and 1860. Britain's methods in her dealing with China have changed radically in recent years, but the hatred caused by the old ones will last for generations to come, and one can hardly be surprised when ulterior motives are still found behind actions which are apparently friendly overtures on Britain's part. It is tragic to see Japan copying so faithfully the methods of the western powers a century ago.

Another difficulty in the situation is the fact that even if an agreement is reached between China and Japan, the South East provinces, including Canton, are not likely to be satisfied. The Central Government is not a representative government because it is not elected by the people and is severely criticised. The South East provinces feel that China is signing away her soul, and I have heard Cantonese up here say that if the agreement is signed they will either withdraw from the republic and form an independent state, or there will be another civil war between the north and south to unseat the present government and vindicate China's honour. I appreciate the central Government's desire to bring an end to the useless waste of life and property that is now going on; but I sympathise too with the reluctance of China to sign one more unequal treaty that will put her at a serious disadvantage with the other nations. Granted China's attitude to foreign powers has been uncooperative and often provocative, yet there is historical cause for this attitude, and part of it can be looked for in the war with Japan in 1894.

Since September 18th 1931[7] there has not been one shred of justice or fair dealing or common decency in Japan's treatment of China. China is completely at her mercy from a military standpoint because she has no well-equipped fighting force, and this arrogant piece of bullying on Japan's part is a revolting thing to witness in an age that calls itself enlightened. . . .

All my good wishes to you and my goodness won't it be good to see you all next year.

Nessie Moncrieff

Shared letter of 10 March 1934:

In the last few years the Nanking Government has devoted a great deal of its attention to demands for the restoration of concessions granted under the unequal treaties, and many have believed that this was a necessary first step to national reconstruction. Students in particular were very convinced of this and anti-foreign propaganda and efforts to re-establish China's sovereignty were rallying points for student thought and activity. At the same time political leaders from Sun Yat-Sen on have laid great stress on rural and land reform. It is very evident that the attention of China is being turned slowly but surely to her great rural economic problems. In the solution of them lies China's hope of real stability and national reconstruction. Even in remote districts China's rural economic structure has been affected by trade with the west and in districts near the treaty ports household industries have been considerably dislocated. In cases where the farmer's supplementary earnings have been removed owing to the production of machine made cloth, paper and so on the lot of the farmer has become infinitely harder

If the standard of living of the farmer is to be raised and the economic life of China stabilised there must be established rural co-operatives, credit systems, better facilities for transport and marketing, and most important of, all improvement of farm production. Experiments are being carried on in a number of places by various organisations; but China is so vast that only the Central Government can cope with the task on a nation-wide scale. Meantime the greater the pressure of public opinion that is brought to bear on the government the sooner will adequate steps be taken to put into practice the legislation that has already been passed.

It is most encouraging to note the steadily increasing interest of students in rural and social reconstruction as fundamental to the solution of China's problems. This is true of non-student groups as well. As someone said of the Y.W.C.A. Convention last year people were more concerned with providing seeds for the farmer than with pressing international problems of the day. It is not to be surprised therefore that the Student Christian Movement lays great emphasis on rural reconstruction. There is never a conference held without some time being given to addresses and discussion on this problem. At the Student Assembly in Shanghai last summer rural reconstruction was one of the problems chosen for special study and investigation and the Student Christian Movement in the Ho Pei province was asked to take special responsibility for this work.

The Ho Pei Union has, since it was first organised, shown a great interest in the rural problem and for some years teams of students have gone out into the country during the winter vacation and spent a week or ten days in the villages. These groups of students were originally called evangelistic teams; but as they began to see that the problem of the farmer was economic and social and not all due to lack of religious faith they have changed the name to rural service teams. Ten days is far too short a period for the students to accomplish anything of permanent value, but the real value of the work lies in the fact that the students are gaining first hand experience of the conditions under which the great majority of their countrymen live. They are beginning to see how great the problem is and to understand that its solutions can be effected only by the life-time devotion of men and women of vision and conviction who are not afraid to face hardships. It is one thing to study rural reform in class room and library and quite another to see a fragment of the problem revealed in the living conditions of the peasant farmers.

This winter eight rural service teams were organised in Peiping and went out to rural centres within a twelve mile radius of the city. Some fifty students have gone back to their studies with a new understanding of country life impressed alike with the extreme poverty of the average farmer, his philosophical acceptance

'The Student Movement Committee has a meeting. The girl with glasses & a hat below me is Vera Liu, our Student Secretary.' Nessie, right back row, also wears a hat. 1933. ATL PA1-o-1191-25-1

of life and his general efficiency in spite of heavy handicaps. Many students are looking forward to some form of rural service as a life-work.

Last month I went out with a group of six students from the American Board Mission Higher Middle School. We went to Tung Pa, a small market village about seven miles north-east of Peiping. We followed a dirt road now running level with the countryside and now sunken to a depth of four or even six feet. Travelling was slow. By cart it was four hours and by ricsha two. Whatever the vehicle, one moved in a cloud of light yellow dust which lay inches deep on the surface of the road and was easily stirred.

Tung Pa is fortunate in that it has a small church room and a resident evangelist. There is also a small girls' primary school supported by the High School from which the girls of our team came. This schoolroom and the two small rooms occupied by the teacher formed our headquarters.

The first business on arrival was to call on the head of the village. The village elder is always one of the wealthier members of the village, a man who is willing to give time and, if necessary, money to the protection and well-being of the villagers. He is head of the local self-government organisation and has to deal with any inter-family disputes which are not serious enough to be referred to the district court in the nearest town.

Settling into our quarters was a simple process. There were brick beds in the teacher's room and five of the girls slept on them. Ordinarily a fire is kept going under these beds and they constitute the only warm spot in the house. When they are cold they are very cold as the girls found out. Vera Liu and I, the team advisers, had taken camp stretchers and these we set up in the schoolroom. The team captain dragged some of the desks together and spread her bedding out on them. A complicating factor in travel in China is that one always has to take one's bedding along. The school room, besides being the bedroom for three of us, was kitchen, dining room, chapel, reception room, and everything else. Chinese houses always have stone floors which are very cold and hard to keep clean. Our only means of heat was a small coal ball stove. The teacher evidently believed in ventilation because there were small squares near the top of the wall covered only in mosquito netting. One of our difficulties was to keep warm. There were only about three hours at midday when we were comfortable.

Here is a description of our last day. We rose at 7.a.m. Our coal ball stoves were dragged out into the court and Mrs. Sung the evangelist's wife lit them for us. This is a long slow process. Not every one can afford to burn coal balls. By far the majority of homes fuel consists of dry leaves, grass and sorghum stalks. This fact helps to aggravate the problem of farm production because every scrap of dry vegetation is removed every year and the soil is so much the poorer. Coal balls are made of coal dust, water and earth mixed together into a paste and spread out on the ground to dry. This paste is then cut into small squares which are rolled in a sieve till their corners are rounded off. The kindling used was dry corn cobs saved for the purpose from last year's harvest. The stoves had to be left outside till the coal balls were red hot. As long as there is any flame it is not safe to have them in the room because the fumes are poisonous. There have been many fatalities in China due to coal stoves.

About 8.30 the stoves were ready and brought inside. Our morning wash had to wait while the water heated. Meantime we had morning prayers and discussed our day's programme. We followed the country plan of two meals a day. This saves time and fuel. It was 9.30 before our breakfast of rice porridge and boiled potatoes was ready though we were more than ready for it. Chinese students do not as a rule know how to cook and our meals were somewhat hit and miss in consequence. Many were the jokes exchanged over the pots and pans. It was a grand way to get to know each other really well and I am sure our team work was better because of the fun we had cooking meals. There was never the slightest doubt of our appreciation of whatever came out of the pot. Two meals a day gives one a keen appetite.

About 10.30 we were ready for the day's work and this was a very good time to begin because the village folk were also through with their morning meal and were at leisure to listen to us. That morning we had arranged to go to a much smaller village about a mile away. This was a group of farmers' homes numbering about twenty families and there were no shops at all. Everything that was not brought round by pedlars had to be bought in Tung Pa.

In this little village we first called at the homes of two of the girls who were being educated in the Tung Pa school. These homes were far above the average in comfort and cleanliness. The families owned about two hundred mu of land (one mu is about of an acre). It is hard to say what the average holding of a farmer is in this part of the country, but the Mass Education Movement's survey of Ting Hsien in this province showed that 55.7% of the holdings are below 20 mu. Many of them are very much less of course.

I wish you could have seen the old lady who received us in the second home we went into. She was most attractive with her fresh blue gown, her rosy weathered face and a red flower in her grey hair. We chatted about all sorts of things as we sat on the kang[8] and sipped tea. Her son is studying at the Y.M.C.A.'s Commercial College and will graduate this year. Conversation turned to a play that the students had acted the day before. It was an adaptation of a famous old Chinese play which shows the hardship endured by a daughter-in-law in a Chinese family. It was very sad and the girls had acted well. Many of the older women and some of the men too had gone away wiping their eyes on their sleeves. Our hostess had heard of the play and agreed that one of the greatest problems in a family is the position of the daughter-in-law. But she said that she herself always treated her own daughter-in-law well, and indeed the serenity and poise of the daughter-in-law as she poured tea for us gave no indication of any of the misunderstanding or harsh treatment which often makes the lot of women so unhappy.

Later she accompanied us on her little bound feet to the meeting-place which was in the court of the village temple. Experience had taught the girls that it was better to separate the children from the adults and hold two meetings; but in this case it proved impossible because the mothers were so interested in what the girls were teaching the children. Of course the children in these villages know most of the old Chinese folk songs and stories so sometimes the girls were hard put to it to find new material. Often they took a well known tune and fitted new words to it as in the case of one simple little song which with much repetition said that good Chinese children wash their face and hands every day, never speak rudely to others, never strike anyone and never tell lies. The number of children in this village was most amazing and made one think seriously of China's over-population problem. Some of them were well-cared for, but others were bundles of rags and very sickly looking.

Part of the work of the teams is to investigate living conditions in the district they go to and this is done largely through talking informally to people and finding out from them the general village conditions, size of families, size of farm holdings, nature of land tenancy, supplementary sources of income and so on. This was done while the children were singing. Such friendly conversation serves as a good introduction and increases the interest of the people in the more formal meeting.

The main address of this meeting dealt with hygiene both personal and public and the training of children. For the former topic gay-coloured posters were shown of children sleeping with the windows open, taking a bath, washing their hands before a meal, cleaning their teeth, using a handkerchief, eating meals containing green vegetables, playing games and the why and wherefore of these strange activities were expounded. I couldn't help wondering how many of the families could afford one toothbrush let alone one to every member of the family. Some of the children admitted that they had baths sometimes in the summer, but a bath a week in winter is an impossibility for most people. With no means of heating the necessary amount of water, no utensil large enough to bath in and a room well below freezing point for several months on end I didn't blame them for being sceptical. Most country people don't take their clothes off all through winter and for a very good reason. I shouldn't myself under the same conditions.

Top: Nessie pulling a colleague in a ricsha, 1931. ATL PA1-o-1191-07-2

Bottom: 'I avoid ricsha fares as far as possible by cycling everywhere. My weekly average is sixty miles.' 1932. Moncrieff family collection

Nessie ready for adventure, 1933. ATL PA1-o-1191-29-3

The work that the students did with the children was particularly good. Everywhere great emphasis was laid on the importance of education. The team had a supply of Chinese stories and other printed material. Wherever a child could read the title he (or she) was presented with a copy of the booklet. Copies of St. Luke's Gospel were also given to some of the more advanced children.

With the adults the inexperience of these High School students was more apparent, and especially in the religious talks. A question that concerns deeply every evangelist is that of how to present Christianity, how to relate it to the thought and experience of the hearers. It needs training and experience to do this successfully. It is difficult for students to make their vocabulary fit country folk. The Chinese language is developing so rapidly that already the language of the students is far removed from that of the older villagers and it is often difficult to express new ideas in older and simpler terms than one is accustomed to using.

The village meeting lasted till about 1.30 when the crowd began to disperse. So we packed up and went back to our headquarters. At 3.p.m. our second meal was ready – rice (somewhat burnt), a dish of white cabbage and noodles, eggs and onions cooked in peanut oil, and of all things a tin of sardines – a positive incongruity in that setting.

The afternoon meeting began at 5.30 in the Tung Pa Church room. The fame of the team had spread widely and at this the last meeting of the week, we were somewhat embarrassed by the numbers that turned out. This final meeting was entirely religious in content. Christianity was presented through sermon, pageant story and song. The stories and pageant were the most popular. They were all in the colloquial speech of the people and were thoroughly appreciated and understood.

An unfortunate incident brought our meeting to an early close. Some soldiers who could not find standing room began to talk loudly at the back. Many people could not hear the girls and the disturbance spread till only those on the front benches could hear anything. Finally it was necessary to close the meeting and in endeavouring to persuade the people to disperse a policeman fell foul of one of the soldiers and had an exciting escape over our back wall – exciting both for him and for us.

This incident served to impress on us how much the village people are at the mercy of the soldiers. The people are always uneasy when there are soldiers about. Only two months before Liu Kuei T'ang with his struggling bandit troops had been through this village and looted right and left and the people were more than usually nervous. We were an extremely thoughtful group as we came back to the city next morning, more understanding of the rural problem, more impressed with the need for rural reconstruction, and more determined to do what we could to help. . . .

Yours sincerely,

Agnes Moncrieff

The final letter Nessie kept from her first term was her reply to one from the chairman of the national committee of the YWCA of China:

9th April, 1934

Dear Mrs. Huang,

Thank you for your letter of March 24th conveying the Executive's decision to ask for my return to China. This experience of living and working in China has been a very happy one and although I do not feel I have accomplished much I should be glad to return after my furlough . . .

I am

Yours sincerely,

Agnes M. Moncrieff

'Lunch on the wall.' Nessie second right, in front. 1931. Skinner family collection

3

Home, Travels and Return to China

1934–1937

NEWS FROM CHINA – MISS MONCRIEFF RETURNS.

> Immensely interested in China and the Chinese, Miss Moncrieff, who returned from a four and a half years sojourn in that wonderful and vast country by the Wanganella yesterday, had much to tell of interest. She had a very delightful tour en route for New Zealand, leaving Peking and calling at Shanghai, Hongkong, the Dutch Celebes, and so to Australia, visiting several towns before arriving at Sydney. Miss Moncrieff spent all her time in Peking in the student department of the Y.W.C.A., which has many University and high school students in touch with its activities. . . . She is in New Zealand on furlough, but hopes to return some day to her Chinese friends who she values very greatly.
>
> *Evening Post*, 30 August 1934[1]

In 1934 Nessie returned to New Zealand on a two-year furlough. This gave her the opportunity to speak locally about her work. She also undertook some international travel in North America, Europe and India, and study in Britain. On returning to China late in 1936 she was stationed in Shanghai. In July 1937 she travelled on holiday to Kuling [Guling, now Lushan], a hill station above the Yangtze River, and was prevented from returning to the coast by an outbreak of hostilities in Shanghai.

Although Nessie wrote regularly to her mother from the beginning of her time in China, the letter below, written at the end of her furlough, is the earliest that survives. Mrs Catherine Agnes Moncrieff was a widow living in the family home at 21 Victoria Street, Carterton. Nessie's father, James Moncrieff, had died in 1923 at the age of sixty-one. He was an accountant and at one time town clerk of Carterton. Nessie's letters home usually end with 'love to all'. This included her older sister Catherine, younger sister Janet, brother Doyle, and twin sisters Dora and Jean.

Most of Nessie's letters were typed in small typeface on thin paper, but sometimes they were written in ink with a flowing style; ampersand usage (&) was not consistent.

Letter home, handwritten on board the *SS Comorin*, en route from Hong Kong to Shanghai, 24 November 1936.

My dear Mother,

We are pounding up the coast of China and are due in Shanghai at 7.a.m. on Monday morning. I'm sorry for the folk meeting us at that early hour. I had an air mail letter from Talitha Gerlach just before we left Hongkong. She is meeting me and I'm going to live, while in Shanghai, at the Chinese Hostel. I shiver at the thought of China breakfasts but I'll probably survive.

Arriving at Hongkong was an awful muddle. We were not expected till Friday morning, but arrived at 1.p.m. on Thursday. Very few people were met & it was a forlorn group of passengers. No one came to meet Tsai Kwei & me & she was very disappointed because she expected her husband whom she has not seen for 14 months. He teaches in Kiangsi & was to fly down to meet her. We went to the Hotel where he had told her to book & he wasn't registered there so there was more disappointment. Then we went up to the Y.W.C.A. & the General Secretary was out at a meeting & not expecting us till the next day. However we went into town again & met her & then went back to Tsai Kwei's hotel. After about half an hour her husband arrived. Great rejoicing!

Much love to everyone,

Nessie

Shared letter from Shanghai, 1 May 1937, from the address of the YWCA of China, 133 Yuen Ming Yuen Road, Shanghai, China:

Dear Friends,

When I returned to China at the end of last year I was given the choice of the International Branch of the Shanghai YWCA or going up to the youngest Association in Taiyuan – the provincial capital of Shanshi. As far as personal inclination went there was no question in my mind. I chose the Chinese interior city, conservative in many ways and yet the centre of what was known for a long time as a model province. A young, small Association with opportunities for industrial and student work as well as regular city activities appealed to me very much and the cosmopolitan city of Shanghai did not seem like China at all. 'The best laid plans of mice and men gang aft agley' and almost overnight, when my boxes were already packed for Taiyuan, the decision was reversed and I had to remain in Shanghai. Miss Jeanne Perkins, who has been the International Branch secretary for ten years, was on furlough and someone has to hold the fort in her place. When the needs of all the cities were considered together it really did seem as if I was the person for the job not because of any special qualifications on my part but because other members of our small staff of city secretaries were all needed elsewhere. Together with my work in the local Association I have some National responsibilities and spend three mornings a week at the National office, and the rest at the International Branch at 999 Bubbling Well Road.[2] You can imagine how difficult it was to adjust to two entirely different sets of problems and even to the physical fact of having two offices two miles apart. The things I needed for my work always seemed to be on the wrong desk in those first hectic days. However the national end of my work I must leave to another letter.

Just over a year ago the Shanghai YWCA and the International Branch moved out together to a new site at 999 Bubbling Well Road. For the first time the two organisations were housed in one building and were therefore able to work in much closer co-operation than ever before. But the new headquarters is two miles from the busy downtown section where the majority of firms have their offices, and the most obvious service of the YWCA to foreign business girls – that of providing lunch room, rest room and library – has had to be discontinued. Even rooms for transient guests are not well patronised so far out of town. Gone are the everyday contacts with a wide group of business girls and the question which faces the committee is along what lines to develop new activities and a new programme.

Of course, some of the old activities moved out with the office of the International Branch and chief among them is the Employment Bureau. Every day girls of many nationalities come to see Mrs. Leitao, our Portuguese Employment secretary. Many of them are easy to place because they are well equipped to work, but too many of them are on the verge of 'unemployability'. The problem is a serious one and made more serious by the peculiar conditions of Shanghai.

In the first place there is practically no vocational training for foreign girls in the city except in stenography. Those whose families cannot send them abroad for training, and there are many such, have perforce to become stenotypists, office assistants, telephone operators, cable clerks and for a very limited number, sales girls. No teachers are trained in Shanghai and no nurses. There are no technical schools or university colleges for foreign girls or boys. The range of occupations is very limited. Chinese men do all the tailoring and Chinese girls fill the work rooms and factories. The girl whose mentality, or whose English, is not up to the standard required in an office has a hard time finding work.

Reports given at the League of Nations Conference held last February in Java to consider traffic in women and children give shocking figures for Shanghai. There are 25,000 habitual and occasional prostitutes in this city of four million people. For a girl with no resources, no training and youth as almost her only asset, the way to dance halls and brothels is tragically easy. The problem is aggravated both

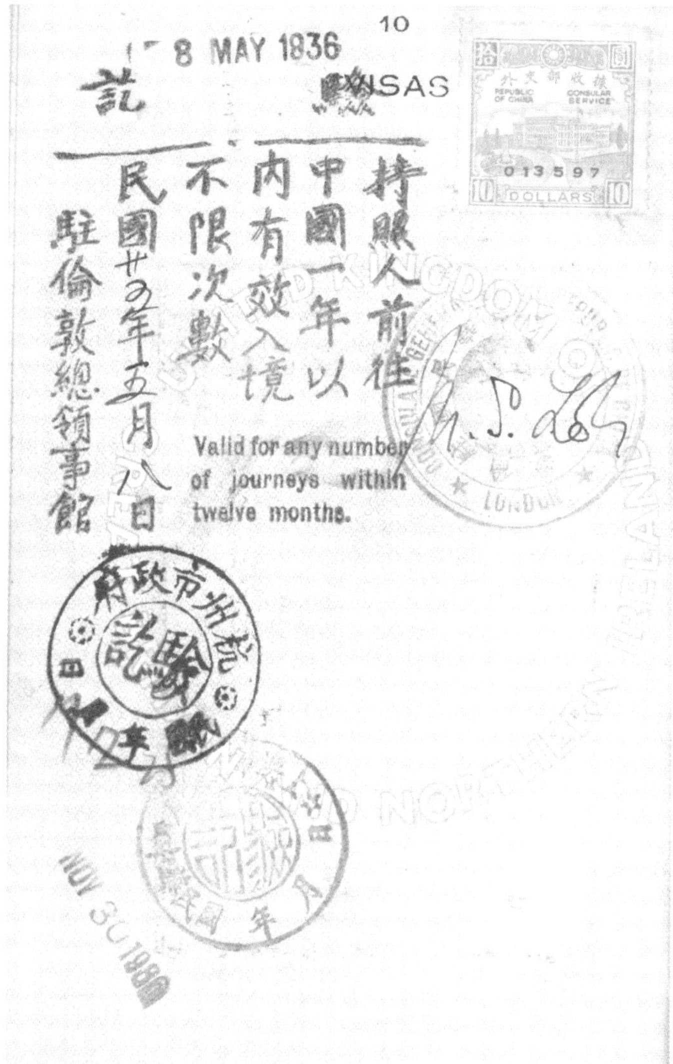

Visa for Nessie's return to China, issued in London on 8 May 1936. Stamps at bottom of page denote her arrival in China. Moncrieff family collection

by the depression and the fact that girls are coming from Harbin and Vladivostok to look for employment which does not exist. In the last twenty years Shanghai has had to absorb 20,000 Russians, most of whom are 'white', into normal and productive occupations and the marvel is that the problem of unemployment is no more acute than it is.

The government of Shanghai is in the hands of three municipal councils. One governing the International Settlement, one the French Concession and one greater Shanghai. Co-ordination of activities is not always easy and as far as social services are concerned it has to be remembered that with the exception of Greater Shanghai there is no national government behind the council and therefore no national resources to draw on. Everything that is done has to be done from the taxes levied on Shanghai citizens by the various councils or by charitable institutions. There are many of the latter in Shanghai; for the most part serving only their own national group, but the YWCA recognises no boundaries of nation or race and endeavours to help all who come. In this situation the work of the Employment Bureau is important because it is constructive and preventative.

It is often difficult to understand the girls who come into our office. Their English is sometimes very limited and with a gleam of hope one asks, 'Do you speak German?' or 'Do you speak Russian?' only to be disappointed. Behind the need for money there is often tragic loneliness and personal problems that need sympathy and understanding. The International Branch aims at being a friendly place for these girls to come to.

There is no use for sentimentality; often one has to be very firm and make these girls face the reality of their situation, but there must be a friendly approach that will inspire confidence. Often a pair of shoes, or a coat or some other badly needed article of clothing increases a girl's chance of securing a job. Such clothing is brought in for Jumble Sales to augment the funds of the Branch, but nothing ever accumulates so we are spared the JS. For some girls there is no solution and Mrs. Leitao says the only time she doesn't like her job is when she sees a girl she knows she cannot help coming up the path.

Years ago a YWCA Helping Fund was started to help girls over difficult days. It is a loan fund and it's surprising under the circumstances how much money is returned. In comes a Russian girl who is trying to make a living selling cosmetics on commission, a hopeless job. She has had nothing to eat for several days and her landlord is threatening to turn her out because her rent is not paid. Or a German girl can get work in another part of China if she can find the price of the ticket to take her there. Or a girl needs to advertise for work and has not got the necessary money. In these cases and many others the Helping Fund is called on.

Sometimes it seems as though the rapidly shrinking fund will not stand the strain of the year's need till Christmas comes and it is replenished by folks who know how badly it is needed. Every case has to be investigated and sometimes, in spite of careful questioning and consultation, there is an awful fear that a mistake has been made and the money lent for a wrong purpose. . . .

Sincerely,
A. M. Moncrieff

In July 1933 Nessie had received a letter from the general secretary of the YWCA of New Zealand, who wrote, 'I was wondering if it would not be possible to put into a little dramatic form some of the happenings; it would make your work so vivid.'[3] The account below seems designed to meet that challenge:

A DAY WITH THE INTERNATIONAL BRANCH OF THE SHANGHAI YWCA 1937

The secretary ran upstairs two at a time. The clock over the information desk was striking nine and her telephone was ringing. She picked up the receiver and took a deep breath. 'Hello!' The day's work had begun.

Half an hour later she paused to take off her hat and ran her fingers through her hair. She had already phoned three girls to go after that stenographer's job with the shipping firm, taken two telephone calls, one for a children's nurse and one for a dentist's assistant ('Good front teeth please') and assured an anxious enquirer that the YWCA did not store furniture.

Meantime the lounge was filling up. 'My sister, she not spik English, you have class, yes?' She enrolled 'sister' in the afternoon class for Russian girls and hoped the teacher would bear up under the strain of another beginner so late in the term.

The next were not so easy. A German girl peddling cosmetics, no sales for days and no food either and a landlord who had delivered an ultimatum. The Helping Fund was slim, but being turned out was the first step to the cabarets and the streets and that must be avoided. Besides, the girl had always refunded in the past and was making a gallant effort to be self-supporting.

A middle-aged woman who had walked four miles because she had no car fare and who protested between sobs that she was terrified of cabarets and preferred poison at fifty cents. Would she use the dollar and go out and apply for the cook's job or would she lie in a store of poison? Well the risk had to be taken. She'd never get a job if she turned up in those shoes. But the Jumble Sale box provided a pair large enough.

'Don't mention Age – I've dyed my hair,' was the jaunty remark of a woman of forty as she went out after a job at a salary just half of what she had earned three years before. 'What happens to women when they are no longer young and attractive enough to suit the general demand?' The secretary deliberately shut her mind to that question and turned to the phone.

Three girls wanted reservations for the business girls' supper the next evening and while she was answering their questions about the programme her call sounded on the other telephone. A dash to the landing. A shipping firm calling – through passengers wanted a children's nurse while the ship was in port so that they could leave their children and go sight–seeing. They would pay a dollar gold a day and all meals, also taxi fare if the girl had to wait till late at night. Why wasn't Margaret on the phone? She needed work more than anyone else and was so hard to get hold of. Besides she had completed the training course for Children's Nurses and had her certificate. A chit for the office chit-boy and off he went on his bicycle.[4]

Now perhaps there would be a moment to open her mail. An up-country hospital wanted a nurse for three months. No one suitable on the files so that must wait. Why couldn't someone make a fuss because there was no nurses' training for foreign girls in the city. Several girls wanted to, and would make good nurses, but short of going to America or Europe there was no hope for them.

Four registrations for the summer camp, which reminded her that a letter must be sent straightaway making application for the camp site definite.

A note of thanks from a girl placed as a stenographer the month before enclosing a contribution to the funds.

A communication from the bank asking how long the clean overdraft was to run. 'What is a clean overdraft and if it is clean why worry?' thought the secretary as she laid it aside to attend to more urgent matters.

In walked two smartly dressed attractive American girls. They had arrived from San Francisco the week before and would like secretarial work. The secretary almost wept. With their recommendations they would soon get work and would write home to their friends and say how easy it is and then more girls will come and somewhere down at the bottom of the scale Shanghai girls who had to live here will be unemployed. Survival of the fittest, but why couldn't the fittest stay in their own country and give the merely fit a chance. But she greeted them with a smile and gave them advice about apartments within their means.

As she ushered them out the Information secretary arrived at the top of the stairs. Downstairs a girl had arrived straight from the boat and no one could understand her. She was a French subject with very little English and had returned to Shanghai, where she had lived fifteen years before because she was getting a divorce and must earn her living. 'But why Shanghai?' thought the distracted secretary. 'She couldn't have chosen a worse place.' No training, no experience, next to no English, 35 at least and only a small allowance for one year. Even the hat trick couldn't produce work for a girl with absolutely no qualifications. The transient rooms were all full too. Still she could have the bed on the landing if screens were put round it and that would do to solve the immediate problem. As to the future unless she could be persuaded to return to France and money could be found for the fare there was nothing for her but the Foreign Women's Home.

Two girls were waiting in the office to join the tennis club and enquire about swimming lessons. A newspaper called. What was the meeting on Thursday and what would the speaker say? The secretary invented a probable speech and hoped there would not be a libel case over it.

It was long past twelve. She shot round the corner for lunch, discovered another social worker munching a sandwich and learned to her horror that fifty resource-less girls had just arrived from the north. Couldn't there be some law to prevent such girls from landing in Shanghai. But what would happen if there was such a law? It wouldn't really solve the problem. They must live somewhere.

The problem was twisting back and forth in her mind all the way down to the customs jetty. Two YWCA Board members were arriving from England and it would be friendly to meet them. They were helped through customs, taken to an hotel and plans made for a visit to the Association the next day. On the way back she bought an outline map of the world to make a chart showing which countries were touched by the International Branch. Thirty–eight in all which shows we really are international.

'Princess Elsa Kederoff' said the card on her desk and there she stood, but surely not quite a princess. She must have work, but knew no English. 'Man want drink, I understand. I work bar, you find, yes?' 'Really,' thought the secretary, 'a princess, a bar and a YWCA. They simply don't go together'. It took her fifteen minutes to find English simple enough to make the princess understand that no bar owners ever rang the YWCA to look for assistants. Another recruit for the English class, perhaps?

'If I would not already be convinced about the value of the YWCA, Shanghai would convince me,' thought the secretary. 'It's little enough we do when you measure it against the need, but we're friendly and we help as much as we can and the girls know we care.' And with that she bundled the unanswered letters and the notes of the day's work into a drawer and went home.

Kuling was a popular summer holiday resort in the hills above the Yangtze River, much favoured by missionaries for its a cooler alpine temperature. The Kuling American School, a boarding school founded by missionaries for their children's education, made its hostel available for accommodation in the school holidays. Nessie travelled there on vacation in the summer of 1937 with her friend Pearl Pollock, an American foreign secretary.

Letter home from Kuling, 9 August 1937:

> My dear Mother,
>
> I feel sure that if I had remained in Shanghai I would have had another letter from you by this time. Air mails come up in a few hours but the ordinary mails are three to four days so I shall have to wait a little longer for my NZ mail. It is raining this morning and there is a lovely soft mist down over the hills. We began the day very hot but there has been a thunderstorm since and Pearl and I are spending the morning with our typewriters going hard. We sound awful going together and what our neighbours think I don't know but the morning is the only time we type so they really can't complain.
>
> I think I wrote last from the boat which we both hated. We had a nice morning in Nanking which I had never seen before. We took a taxi and went out to see the Sun Yat-Sen tomb which is the showplace in Nanking. It has been built on the slopes of Purple Mountain which is a few miles from the city and the road out there is planted on either side so that it is like driving through a huge park. The tomb is white with blue tiles like the Temple of Heaven in Peiping and there are flights and flights of steps up the central building. The view from the top is lovely.
>
> Nanking city is a mess. It is like nothing I have ever seen. It had to be built up so quickly to house the government when it moved down from Peiping and there seems to have been very little system to it. Some of the new buildings are in the old Ming style like the palaces in Peiping and some are quite modern. They are all mixed up with the old Nanking, parts of which are very old with narrow streets just like any other Chinese city. We went to see Spirit Valley too, which has very lovely walks and temples and a view. We were told to be back at the boat at 2.p.m. and were, but the old thing didn't move till 7.p.m. and all that time we had to try and put up with the heat and the noise of unloading cargo and no chairs to sit on. Shanghai was visited by the worst typhoon for years while we were on our way up river and we certainly benefited by it. It blew us up the river and the wind was very strong even though it was following. If it hadn't been quite as bad the trip would have been too hot for words. All the same we were mighty glad when we woke up at 6.a.m. to find ourselves tying up at Kiukiang.
>
> The China Travel Service organises the trip up the hill to the last detail. A bus left their office at 7.30 and after a trip of about eight miles we reached their station at 850 feet above sea level. There we took chairs. It was pouring with rain, but after a while we had a marvellous view down on to the plains. Then we went into dense mist which completely cut out the views so that we could

Pearl Pollock (left) and Nessie (back) with their Chinese teachers at 17 Hsiao Po Ko Shih, Peiping. 1931. ATL PA1-o-1191-06-2

only see about twenty feet in front of us. Higher up it came on to rain again and we saw nothing of our surroundings at all. We passed through a shopping street and started downhill till we came to the American school. The down grade was a lot easier for our bearers. A hundred and sixty pounds [72 kg][5] is the four-man limit so I had to have six men to my chair. We arrived about 11.a.m. very hungry because we had had no breakfast and wet through as to our feet. Our baggage had not been properly covered so we had to unpack straight away. The management brought us tea and toast and we had baths and felt better. It rained cats and dogs all day and as we were not supplied with water proof footgear we had to stay in.

The next day we went up to the shops commonly called 'The Gap' and bought awful looking Chinese galoshes which will keep the water out pretty well but will not be very comfortable to wear. Nobody is very communicative round here and there is no map in English so we have not yet found the best walks. We know the way up and down the Gap pretty well as the P.O. is there and the China Travel Service and the banks and the shops. . . .

The shops up here are simply wonderful considering that every single thing has to be carried up. Next year there may be a funicular railway but at present there are about two thousand chair men who spend their days coming up the hill with load after load. The chair men sometimes do as many as three trips in one day and the road is very steep in parts. The Chinese have not yet learned to zigzag and have put in stone steps and the result is shorter but a much steeper path. We have been for one or two nice walks but so far have not managed to get high enough to really see the lie of the land. We keep hearing people mentioning different valleys but their instructions how to get there are so vague as to be almost useless.

I had a surprise this morning in the shape of a visit from Miss Lenwood. I had heard that she was here this summer but could not find her name registered at the Bureau of Information so concluded that the trouble in the north had kept her away. However she had been here since the end of June. Her problem is how soon she will be able to get back to Peiping now that it is in the hands of the Japanese.

Things look very serious here still and no one knows whether there will be a war or not. There has been nothing untoward at Shanghai, but panic has seized the Chinese who live on the north side of Soochow Creek and they have been crossing over into the International Settlement and the French Concession in tens of thousands. The influx has been stimulated by household removal firms and house agents who own property on the south side. Rents have gone up a hundred and two hundred per cent and the agents benefited while the going was good. The Japanese, with the exception of the Consul, have all been evacuated from Hankow and the Japanese Concession is quite deserted as far as the Japanese are concerned. But, although the Chinese are protecting it and all Japanese property, the Japanese have made it clear that they want it back and the Chinese are not to hold it permanently. Isn't that a queer business? I can't imagine any other country but China being so accommodating. Whispers came yesterday to the effect that Nanking is showing signs of wanting to compromise again and not embark on major operations against Japan. It would be an awful come down after all their manifestos and so on but on the other hand war would be awful.

The localised fighting in north China has brought death to thousands and the Japanese have deliberately destroyed universities and schools. They have behaved like utter barbarians. . . .

Love to you all,
Nessie

Pearl Pollock, a foreign secretary for the YWCA of America in China from 1929–1943, is featured in photos and mentioned in several letters. She was three years younger than Nessie and they became good friends in their early days in Peiping. In 1937 Pearl was with the national YWCA's rural department in Shanghai.

Letter home from Kuling, 15 August 1937:

My dear Mother,

I don't know when this letter will reach you as there is no mail down to Shanghai at the present moment but I will write all the same. Pearl and I are still perched up at Kuling in perfect safety while Shanghai is being bombed and the most awful fighting is raging there. It seemed to come so quickly when it did come. We wrote by air mail to ask if the National Office would like us to return and their answer came that they would let us know in a day or two, and in a day or two Japan had massed over twenty gun boats in the Whangpoo at Shanghai, landed reinforcements that brought their troops up to 9,000 in Shanghai city, the British and American Volunteers had all been called out, the river service had been interrupted by the laying of mines between Nanking and Chinkiang and the bombing had begun.

There is at present no way now of us getting to Shanghai as the Japanese hold the North Station, and no air passengers are being accepted. The railways are all being used for movement of Chinese troops and the China Travel Service assures everybody there is nothing to do but wait till it is all over. We both would like to be in Shanghai lending a hand to the relief work that the Association is doing but there is no way of getting there so we are cooling our heels and foaming at the mouth both at the things the Japanese are doing and at our own enforced inactivity.

The last two days there has been no news through from Shanghai, even by air and what we heard this morning had come by radio via London. The Chinese are putting up a much better resistance than they were able to in 1932 and the rumours say the chances are even at present. The Japanese seized the P.O. but the Chinese have got it back. You remember it is just across the road from my flat and I am wondering if my roof garden was used by snipers on either side. Lydia Johnson was occupying the apartment when I left and when the American and British consuls ordered all their nationals to leave. I am hoping that Lydia took some of my possessions with her. Otherwise I won't have much left. I have all my winter clothes and some shoes in cold storage, also my fur coat. Also some books and a box of bedding are at the YWCA and of course I have a good many of my summer things here with me, but I stand to lose a good deal all the same; all my spring things including a good many dresses and a coat I bought in London and the few housekeeping things I possess, some lightweight blankets and some pillows. However what I lose is of minor importance when buildings are being bombed wholesale and people left homeless. There was a most tremendous exodus of people from that section of the city going on for about two weeks before we came up and Talitha told us in a letter that houses that have not been rented for years are now rented on a year's lease.

More British reinforcements have been sent from Hongkong to assist in the defence of the Settlement and the whole city must be a complete mess. Now that news has ceased it's very hard to sit and wait and not know what's happening. I don't know how long it will be before we can get back to Shanghai.

Meantime up here it rains and rains and the temperature has dropped and no one has winter clothes with them. I haven't even a silk dress with me and the last two days have been lamenting the fact that I did not put in a pair of knickers. I have nothing but scanties and they are very draughty. You can get warm walking but you can't walk far in this rain without getting pretty wet. Everyone is knitting and I have joined the company. So far relief work has not been organised so I am knitting for myself and have completed an orange jersey to go with the black skirt in Shanghai, which I may never see again and now I have begun on winter vests. The wool is very fine and so are the needles and whether I finish one by winter remains to be seen, but we have plenty of time at our disposal and of course there's the possibility that we may have to remain here till Christmas. It all depends on the Japanese. There was news this morning of a bomb having fallen in the Settlement and killing two hundred people.[6] The Settlement must be jamb full and the streets much more crowded than usual which says a good deal. Two Americans were killed according to the report. If only we could see a newspaper it would help, but the air service, even for air mails seems to have been dislocated. . . .

An earlier trip using chairs when based in Peiping. 'Starting down T'ai Shan.' Nessie third right, back of photo. 1931. ATL PA1-o-1191-12

I am hoping this letter may be sent via Hankow and Canton. If it isn't it will be a long time on the way. They say that trains are still running on that line though no one knows how soon the rolling stock will be commandeered for other districts. We are really refugees too, though in much better circumstances than those in Shanghai. Food supplies may give out, or rather supplies of imported things such as butter and tinned goods and coffee but I don't suppose we shall suffer much. It seems awful to be so safe and comfortable while everybody else in the YWCA is living under such a strain.

Much love to you all. . . .

Nessie

Letter home from Kuling, 22 August 1937:

My dear Mother,

. . . As you see we are still at Kuling and wondering how much longer we shall have to remain here. It has been a desperate week in Shanghai and untold damage has been done. As far as we can see the Chinese are getting the better of it on land and the part of the city occupied by the Japanese is getting smaller and smaller. This morning's news said that reinforcements had arrived from Japan but there was no place they could land so they were remaining on the gun boats. The Chinese hold Wayside Wharf which is one of the main Jap. wharves and the Japanese hold the Jardine Wharf nearer the Creek. The space occupied by the Japanese is so small that big guns are not possible and hand to hand fighting has to be resorted to. I have heard people say that the Japanese are terrified of the Chinese big swords so perhaps the Chinese will continue to get the best of it. I sincerely hope they will. The Japanese are occupying Broadway Mansions, which is a thirteen or fourteen floored apartment building in North Soochow Rd. It must be a fine point of vantage but they can't mount big guns in it because it would not stand the vibration. There have been several enquiries as to its permanency since it was built because it is such an immensely high building for a mud foundation.

Planes are still ranging all over the country taking pot shots at airports and anything they don't like the look of. Kuling lights are a grand beacon for raiding planes so whenever a report comes through that planes are coming over we have to sit in darkness till they have passed. Last night was full moon and we took our supper away out to the Nankang Pass. We had hardly more than settled when a soldier came along and politely informed us that planes were in the vicinity and would we go inside the little pavilion there or go home early. His report did not alarm us in the least, but the fact that he had his finger on the trigger of his revolver all the time he was talking to us raised our hair. He was not pointing it at us fortunately but he was evidently expecting the plane any moment. It was a most wonderful spot to watch the sun set and the moon rise. We were on top of a ridge that ran practically east and west and the clouds at sun set were riotous to say the least of it. Then to the west the moon shone over Poyang Lake and made a stunning path of light across the water. The mountains fell away to the Lake very steeply so the view of the valley and the lake was lovely. We could see a little white steam launch tugging three or four barges across the lake and an occasional white spot of a sail. . . .

We still do not know what we are going to do. This morning I sent an air mail letter to Nell Elliott at Hongkong to ask if there was a job of work I could do there if I went or whether Hgkg was so full that I would only complicate the refugee problem. . . . If only we could get news of the folk we know or could relieve them for a while while they come up here to recuperate, we should be a lot happier. This last week has been one of the longest on record.

Much love to you all and I hope I will have happier news to write next week.

Nessie

The monthly YWCA publication *The New Zealand Girl* featured an update in their October 1937 issue:

MISS MONCRIEFF WRITES FROM CENTRAL CHINA.

A letter has been received from the American School, Kuling, Kiangsi, dated August 26th in which Miss Moncrieff says:

'Yesterday we received an air mail letter from the National Office in Shanghai. It had been written on August 13th, which was the day fighting broke out in Shanghai. As a matter of fact they were in the middle of a meeting to discuss the emergency programme when the first guns were fired. They asked us to return at once to Shanghai. The letter has made us more restless than we were before, because Miss Pollock and I would both give a great deal to be in Shanghai with the others, working at relief. There is, however, absolutely no way of getting through. We thought of going through to Hongkong as Wuchang and Hankow did not want us, but Hongkong is now overcrowded, and refugees are being sent on to Singapore. Yesterday we heard that they were no longer allowing foreign nationals to land, which means that Pearl Pollock would not be admitted,[7] so I fear there is nothing for it but to stay in this part and hope that some day money and letters will come. We get nearly desperate sometimes with the uncertainty and the lack of news, and being cut off from the others. What it must be like for those who are living and working in that inferno with food shortage, hundreds of thousands of refugees, blazing fires and almost continuous bombing and shelling, we just can't imagine.'[8]

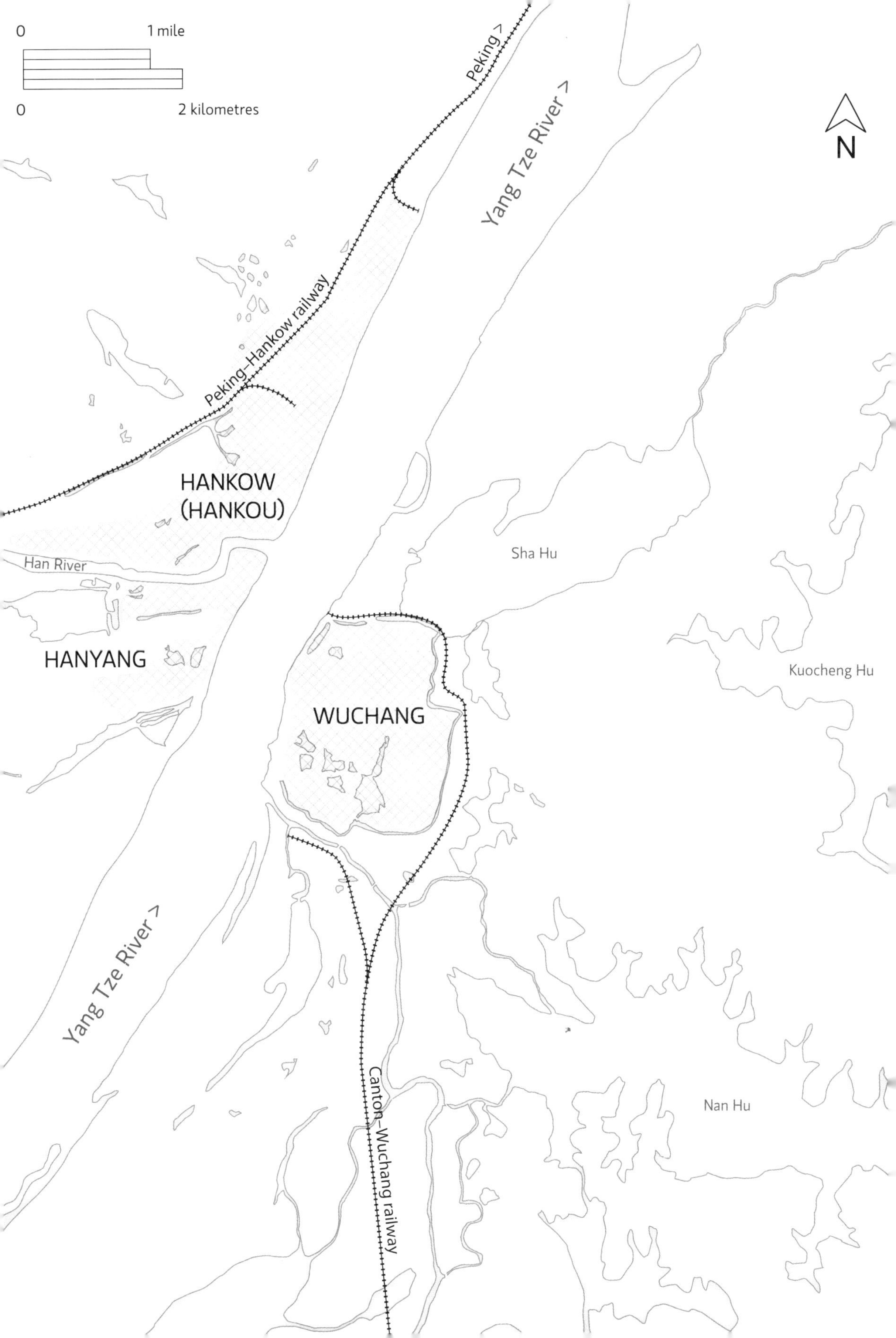
0
1 mile
0
2 kilometres
N
Peking >
Yang Tze River >
Peking–Hankow railway
HANKOW
(HANKOU)
Han River
HANYANG
WUCHANG
Sha Hu
Kuocheng Hu
Yang Tze River >
Canton–Wuchang railway
Nan Hu

4
Hankow
September–December 1937

From Kuling, Nessie was redirected to Hankow, where she arrived at the end of August 1937. There she worked with the International Red Cross, organising medical supplies for distribution to hospitals and relief centres, while at the same time carrying out her YWCA responsibilities.

Letter home from the YWCA, Hankow, Hupei, China, 1 September 1937:

> My dear Mother,
>
> . . . On 25th August we had [a letter] dated the 13th [August] and in it Tsai Kuei asked us to go back to Shanghai. We felt even worse than we had done before but of course there wasn't any way of getting down. Then on the 28th we had another letter written on the 21st telling us not to come, but to go to Hankow and Wuchang and perhaps Changsha and see if we could make ourselves useful in the Associations there. That evening a telegram which they had sent on the 17th arrived. Papers began to come through from Shanghai and we almost felt in touch with the world again.
>
> Meantime there has been a very bad air raid on Nanking lasting four hours and the consuls there had ordered the evacuation of all British and American women and children remaining. We knew the boats would be crowded, but we decided to go to Kiukiang and try there first. We sent our baggage on by coolie and left at 2.p.m. on Sunday to walk down the hill. We had seen nothing of the path on the way up because of the heavy rain and were disappointed that a heavy mist blotted out the view completely on the Kiukiang side. However in time we got down below it and had a lovely view of the plain and the dirty old river. The road down is paved with very unevenly cut stone most of the way and is very trying. There were some lovely falls and pools and the bamboo groves as we got lower down were beautiful.
>
> We found our baggage at the bus station and were in plenty of time for the 6.p.m. bus. Just before we reached Kiukiang the bus road disappeared under flood

waters and we had to take to sampans. A Chinese Travel Service agent was there so we put ourselves and belongings into his hands and he put us into a sampan. It took us about three quarters of an hour to get to the China Travel Office and it was really a very interesting trip. I had not seen flood conditions in China before. Ever so many of the streets were simply flowing rivers and the people in the poor houses which had no upstairs were living on improvised platforms in their rickety houses. I couldn't help wondering what happened when anything was dropped on the floor. Some of the shacks were very rickety and when we bumped into one I wondered if it would collapse on us. We rowed up the small river that flows into the Yang Tzu part of the way and I wondered why we had left it till I saw the bridge. The water was so high that the sampan could not go underneath. There was a lovely evening light as we came along with a sunset attached. The mist had cleared off the mountain and we could see the path away at the top which we had walked along a very long time before.

When we reached the office we were told that the 'Suiwo' [Yangtze steamer] would be in at 2.a.m. and then the Chinese Travel man proceeded to ring up various places to see if we could get a bed for the night. We finally decided to go to the French convent hospital because they were not on the telephone and could not tell us that they had no room. The man took us out the side entrance of the office and we walked along a sort of duck walk till we came to some ricshas which, for a consideration, pulled us through the water to the convent.

The little sisters were all a bustle. They were having the thrill of their lives looking after hordes of travellers and refugees. They told us of having to house 42 Italians who had been evacuated from Nanch'ang factory where they assemble the aeroplanes.[1] Evidently everyone departed after a particularly vicious air raid.

We sat in the hall and proceeded to let thousands of mosquitos have an evening meal and finally the sisters told us that two people they had prepared for were evidently not coming and we could have the room. It was just big enough to hold two beds and us. Just when we were beginning to gnaw the sheets they told us our dinner was ready. I don't know whether it was typically French or just war-time but everything seemed to come at the wrong time. It was deliciously cooked and when the Mother Superior came and asked if we would like wine I assented before Pearl had time to think. It was very good. The coffee was a bad mistake. I sipped mine first then took it in a gulp as I have often taken cascara [a laxative]. It tasted about the same. The mosquitos had meantime told all their relatives about us and we were thoroughly chewed by the time the meal was over.

Then we retired to our rooms again. You couldn't sit still for a moment because of the mosquitos. They were plain awful. We used our umbrellas as a weapon of defence and by half opening and shutting them again very quickly kept off the mosquitos and fanned ourselves at the same time. The bath was hard to manage because the water wouldn't run away on account of the flood but we managed with numerous basins and went to bed early. It was impossible to keep dry in the heat and my night gown was a wreck in no time.

At 11.p.m. there was a loud knock at the door and the China Travel man appeared again to say that the boat was in and there was no room, but would we like to go and see. We dressed and threw our things in to a bag in record time and leapt madly from bench to bench in the convent garden to some ricshas waiting in the street and were pulled round to a raised wooden walk made of planks on the bund.[2] We had difficulty passing people going in the opposite direction because it was so narrow but we finally reached the pontoon which led to the ship. There was no first class gang plank but we scrambled on at river level and fought our way through the third class quarters. I have never seen anything like the mass of humanity. There was hardly a square inch of space anywhere. People were lying everywhere. We just managed to get by without treading on faces and hoisted ourselves up to the second class level. Our shrewd agent had a sampan bring our baggage round from the office to the pontoon and it joined us there.

When we got to the second class saloon the door was shut upon us and curtain drawn. No amount of knocking would open it till I found a window and the sight of a foreign face there brought a steward to open it. When he found that we were new passengers he went pale with fright and told us to go immediately to the purser. So we fought our way over more faces up to the first class quarters and found the purser. He was not at all pleased to see us and said that he had orders from the captain not take any more passengers. We stood and looked pathetic and helpless and said all we wanted was standing room and finally just as I thought we would be ordered off the ship he caved in and told us we could sit in the saloon. One kind lady offered us her cabin to wash in and we refrained from mentioning that we had already had baths because we were being allowed to remain only because we had nowhere to spend the night. We hadn't by that time either. We knew we had taken a risk when we left our room. Finally two long cane chairs were produced and a blanket apiece and we spent the night on deck in them. There was a cool breeze on deck and we were not as uncomfortable as we might have been. Lack of a place to wash was our chief problem and of course we had to sleep in our clothes which was not so good. There were a hundred first class passengers and the ship holds only thirty so it was a pretty good jamb. Meals were in three relays and there was plenty to eat but it was a bit rough. We left Kiukiang about 12.30 p.m. next day. We sat on our chairs all day in case anyone got them and went to sleep fairly early in the evening. I woke for the last of many times about 5.30 a.m. just as we were reaching Hankow.

We didn't know where we were going to stay but about 7.30 we picked up a bag or so and found our way to the Y.W.C.A. Miss Ch'en had arranged for us to stay at the Lutheran Mission Home but they had taken thirty people off the Suiwo and by the time she informed them that we had arrived they were full up. We had a bath at the Association but had to get back into the same clothes we had slept in for two nights. It was the longest and hottest day I have known. Later Miss Christensen sent a note to say we could go that evening to the Home and we were duly relieved. . . .

Much love to you all,
Nessie

Hankow, along with Wuchang and Hanyang, makes up the city of Wuhan. Hankow, on the northern bank of the Yangtze, was the terminus of the Shanghai to Hankow railway, while Wuchang on the southern bank was the terminus of the Canton to Wuchang line. A regular steam ferry service sailed between the two cities. Hanyang is also on the northern bank, but across the Han River.

Nessie mentioned she and Pearl had found accommodation at the Lutheran mission home. In her 1985 interview she said that 'The Lutheran mission had an enormous six-floor boarding house-cum-offices-cum-everything else and everybody who went through Hankou in the way of foreigners – and some Chinese too – stayed in the Lutheran mission place.[3]

Letter home from Hankow, 12 September 1937. Across the top is written 'Use this address: C/o Miss Nell Elliott, The Bishop's House, Hongkong.' Nell Elliott was a Canadian YWCA secretary working in Hongkong whom Nessie knew. She was able to have Nessie's mail brought up to Hankow by various people passing through Hongkong on their way north. For the next two years this was the address Nessie had her mail sent to and mostly used at the top of her letters, but with 'As from Miss Nell Elliott'.

My dear Mother,

Here it is a month to-morrow since the fighting in Shanghai began and we are no nearer the end. I am wondering if any of my letters to you have got through. They have been very slow on the way from Hankow to Canton I know and I expect you will be wanting regular news. I had a mail from New Zealand on the 8th. It had of course come via Shanghai and was a record from there. The Shanghai postmark was Sept. 4th. Your letter was written July 25th, which wasn't bad considering how slow and irregular mails are between Hongkong and Shanghai. Any boats that get into Shanghai have to pass up the river and there is usually an exchange of compliments going on between the Japanese war ships in the river and the Chinese guns on one shore or other. The boats have to run under the firing at times and it is not a healthy sport. American ships have been forbidden for the time being to make Shanghai a port of call but British ships still dash up and down every now and then. The 'Central China Post' does not give us much news and under war conditions papers are not accepted at all by the P.O. I would give anything to see what the foreign papers are saying, but haven't a hope till the war is over and foreign observers give five years as an estimate.

Japan seems to be working very hard at present to involve Great Britain. What with shooting the Ambassador [Sir Hughe Knatchbull-Huggessen],[4] and searching British ships and seizing customs launches in British waters, it's a wonder Britain hasn't told her where to get off long before this. If other nations joined in and a world war developed people might forget in time what a fool Japan has made of herself and her 'face' would be restored. At present she hasn't a feature left. It has evidently been a considerable surprise to her to find what a strong resistance China can put up and a front line 300 miles long in the north doesn't look as though she is getting away with it too easily up there either.

I wish some of the other nations would organise a boycott of Japan. That would bring her to financial ruin before so very long and she simply couldn't carry on. With full moon coming next week we are expecting more air raids up here, but maybe she has as much as she can at the present. She seems to be preparing to attack the south. Her objective is to cut the Hankow–Canton railway because ammunition is pouring along it. I hope she doesn't succeed.

Yesterday was a red letter day. I went over to see Pearl at Wuchang in the afternoon and was invited to stay to dinner. THEY HAD FRESH BUTTER. I could have made my meal of bread and butter, it was such a treat; I hadn't tasted decent butter for weeks. The Hazelwood Co. is trying to get some up from Canton by rail but there are no refrigerator cars on that line so I don't know whether it will keep unless they supply containers for it to travel in. It is much cooler than it was and I can bear a sheet over me most nights but the maximum temperature is still around 86 degrees [30° Celcius] and it drops only ten degrees at night.

This afternoon I went for a long walk through the Japanese Concession. The Japs all evacuated from here about five weeks ago and the whole place is deserted. It is quite uncanny walking through it. All the shops are boarded up and the doors sealed; the houses are all empty and the gates padlocked. Many of the houses have shrubs on the balconies. They were evidently put out to get what moisture they could and they are all brown and dead. It really is a mournful sight. I believe that many of the Japanese merchants were furious at having to evacuate. They don't approve of the war at all and think the military leaders are making a bad mistake. So they are. They say over and over that they are trying to induce

Key colleagues at the third national convention of the YWCA of China, held at the Shanghai Baptist College, August 1933. From left: Eleanor Anderson (née MacNeil), of Australia, a previous foreign secretary YWCA of Australasia; Nell Elliott, foreign secretary for the YWCA of Canada in Hong Kong; Ting Shu-ching (1890–1936), general secretary for the YWCA of China 1926–1936; Marianne Mills, secretary for the World YWCA; Sarah Lyons, executive director for the foreign division of the American YWCA; Agnes Moncrieff (Nessie), foreign secretary for the YWCA of New Zealand in China. Note the white shoes of foreign secretaries. ATL P-A-Coll-7741-1-4

China to be friendly to Japan. They don't seem to realise that it can't be done with big guns and bayonets.

Someone was describing the other day an incident that is typical of this war. A lone Chinese sniper was picking off Japanese one by one spending about 70 cents a shot. The Japanese were replying with their heaviest guns spending hundreds of dollars. Then after a silence the Chinese sniper would start up again and pick off the Japanese. Boom would go the big guns in return and still the sniper would carry on. The Japanese are not very good marksmen except when they are bombing refugees and civilians. They destroyed a whole train of refugees the other day, five carriages full of women and children. Three hundred were killed and five hundred wounded seriously. There wasn't a single soldier on the train. How's that for a massacre. They kill Red Cross men too when they are trying to bury the dead. It's an ugly war alright. . . .

Lots of love to you all,
Nessie

Letter home from Hankow, 19 September 1937:

My dear Mother,

Well here I am still in Hankow and still wanting desperately to get back to Shanghai. The war is still on though in Shanghai neither side seems to be making any advance. The Japanese seem to be gaining a little ground in the north. I wonder how long they can keep up this fighting. Japan must be getting nearer bankruptcy every day. That's why they would like to end the thing speedily, but the Chinese want to prolong the fighting because every day they can postpone a Japanese victory means the Japanese are a day nearer to economic collapse. If Japan begins to feel the effects of war and really wants to stop it she is not likely to impose such terrific demands on China. . . .

Did I tell you that I had offered my services as an assistant in the office of the International Red Cross that has just been started here? It is a most interesting group and I am enjoying the work and the contacts it is giving me. So far I have done mostly typing. Long lists of drugs which I have never heard of before with their quantities, measurements and costs. It nearly drove me crazy, because one mistake in figures might have made a big difference. The job is not quite finished because Dr. Maxwell dug up some more figures today that have to be copied.

Even if we don't have adventures ourselves we certainly meet people who have them. Yesterday morning at breakfast I sat next to a young American girl who had just come down from Tatung. Her home is in Manila and a year ago she went to Peiping. Up there she has been teaching English in the Y.W.C.A. Evidently she went up to Suiyuan[6] for the summer and while she was there the Japanese started up their monkey tricks. She was by herself and didn't understand or speak Chinese. In Tatung she knew a Chinese official and he heard that the general up there was sending his wife and family south on a motor truck by night. The official wangled a place for her on the truck and she got out to Taiyuan that way. Of course there are no foreigners left in Taiyuan now, but she managed to get on to the railway junction, Shihchiachung. There she stayed in the Railway Hotel quite close to the station. She had a letter of introduction to someone in the British-American Tobacco Co. and though again all foreigners had gone, a young English-speaking Chinese advised her to move from the hotel to the B.A.T. compound. Two days later while she was still waiting for a train south the station was bombed and the hotel where she had been staying collapsed. You can imagine the nervous highly-strung condition she is in. She is going on to Hongkong, but all her money and clothes are in Peiping and I don't think she has the price of a fare back to Manila. Tonight I sat next to an old lady who has just come down from Kalgan. It has taken her about ten days to make the trip and I bet she could tell some tales if she would. I asked the young American how she got on for food and she said, 'Fortunately you can always get hardboiled eggs in China.'

The trains leave for Hongkong every Monday, Wednesday and Friday and they are all crowded every time. Most of the missions are evacuating anyone due for furlough this year or next and any old or sick people. In places which are likely sooner or later to be the scene of fighting the women with children are leaving and men and single women are staying. . . .

Much love to you all,
Nessie

The International Red Cross to which Nessie refers was not the organisation based in Geneva. It was formed by a group of missionaries and diplomats in central China with Hankow as its headquarters to ensure that supplies sent from friendly countries were distributed for the relief of wounded Nationalist soldiers and civilians.

In a letter to the YWCA of New Zealand general secretary on 12 October 1937 Nessie wrote:

I am enclosing a general letter. . . . I have sent a copy of it by air mail to my sister [Catherine] in Wellington, hoping she would get it into the 'Evening Post'. I told her to pass it on to you if she could not do anything with it.

CHINESE SCENE: DEEPLY-STAINED LAND.
Y.W.C.A. OFFICER'S LETTER
'WHEN WILL IT ALL END?'

Writing from Hankow on October 10, Miss A. M. Moncrieff, M.A., representative of the New Zealand Y.W.C.A. in China, presents a striking pen picture of the feeling of tension existing in China and the destruction and suffering that have arisen from the activities of the Japanese there. Miss Moncrieff formerly spent five years in Peking and also travelled in New Zealand for several years for the New Zealand Student Christian Movement. Miss Moncrieff writes that she was out of Shanghai, on holiday in Kuling, when the 'storm' broke, and was not able to get back. She was cut off from news of Shanghai friends and from all financial resources for about three weeks, and had to travel to Hankow under refugee conditions. Apart from this and from having to face the autumn with nothing but the very lightest summer clothes and, with the knowledge that many of her possessions were in the fighting zone in Shanghai, she had not had to suffer any hardship. No place in China was absolutely safe, but Hankow was comparatively safe and had not had to endure the bombing that Nanking, Canton, Taiyuan and many other places had experienced. Although, says Miss Moncrieff, she is not in the least resigned to being in Hankow and feels that she is needed in Shanghai the National Committee and staff see the wisdom of keeping some national secretaries in the field, hence the reason for her being at Hankow.

UNCERTAINTY AND INSECURITY.

'I have to admit that life is not easy even here in Hankow,' Miss Moncrieff continues. 'My imagination does not help me to picture what it is like in Shanghai! There is a certain nervous tension, a sense of something awful hanging over one, and sometimes an insane desire that what is going to happen, whatever it may be, will happen quickly. The newspapers are a daily reminder of the appalling things that are happening all over the country. It is impossible to speculate what the outcome of the war will be, and no one would care to bet on when it will end. I suppose it takes time to get accustomed to living with uncertainty and insecurity. I find I do not like air raids. It is difficult to believe that humans are deliberately bringing death to other humans. A doctor asked the other day what I thought occupied the minds of bombers as they approached a defenceless city to drop bombs on it. The planes which bombed Hankow and Hanyang were over the cities at most fifteen minutes, and in that time they injured over a thousand people, all non-combatants. Of these, between three and four hundred were killed or died of their injuries. The objective of the attack was presumably the arsenal at Hanyang, but the most congested areas of Hanyang and of the native city of Hankow suffered terribly. There is a fairly large river, the Han, flowing into the Yangtze between these two cities so it does not say much for the aim of the Japanese that Hankow was hit. Whole blocks of buildings were destroyed, and most of the victims were women and children, as the men were still away at work in other parts of the cities. I mention these facts because I read in the Central China Post the other day a report that the Japanese Chamber of Commerce in Sydney had cabled the Chamber of Commerce in Wellington stating that reports of a Japanese bombing in China were 'false propaganda of the Chinese Government'. That is not so. The Chinese Government has no need to indulge in any campaign of propaganda. The facts themselves are hideous enough to beggar description.'

DETERMINED CHINESE.

'I know from my own experience here that newspaper accounts do not do justice to the terrible scenes that follow an air raid. In many cases there has been no object of military importance in the neighbourhood where the bombs have fallen. Hospitals, refugee trains, and camps, congested residential areas and educational institutions have suffered most heavily. I cannot see how a train of lighters crowded with refugees being towed up the Soochow Creek away from Shanghai could be mistaken for anything else. It is hard to believe that the bombing of non-combatants is deliberate and yet all the evidence points that way. The only reason one can see behind such action is a desire to terrorise the Chinese and break their morale. The bombings are having the opposite effect. The more ghastly the outrages, the more determined are the Chinese to resist to the limit even though "the land is stained with the blood of our people". And believe me, this is no empty phrase. The land is already deeply stained.'

DISCONTENT IN JAPAN.

'What one hopes for of course is that the Western Powers will apply sanctions against Japan as a protest against the savage and brutal methods that are being used. War has not been declared, diplomatic relations have not been broken off, and yet Japanese planes are free to wander over China where they will and reduce cities to a shambles and non-combatants to groaning masses of mutilated humanity. Turned back from Nanking, they bomb Wuhu, turned back from Hankow, they bomb Nanchang. The September number of "Current History" states that the check on Japan will come, not from China, nor from the Western Powers, but from within Japan due to the cost of war and the adverse balance of trade. There are already signs of a growing discontent in Japan. The conflict between military and industrial interests is an old and bitter one. This war is in itself a proof that for the time being the military point of view is in the ascendancy.

The end of the war is not yet in view; but the cost to Japan is indicated by the fact that already forty of the Mitsubishi factories have had to close down because of lack of raw material and that trade contracts to the value of 7,000,000 yen have been cancelled by the Dutch East Indies. Moreover, the term of service for Japanese soldiers has been extended, which leaves one to suppose that even with conscription in force Japan is finding it difficult to provide the manpower for almost 300 miles of front line. If the brake on the ruthless aggression of Japan can be an economic one, so much the better.'

IN HANKOW.

'The situation in Hankow is an interesting one. You will have read in the papers of the landing of Japanese marines in the concession here late in July. On August 3, after a period of intense military activity in the Japanese concession, all Japanese citizens were evacuated. One thousand marines, who had been guarding the concession, embarked on gunboats and sailed down the river, taking all their military equipment with them. Before they left the Japanese Consul-General requested the Hankow municipal authorities to take over the protection of the Japanese concession. The Japanese idea was not to restore it to China but to reoccupy it when their "punitive expedition" to "defend Japanese life and property" was at an end. Meantime, the Chinese undertook to protect this section of Japanese property. As soon as the Japanese marines left, fifty Chinese police marched into the concession and took their places on point duty. The concession, 32 acres in extent, is now a deserted city. All gates and doors are locked, barred, and sealed, all windows shuttered, and the streets uncannily silent. The first work of the police was to raid opium dens and workshops for the making of counterfeit money, establishments which they had known for a long time existed in the Japanese concession but which were carried on under Japanese surveillance in a part of the city that Chinese police were forbidden to enter. Underground passages, secret cupboards, and storerooms were found full of counterfeit money and stores of opium. Counterfeiters and opium dealers had all fled, but their stocks and equipment were confiscated. The opium trade here is dead since the Japanese left! Only once have the Japanese revisited Hankow. They came in bombing planes. In contrast to the peace and security of the Chinese-guarded Japanese concession in the eastern section of the city is the mass of debris from destroyed Chinese homes in the western section. Japanese houses stand empty in the east and in the west homeless Chinese refugees gaze bewildered at the ashes of what once were their homes. Hospital supplies are strained to the limit in the west, Japanese hospitals stand silent in the east, their stores of essential drugs, now so badly needed, untouched. A more telling contrast could not well be imagined.

On the one hand the utmost restraint, on the other wanton destruction of life and property. Even after the raid there was no attempt on the part of the Chinese to retaliate by looting and firing Japanese property. In Shanghai thousands of dollars' worth of iron has been seized from the little metal shops of Hongkew. In Hankow stocks of food and other essentials remain untouched in Japanese stores and godowns.'

TRADE AT A STANDSTILL.

'Trade in the Yangtze Valley is almost at a standstill. Stocks of imported goods are very low and already some of the provision stores which have dealt only in foreign foodstuffs have closed down. Butter was unobtainable for a while. A little is now coming in by air from Hongkong. In Hongkong it is 80 cents a pound. Here it is 20 dollars 50 cents (about 3s 2d). Klim,[7] once 2 dollars 60 cents a tin, is now 4 dollars owing to the extra cost and risk of freightage from Hong Kong. Coffee and sugar are almost unobtainable. Cereals, except for Chinese puffed rice, are out of stock, and tinned milk is an expensive memory. A few commodities are coming out of Shanghai by motor-truck to Soochow, train to Chinkiang or Nanking, and river boat to Hankow. Second-class mail which for a long time was not accepted by the Post Office is also beginning to trickle through. There is still no parcel post except for essential drugs and other necessities. After the last air raid the hospitals were so busy that another 50 patients would have exhausted supplies of linen and dressings. There is no supply of ether or chloroform in the whole of Central China and with one hundred cases of cholera among the wounded soldiers brought in from Nanking, the Hankow Health Department has sufficient serum for 2000 injections.' Miss Moncrieff refers to the setting up of an International Red Cross committee for Central China and the appeals for medical supplies that have been made to other countries. Some hospitals have already had to close down because of lack of supplies. Miss Moncrieff proceeds, 'Some, near the fighting zone, are crowded with wounded soldiers and sick refugees. Mat sheds have been put up in hospital compounds and resources are severely strained. The Red Cross committee is attempting to co-ordinate the work that is being done by Chinese and foreign organisations to produce a supply of bedding, linen, pyjamas, dressings, and bandages for use in the hospitals of Central China especially in these three Wuhan cities (Hankow, Wuchang, and Hanyang) which are having to house thousands of wounded from the Shanghai area.'

UNITY AT A PRICE?

'I marvel at the spirit of the Chinese which can endure so calmly the ravages of a war that is destroying much of the fine, constructive work of the last ten years. The stately Ming buildings of the Civic Centre at Shanghai are damaged

> beyond repair. The Jukong wharf, one of the finest in the East, and opened only a few months ago, is gone. The modern buildings of the Health Administration Service in Nanking and the model Central Hospital are unusable. Nankai University in Tientsin, Tung Chi University in Shanghai, and many other schools and colleges have been completely destroyed, innumerable Chinese factories and industrial plants have been bombed and gutted by fire. What the Chinese say is, "When we have got rid of the Japanese we can rebuild." Out of this terrible conflict has come a unity that China has not known for a long time. Communist, Fascist, Conservative, and Liberal, all have rallied to the service of China and put themselves under the orders of Chiang Kai-shek. Unity, yes, but at what a price!'[8]

The March edition of *The New Zealand Girl* had an article from Nessie under the title 'From Friends Abroad', dated 29 November 1937:

> Nothing could have looked more unpromising than godown [warehouse] No 4 lent by the Arnold Trading Co, a British firm in Hankow, for the storing of reserve supplies of the International Red Cross Committee for Central China when Dr. J. L. Maxwell, the General Secretary, introduced me to it.
>
> That was over two months ago and now everything is in full swing. The godown is no longer empty. Every day supplies come in and supplies go out. In one corner there is a huge pile of straw given by the Farmer's Co-operative Assn for stuffing pillows and mattresses. Close by are bales of absorbent cotton and surgical gauze. Our cupboards are full of sheets, pillow cases, bandages, slings and hospital suits which overflow on to temporary shelves made by stacking trestle beds one on top of the other. One end of the godown is piled with splints of every size and description from the big Thomas leg splints to two and a half inch finger splints. Some have already been padded by the working parties of women who have been steadily at work since the beginning of the war. Piles of crutches bring to mind the amputations that are often so necessary. Five first-aid stretchers were among the last lot of things to come in. Tetanus anti-toxin, unprocurable for so long, is stored away in a dark corner alongside cholera vaccine which will alas! be so necessary next spring. There is no difficulty in finding 'chill room' for these. The godown is like a vault. Bales of Chinese quilts, padded with cotton, are piled high ready to go out to up-country hospitals. Near them are several hundred padded suits of clothes for convalescent soldiers.
>
> The shelves of drugs are by far the most interesting. They are arranged in alphabetical order regardless of whether they are tinctures, acids, crystals or what not. Opening up a consignment of drugs has its excitements. Sometimes they are delivered before the invoice arrives and a list has to be made as we go along. A tin of asprin tablets has no indication of the number inside. A case contains a tin of

Interior of the godown (warehouse) of the Arnold Trading Company, Hankow, November 1937, when used by the International Red Cross Committee for Central China as their depot for receiving and despatching medical supplies for the relief of wounded soldiers and refugees in the Sino–Japanese war.

Top: Cases waiting to be unpacked, sorted medicines on the shelves. Note stamped-on crate in the centre, 'FROM THE LORD MAYOR OF LONDON'S FUND FOR THE RELIEF OF DISTRESS IN CHINA.' Moncrieff family collection

Bottom: Drums of liquids, and splints in background. Moncrieff family collection

cod liver oil and another of castor oil and neither is labelled, a tin has two labels, one Lysol and one castor oil. Something has leaked on to the carbolic acid label and the amount has been obliterated. Several hundred ampoules of adrenalin solution or digitalin packed in cotton wool have to be counted. The whole thing has to be valued for the insurance firm and for the Red Cross accountants.

Keeping the records for these supplies is rather like keeping accounts, though one is handling 'things' not cash. Everything has to be entered on filing cards and I often wonder when the final day of accounting comes, whether the stock will really tally with the records. Once a week a complete list of everything in the godown down to the last asprin tablet and the last cotton swab has to be sent in to the General Office so all the records have to be kept up to date.

Life is certainly very full and interesting, a trifle too full at times. There are often times of discouragement and sometimes I feel apprehensive about the future but always I am immeasurably glad that I am here and able to take my share of the responsibility and work. It is marvellous too, to know that there is so much sympathy and support among New Zealand friends. The situation needs the thought and prayers of all peace-loving people.[9]

Letter to Ethel Law from Hankow, 4 December 1937.

Ethel Law had been general secretary of the YWCA of New Zealand from 1927–1930 and had been deeply involved with Nessie's training and departure for China. She and Nessie were good friends; both were ex-pupils of Wellington Girls' College, members of the SCM, MA graduates of Victoria University College and then teachers. Ethel had recently returned from six years with the YWCA of Canada to resume her former position as general secretary, which she held until 1947:

Dear Ethel,

. . . Hankow is now a city of refugees. A newspaper report said that its population had been increased by 300,000 in one week. The crowds on the streets make that figure seem a low estimate. People are still pouring in from down river ports and boats come in with loads of four and five and six thousand passengers. The refugee problem is becoming serious and before very long I feel that the Y.W.C.A. will be planning a camp of some kind for women and girls.

Last week came a telegram from Shanghai saying that four of our national secretaries had left for Hankow via Hongkong. We are to open a temporary office here as communications between Shanghai and the rest of China are exceedingly difficult. Letters are now coming to us by boat to Hongkong and air to Hankow. For a few days even radio and telegraph were not functioning. Now they are all under Japanese censorship.

Our feelings about the arrival of more national secretaries in this area were very mixed. It will be great to see them and get news, but it is unwise I think, for anyone who need not come, to come to Hankow at present. The situation here is a very difficult one and the hopeless overcrowding is a source of danger. We have written to the secretaries in Hongkong describing the situation here, because we felt it would be awful to let them arrive in Hankow without knowing anything about the general conditions. With the enormous crowds here there would be no possibility of an evacuation in the event of a panic. The boats that go up the river are very much smaller than those that come up here from Nanking and are already booked up to January. In the evacuation of Nanking the government commandeered the railways and no one was allowed to leave on them except troops and government officials. The same thing would happen again if Hankow were to be threatened. Everyone in Hankow except a very few would have to remain here and face whatever comes. Personally I would much rather stay here than attempt to travel under refugee conditions. Not long ago the British Consul-general asked for the day and night phone numbers of all British subjects. I imagine that means that an effort would be made to evacuate us in case of danger. It would be very difficult to make up one's mind to go leaving the Chinese staff behind to face the worst. I do not want to have to make that decision.

For a time I have felt very discouraged. There were signs the morale of the Chinese troops was not what it had been and I believe the evacuation of Nanking was carried out so suddenly because a very critical situation had developed during the retreat from Shanghai. The Chinese air force was almost completely demolished during the retreat from Shanghai and the constant bombing of the Japanese was enough to discourage the bravest. However more planes have come in from Russia and things are much better all round. I can tell you that even 'neutrals' appreciate the heavier droning of the new Russian bombers that we are now listening to every day. We felt that if the Kiangyin Forts[10] fell and the boom across the river was broken the Japanese might be up here in a few days. However the Kiangyin Forts are still in Chinese hands and the boom is still intact.

Another boom has been thrown across the river at Chinkiang and a third has been prepared near Kiukiang. Even if the Japanese cleared the river I feel it would be poor strategy to send their ships up here unless they could be supported by forces on land. The Chinese could place a boom behind them and cut them off from supplies. With the river getting lower every day it's difficult to get any but very small gun boats up as far as this. It looks as though we are not in any danger of Japanese bombardment, except from air. However it is not a situation one can bet on.

There are however two other factors in the situation that are rather serious. Thousands of wounded soldiers are being brought up to this area and no provision has so far been made for discharging them. They are not disarmed when they are wounded and when convalescent are not sent home or drafted back into the army. No money is so far available for them and they could become a very serious menace to the peace of the city. We do not have here the efficient police force of the Settlement in Shanghai though for ordinary things no criticism can be made of the police force.

If the numbers of refugees continue to increase and no provision is made for the needy there may be serious rioting. Many people have left Nanking with only the price of their boat fare. Moreover the strain on the food supply is bound to be felt before so very long. . . .

Nessie continues on a new page:

Dec.6th

Kiangyin Forts are already in Japanese hands and though the boom is not yet broken it looks a matter of time only. The local Air Defence Headquarters has issued a proclamation 'advising Chinese civilians whose professions do not warrant their continued presence in the city, to evacuate to the surrounding districts or ports along the Yangtze Valley.' This is, I gather, not because of immediate occupation of Hankow by Japanese, but because with the terrific increase in population there would be a corresponding loss of life in air raids. I hope some of the folk staying in our Hostel will move on and make room for others.

Yesterday I went down to the A.P.C. [Asia Pacific Cargo] installations to see some friends. The installation is about six miles from here down the dyke road. I was tremendously interested to see all the activities down there. The trains that have come from Nanking, or rather from Pukow on the north bank of the river opposite Nanking, seem to be lined up waiting to discharge their cargo. There are almost miles of trucks piled with every conceivable thing. I saw motor cycles and hundreds of bicycles, and armoured cars and camouflaged trucks, cases of Shell motor spirit, cases of ammunition, trucks of machinery of one kind and another, furniture, hundreds of iron beds with folding legs, and enough stuff piled alongside the road to make motor traffic almost impossible. The dyke has been cut in two places and light trucks run down to the river's edge. Freight and rolling stock are still being taken across the river to the south side. I have no idea what it all means or where it is all going. It certainly gave me the sense of a country at war more than even the air raids have done. Some of the carriages are Blue Express from the Tsinpu line and had no window glass left. They may have been on the Blue Express train that was bombed some time ago.

Yours affectionately,

Nessie

Letter to Ethel Law from Hankow, 12 December 1937:

Dear Ethel,

The situation has not changed in any essentials since last time I wrote. Things if anything are a little more tense here. The garrison commander has placed the Wuhan cities (Wuchang, Hankow and Hanyang) under martial law and there are hoardings up carrying information of what conditions are to be enforced.

The Battle of Nanking has begun in real earnest. Civilians are massed as far as is possible in a Safety Zone from which the Chinese have removed all military supplies, guns and other defence works but which the Japanese have declined to recognise. Chiang Kai-Shek and Madame have left Nanking and are presumably here in Hankow, but there is nothing in the papers as to their whereabouts. Their apartment is on the Bund just in front of the Lutheran Building and we have all been interested in the construction of an underground shelter in the yard. It is said to have cost $20,000.00.

The British Consul has issued a notice of the scheme for concentration of British subjects in danger. There is, of course, no immediate danger, but they are prepared in case. The points of concentration are the A.P.C. Building and the Hongkong and Shanghai Bank. We have been advised to buy beds and have them stored at the Navy Canteen in case the period of concentration is a long one. I have bought a camp stretcher but it is stored in my room and I do not intend to go to a concentration point unless the Chinese Defence authorities ask all foreigners to leave, as they did in Nanking. If the Lutheran Home were closed I do not know where I could live but I suppose that if things got really serious as that there would be room at the Y.W.C.A. because people would move on from there.

On Friday a special train left for Canton with over a hundred foreigners on board. I hear another one is to leave next Friday. There has been no suggestion from the Consulate that anyone should evacuate, but naturally women with children are getting out if they can. I am glad that some are going. It leaves the rest of us a little more space to swing the proverbial cat. . . .

I have just come up from supper and Dr. Maxwell has brought us the very disconcerting news that the Japanese have fired on the HMS 'Ladybird' and the HMS 'Bee' at a point between Nanking and Wuhu. The two gun boats returned fire and one officer was killed. This is deliberate provocation and terribly serious. I feel it cannot mean anything but war with Britain. The general interpretation of these attacks on British boats is that Japan realises she can not get out of the war with China without considerable loss of face and she thinks that if she can provoke other nations and make a world war of it she can save herself. I imagine she thinks that Italy and Germany are solidly behind her and that she can afford to challenge Great Britain.

Oh Ethel, I cannot bear the thought of this war going further. Even at this distance I have seen enough of the suffering and misery and panic and all the other things that war does to people. What is going to be the end of it all? How can war be prevented when some nations are keen on fighting? . . .

My love to you,
Nessie

Letter to Eleanor Anderson from Hankow, 17 December 1937.

Eleanor Anderson of Chengtu was, as Eleanor MacNeil of Australia, Nessie's predecessor in China from 1915–1926. Although now married to a missionary doctor, Eleanor continued to work for the YWCA of China in Chengtu, where they were stationed and which lay outside the reach of Japanese occupation:

My dear Eleanor,

. . . It is a funny business sitting around here waiting for the blow to fall. When and how is of course a matter for speculation. The papers have lulled with a false sense of security by telling us that Canton would be the next point of attack. This morning's paper says Hankow is in for it next. It makes all decisions difficult. For instance there is no reason why we should leave Hankow at the present minute and yet we know if a general evacuation was attempted when attack became imminent there would be no way of getting out. Communication and transport are much too inadequate for the swollen population of these three cities. I don't mind myself for one scrap. I'd be peeved to go if anyone told me to go because I would enjoy waving a British flag, in bad repute though it is, over the Y.W.C.A. if the Japanese came. But I cannot bear the thought of these young national secretaries being caught here. Privately I think there is far more danger from convalescent soldiers and retreating Chinese forces than there is from the Japanese. We have tens of thousands of the former already and no one seems responsible. There were some ugly incidents a while ago before martial law was established and there is a general expectation of serious looting if the Japanese do come upon us.

Meantime a committee called by the Chamber of Commerce here are organising a 'guaranteed' train to take several hundred women and children through to Hongkong. I think everyone who hasn't a job ought to go. For one thing it will ease up the food shortage. The British consul has issued instructions for concentration if a crisis arises and we have been invited to send camp stretchers in to the Naval Canteen ahead of time. I don't see myself concentrating if it means leaving this national group to face the situation but I am making no stupid declarations about it because there are circumstances in which it might be better for foreigners to concentrate.

Love to you both.

Nessie

Letter to Ethel Law from Hankow, 19 December 1937:

My dear Ethel,

. . . I hope to remain here to serve the various groups as long as it's possible and then if the Japanese take us I may be able to wave a British flag over the Y.W.C.A. and act as a buffer. At the same time I have told the girls that if the British Consul orders an evacuation I will have to go. There is no choice, according to reports that is, for a British subject. I must find out for certain about that. The Lutheran Home where I am staying is just on the edge of the French Concession and an attempt is being made to bring it within the French protected area in case of trouble. This is a matter that has yet to be discussed with the Chinese and French authorities and I have not heard the results of the discussion yet.

Attempts to run a 'guaranteed' train through to Honkong have failed. With the prospect of fighting around Canton the Chinese can't guarantee it and I understand the Japanese won't. On the strength of that the H.M.S. 'Capetown' left with less than twenty-four hours' notice for Shanghai taking about 50 British women and children as passengers. It is probable that 'Woosung', a Butterfield and Swire boat, will run through to Shanghai this week with a party of evacuees on board. It can take up to five hundred, but I do not know how many are going. The river is getting so low now that it is doubtful if the 'Capetown' will get through. She has a draft of seventeen feet. Last night rumours were rife that she had gone aground, but there is no word so far of any mishap. It remains to be seen whether she will be fired on by the Japanese.

People think we might be alright for another month or so, but if Canton is taken I may not be able to get word through to you. Mail goes by air from Chengtu to Yunnan and down the French railway through Indo-China. . . .

We were very disappointed that Nanking fell so easily but I really believe that Chiang Kai-Shek knows what he is about. The specialty of the Chinese Army is guerilla warfare and that is difficult on the plains. If the Japanese can be lured into more difficult country it will be much more expensive for them in both ammunition and money. They cannot use the trucks and tanks which put the Chinese at such a disadvantage. Also foreign military opinion seems to be that Nanking is impossible to hold from a military point of view and Chiang was right to withdraw his troops while there was still a way out. They would all have been sacrificed if he had continued to resist. I hope there is truth in that. General Chiang is a great strategist and he ought to know his China, he has fought over it sufficiently.

At the beginning of the week all the Italian aviation instructors and engineers in charge of assembling aeroplanes were withdrawn and I heard yesterday that all consular officials all over the country have been ordered out by the end of the month. I do hope that is not true and yet I fear it is. It looks as though Italy is to assist the Japanese as she assisted Franco in Spain. Some say that she is already assisting, but I cannot vouch for the truth of that.

Letters are taking three weeks to come by ordinary mail from Shanghai and I suppose second-class mail will take much longer. I do miss foreign papers and periodicals. We don't even get Shanghai papers now and anyway they are useless as they are so thoroughly censored by the Japanese.

Greetings to staff and committee members.

Love,

Nessie

Letter to Ethel Law from Hankow, 29 December 1937:

My dear Ethel,

The last international train leaves tomorrow and we know we are in for it and I am trying to get mail out as far as that by a friend who is travelling on it. It will save a little in postage. The new boom in the river prevented the 'Woosung' from going down to Shanghai and a train load of 264 people went down last Thursday. Almost as large a group is leaving to-morrow. We have had notices that this will be the last train, so we realise we are in for it whatever comes. Of course there will be ordinary Chinese trains, but booking on them are very heavy and they are not 'guaranteed' against Japanese bombs as the international trains are supposed to be. The worst part of the business is not the actual danger we may or may not be in but the suspense of not knowing what is going to happen or when it will happen. It is a bit like being under a death sentence without the faintest idea of when the execution is to take place. . . .

The most horrible reports of what has taken place in Nanking since the Japanese occupation are beginning to get through. Evidently a large part of the J. army ran completely amok and there was looting, massacre and rape on a colossal scale. I will enclose a newspaper cutting which is one of our sources of information. There have been other sources and the fact that the League of Nations and other groups are trying to make investigations shows it is no fairy tale. Wounded soldiers and hospital attendants have been amongst those massacred and even the Safety Zone was entered for looting etc. It destroys once and for all any notion we might have had that the Japanese Army could maintain control of a situation or guarantee order.

Affectionately,

Nessie

5
Hankow and the Godown
January–March 1938

Nessie continued her work with the International Red Cross in Hankow until the end of March 1938, when she was called upon to devote herself full-time to YWCA affairs and on occasion travel to other centres.

Of the letters Nessie wrote to her close friend Eva Skinner in Dunedin, only those written in 1938 and 1939 survive, although she had written to Eva from 1930. Like Nessie, Eva had been a student at Wellington Girls' College, though eleven years ahead of her. Eva served several terms on the board of the Dunedin YWCA. She and Nessie had great rapport, as is obvious from the affectionate tone of the correspondence.

Letter to Eva Skinner from Hankow, 2 January 1938:

> Dear Eva, I am not in the least in a letter writing mood and my typewriter is not behaving properly. There is something wrong with the ribbon. It is a Remington ribbon in a Royal machine and there seems to be an incompatibility that is ruining my spelling. I am not really the least in the mood for anything. I slept from 1.p.m. to 4.p.m. and it was altogether too long. Not even two cups of coffee have restored my sprightly intelligence. There were very few in to afternoon coffee this afternoon. I sat at the table with an Austrian doctor who is sent here by the League of Nations and is here for a day or two before returning to the wilds of Hunan; a member of the professorial staff of Nanking University who is endeavouring to find a passage to take him up to Chengtu where the University is going as fast as it can to find boats to take it, and a Tibetan who is the adopted son of a French woman explorer and who is returning to Tibet via Chengtu as soon as he can get a ride up the river. He by the way is a Living Buddha. What do you think of that for an afternoon tea party? . . .
>
> Letters are beginning to leak through from Nanking and Wuhu. I don't know how, but they all tell of atrocities that are absolutely unbelievable. Jewellery and girls are what the Japanese want and I could wish that we had all our young secretaries well and truly out of this section of the country.
>
> I don't see how the Japanese can get up here for another month or so at the

earliest and I don't really think they want to come as they will be much more at the mercy of the Chinese forces when they are as far inland as this. From a military point of view it would just be plain silly. The Chinese have decided that they will fall back on guerilla warfare which is really their special line and which is peculiarly irritating to the Japanese. All the students are clamouring to be taught guerilla methods. The ex-communists, the eighth route army[1] have had a great deal of success with guerilla warfare and of course it is specially suited to mountainous country.

The burning of the Japanese property in Tsingtao was done, I think, to create a diversion when it seemed that the Japanese would concentrate on Canton and it has been successful. There is a great deal of fighting going on up there. The fate of Shantung is probably sealed, at least for the meantime. The awful thing is that there is no retreat from Shantung if the Japanese hold the railway as they are trying to do. I do not know how far north they have gone from Nanking but it looks as though they are trying very hard to get south from Tsinan to link up with their forces moving north from Nanking. They may succeed, but I do not think that they will strangle the country as much as seizing Canton would do.

Shanghai National Office has decided to send two secretaries round here. I think they are crazy. This decision has been made without waiting for our letters telling them what the situation is like. It is so utterly silly to try and make too many plans when the situation is so very critical. I am completely out of patience with the whole gang. I suppose my nerves are beginning to feel the strain too or I would take things more philosophically. But it is idiocy to pile people up here when there is no way out in case of an emergency. This is a death trap for the Chinese and since we know what happened at Nanking we have no right to be sending Chinese into it.

I am going to have a busy time at the godown next week, or rather this week. 186 cases of drugs have arrived in Wuchang and are probably being delivered to-day. Think of the task of opening them and dividing them up into five pound and seven pound packets. I am going to have three men to help me I think. Now that the schools and colleges have closed for the winter vacation there are a number of people who like a job of work. I need the assistance badly. The thought of all those cases has been keeping me awake at night.

There are 120 more on the way and all the hospitals from all over the country will be sending in orders for drugs that will have to be filled before we have finished unpacking. Packing is such slow work. The coolies are stupid at it and I have to supervise it very carefully especially when there are bottles of liquids. This is far more than a 2 hours a day job. It always has been, but it will be almost be a twenty four hour job for the next month. . . .

Lots of love. Write as often as you can. I do love letters. They take me out of this situation for a breather and that is the best kind of rest there is.

Nessie

Letter to Eva Skinner, handwritten from Hankow, 9 January 1938:

Well dearie, here's a letter by hand for a change. My typewriter is being overhauled. I am enclosing newspaper clippings of our two air raids last week. In the second raid I watched the 15 Japanese planes that flew over this way. None of the anti-aircraft shells seemed to go high enough. Eleanor Booth came into my room later in the day & showed me a jagged piece of a 3 inch shell that had fallen about three feet from her. Rather too narrow a squeak. She had no business to be outside at all. . . .

To-day is a perfectly beautiful blue sunny day and it is impossible to think of death & destruction; but this morning's paper brought the first news of what happened in Hangchow over Christmas. Three days & three nights of looting, wanton massacre & rape. Someone said the other day that the finished methods of the Japanese makes the looting of the Chinese bandits look like a clumsy bungle. One letter from a member of the American Church Mission in Wuhu said what the Japanese wanted most there was jewellery & women. They just shoot every one they see on the streets. I can't bear even to think about it. It will happen here too before so very long. The only thing that can save Hankow is interference by a third power. With feeling running as high as it is in America & in Great Britain I wonder how much longer those two countries can remain out of it. I hate to think of the devastation of another world war but really & truly what is the use of going on with anything if mad military machines like Japan are to be allowed to overrun the earth. . . .

Last week was hectically busy. We had to get equipment for a new hospital of 350 beds to a Red Cross train en route for Chengchow in less than 48 hours. It was terrific. There were altogether 86 cases, bales, bundles & what not. The military are preparing to make a 'strategic withdrawal' south of the Yellow River & that will mean falling back on Chengchow & perhaps further south. A Chinese military hospital in a cotton mill in Chengchow approached the International Red Cross field agent to see if he would take the hospital over. It is to be an annexe to the Baptist Mission Hospital there. Dr. McClure wrote off post haste for equipment & at the same time decided it was necessary to get a protection order of some kind from the Japanese command in case they occupied Chengchow. On Dec 30 he had a Chinese military escort up to the front lines & from there planned to make a dash across to the Japanese lines. He had no bullet proof jacket & expected to be gone five days & was to telegraph on his return to

Left: The Skinner family of 'Rustat', Dunedin, 1933. From left: Dr H D (Harry), Eva and Richard (Dick) Skinner. Skinner family collection

Chengchow. Nothing has come through as yet.

Meantime we packed up 1400 hundred sheets, 700 draw sheets, 700 pillow cases, 350 padded quilts and an equal number of pillows, mattress covers, towels, quilt covers, oil sheets and masses of bandages, dressings & swabs as well as an enormous number of splints, bed pans & so on & got them on to the train. I was simply exhausted next day but there was no rest because the 186 cases of drugs that were part of the Lord Mayor's fund were already in the godown & waiting to be unpacked. I now have four men helping me & every afternoon we measure out cwts., of asprin powder, bismuth, calcium lactate, barium sulphate, zinc oxide etc. into 1lb, 2lb or 5lb packages. All the cases that have to be opened up immediately are open & we have five huge drums still to deal with. Three are Lysol, one is Lanolin & another Izal. One hundred & twenty more cases are on their way up from Hgkg, but except for the drums of castor oil & one large mixed case, they don't have to be opened just yet. This week the orders will come into the godown & we shall be assembling drugs & packing them to be sent out to up-country hospitals. I see no let-up for weeks ahead.

Tsai Kuei & Lil Haass have wired through the American Consulate outlining a plan for them to fly here from Hongkong & then on by air to Szechuen & Yunnan. I have wired back approving the plan in general. Things are rather difficult because the Chinese staff who have just come round from Shanghai don't see the possibilities of the situation here & refuse to see how difficult transportation will be if there is the slightest flurry. We (Pearl & I) saw what happened when Nanking evacuated, but our attempts to be realistic about it are interpreted as a 'save your skin policy'. Some of the things that have been planned by the group as a whole are sheer lunacy, but the Chinese don't see it. For instance Pearl & Li Keng, another rural secretary, have to start out to-morrow morning at 4.a.m. to take a day's journey up the Han River & then about 16 miles overland through bandit country to investigate the possibilities of starting YWCA rural propaganda work out there. The American Consul does not want Pearl to go but does not actually forbid it as she expects to be back in a few days. If it seems to be a good spot to start such work Pearl & Li Keng will come back & then proceed to take a group of students back there with them & start work. This is all against Pearl's better judgment, but further protest from her or a flat refusal would be terribly misinterpreted.

I do wish we had a responsible committee of older Chinese women behind us here in Hankow. When Tsai Kuei & Lil come through I shall talk to them a blue streak. I don't believe in general paralysis because of attendant dangers, but such horrible things are happening all the time out in sections of the country like that. Please keep this under your hat. I shouldn't be criticising so freely but really

I'm losing patience. These people from Shanghai have been through so much there that they all need holidays before they can think straight. They did have the protection of the Settlement & they can't realise that there is no protection at all in these remote country districts. I am much more alarmed for the young Chinese girls than I am for Pearl, though I shall be most devoutly thankful to see her back safe & sound. I wish I could get all the Chinese National staff out of this section and safely up river. I have no desire to move myself & there will doubtless be no need, for foreigners do have a better chance unless America or Great Britain declare war & in that event, I believe J's armies would have to be withdrawn from the interior to meet the problem of defending their own country. I could wish that life had fewer problems.

Lots of love. I will be back some day but this war won't be over for a long, long time.

Nessie

Letter to Ethel Law, handwritten from Hankow, 9 January 1938:

My dear Ethel

. . . I seem to understand less & less the problem of suffering as I go along. I avoid thinking & turn to hard & exhausting work. I even try to avoid feeling – when I can. This sounds like an escape method but I could not keep sane if I let myself think too much. Five months of the most appalling & unnecessary slaughter & no end in sight.

We have had the first news today of what went on at Christmas in Hangchow. Three days & three nights of massacre, looting and rape. We know now that it is not the horrible result of soldiers getting out of hand but part of a deliberate programme of victory. This morning after Communion Service I went to breakfast with Miss Dexter of the American Church Mission here. We were trying to see a way though this situation but could not do it. One can only hope that out of this welter of destruction will come something finer than we even dare to dream. Meantime there is lots of work & for that I am truly thankful. The Red Cross godown has kept me particularly busy this week . . .

Last week we had two more air raids. This section of the city was not bombed, but there were fires on the air field both days & several planes destroyed. It is so long since the last serious raid that we had almost given up expecting them.

With love,

Nessie

Letter home from Hankow, 16 January 1938:

My dear Mother,

. . . Things are jogging along here. The godown keeps me fully occupied. Two hundred cases of drugs came in last week in two lots, but I have not done anything with them yet. This morning Dr. Maxwell had a telegram saying that 186 more cases were leaving Hongkong. With so many foreigners away from Hankow it is very difficult to get someone to give full time to the job helping me. I think the Red Cross is going to ask the Y.W.C.A. if they can spare me for full time work. I hope they will agree as it is too hard to be carrying two jobs like this. I really don't look as ancient as I do in the pictures I am enclosing. Don't you like the office Mr. Baker made me? I hope the snaps won't make the letters too heavy. It is difficult to send anything extra when letters have to go to the coast by air.

Tsai Kuei and Lil are to arrive Wednesday next and I imagine the question of moving our Branch office will come up for discussion again. It may be wiser to move to Chungking or Chengtu especially if it appears that the Japanese will attack Hankow. Don't get agitated about my being so far inland. There is an air service from Chungking to Hongkong and it only takes the best part of a day to fly down. I have always wanted to see the Yang Tzu rapids and maybe I will have the chance. Of course it has not even been discussed yet and even if the office moves it may be best for me to remain here. There are plenty of gun boats to look after the foreigners if the Japanese do come.

The Japanese are certainly beginning to pay us more attention. We had another air raid here last Tuesday. It was the first morning we had in our new National Committee office and by way of a house warming it was not so hot! The building is quite close to the Lutheran Building, only three blocks away, but not nearly so well built and the bombs shook us much more. Anti-aircraft guns were busy and as our office has a good deal of window space we moved into the corridor while the fun lasted. I had a few peeps out and saw about twelve of the planes flying in formation over the city. Some petrol on the air field went up in smoke but the building was too low for me to see the fires as I can from my bedroom window.

Yesterday morning I was awakened by the alarm at 6.50. It was pitch dark but I fumbled into my clothes and waited. We had breakfast and about 8.15 the urgent alarm went. I came up to my room and waited but the only planes up were the Chinese and then just before 9.a.m. the all clear sounded. I went along to the office and about 9.30 started down to the big Chinese street to visit the bank. I was almost at the bank when the alarm went again and I made a beeline back to the office. The Chinese street divides the Chinese city from the part of town where the foreign firms are and I felt safer in the office.

It was most interesting to be out on the streets. The foreign and ex-foreign concessions run in a narrow strip about five blocks wide along the river and behind them is the congested Chinese section. As I came along a street parallel with the river literally hundreds of Chinese were pouring out of the Chinese section down all the cross streets to the big godowns on the Bund where they are allowed to take shelter during raids. There were crowds and crowds of them and at every intersection the police were waving their arms wildly in an effort to stem the tide while motors could pass. It was most exciting. I got back in plenty of time and later in the morning the all clear sounded again.

What had happened was that fifty planes had been sighted heading for Wuhan, but somewhere down the river they divided into three groups. One made for Nanchang, one for Changsha and the third to various points north and north-west of Hankow. An important station up the line, Hsiaokan, about forty miles from here had twenty bombs unloaded on it.

I heard that the railway was damaged but the newspapers are not allowed to print reports of actual damage. At 11.30 I set out again and got my money safely in that time. By lunch time I was pretty tired. The excitement of raids even when they don't come is quite tiring. . . .

Lots of love to you all,

Nessie

Letter to Eva Skinner from Hankow, 23 January 1938:

Eva dear,

. . . Tsai Kuei and Lil Haass have arrived and we have had one morning discussing the affairs of the Y.W.C.A. and particularly the affairs of the Branch office. It seems possible that we shall move to Chungking, but the final decision will not be made for another week.

Pause while I gaze out the window at the Soviet Consulate ablaze. Dirty work I imagine. I wouldn't be a bit surprised if <u>Someone</u> had been paid by the Japanese to do it. It is just about true to their form. Pearl and I are going out to have a look see but she has to dress first so I am getting a few more lines down. We certainly live in exciting times. If it is not one thing it is another. I have had long interviews

Well that was some fire! The building is properly gutted and I don't think a thing can be saved. It is in the French concession so I suppose the Chinese cannot in any way be blamed for letting a fire like that break out.

As I started out to say I have had long interviews today. Two hours this morning with Tsai Kuei and two hours this afternoon with Lil. The Red Cross has written asking that I be allowed to give full time to them for the next two months, but I don't think it will be possible. It seems to me to be a very necessary job and I don't know who they will get to carry on in my place. I say I cannot possibly give it up without at least a month's notice, but I don't think the Y.W.C.A. will be willing to give me as long as that. I would like to hold it at least as long as the end of next month and then go up to Chungking with the Branch Office till the end of summer. Then of course I would like to spend my holiday with my cousins on Mount Omei[2] and after that come down to one of the coast cities where it is not safe for Chinese secretaries to be without a foreigner. As I said to Lil, I think our job will be chiefly in the occupied cities keeping things together and living in Association premises under foreign flags and letting the Chinese staff cope with the building of the Association Movement in the part of the China which is left unoccupied. Lil has a very clear head and she sees further than most of us into the future.

My heart turned clean over at some of the things she said and yet I know that there is every likelihood she is right. Maybe if this goes on long enough we shall develop a technique or an attitude that leaves us serene under the maximum of insecurity and uncertainty, but that time is not yet. It is easier at present to keep your eyes tight shut and live from day to day and that is colossally stupid too. Where is it all going to come out?

I read a letter today from a Ginling College staff member who has remained in Nanking all through the occupation and looting and massacre and rape. It is what she doesn't say that turns you cold. The letter was written on Jan 4th and 5th and even then the hideous conduct that began on December 15th was still going. I don't ever want to have to see Japanese again and how will I manage to live and work under the constant strain of their irritating inspections if I do go back to a coast city. Well, I don't have to look far ahead as that. I told Lil today that I didn't know if my disposition or my discretion would be up to that. . . .

Lots of love,
Nessie

Nessie's cousins were Jesse Moncrieff and his wife Virginia (Vee). They had gone from the USA to China in 1915 as missionaries with the American Baptist Foreign Mission Society, based in Chengtu, Szechuan, West China. Jesse and Nessie's fathers were brothers.

Letter home from Hankow, 30 January 1938:

My dear Mother,

The Japanese are getting peeved with Hankow because we have so many anti-aircraft guns placed around the city to fire at them when they bomb us. So they have threatened to bomb all the residential sections of the city as well as the air field unless the guns are removed. Did you ever hear of anything so ridiculous? Do

Top: Nessie in Hankow, on secondment from the YWCA to the International Red Cross Committee for Central China, working with a clerk in the office made for her in the godown. On the left are the shelves made from trestle tables. January 1938. Moncrieff family collection

Bottom: Another corner of the Hankow International Red Cross godown, with Chinese quilts padded with cotton needing to be packed. In the background are packed boxes of medicines yet to be despatched. January 1938. Moncrieff family collection

they suppose that the Chinese have no right to defend themselves from Japanese raids! We had another raid or so last week. It interferes with work when you are not allowed to go on the street. The favourite hour is about 9 or 9.30 a.m. and the alarm stops us from getting to the office. . . .

It wouldn't be so bad to have a glimpse of peaceful old NZ though how I shall ever manage to live again without the excitement of war, I don't know. Even the thought of going to Chungking makes me realise how dull it will be without the weekly air raids.

Lots of love,
Nessie

Letter to Eva Skinner from Hankow, 6 February 1938:

Dearie this is going to be a horribly dull letter. . . . Last night we went to a movie then to supper at the Navy Y [YMCA] and the late night has been too much for me. I am a silly fool. We should be over at the Navy Y now listening to an American Communist Miss Agnes Smedley lecture on conditions in Shansi. She has been with the 8th route army, the ex-communist group up there, and has the most interesting material. But I know I could not sit through anything this evening. I meant to get all sorts of letters, but have hardly done a thing. At the movies I met a young Chinese lad who was a student at the Customs College when I was in Peiping. He is in the customs service here, was evacuated from Chinkiang on the river below Nanking just in time. I made the mistake of asking him where his family is. He literally doesn't know. Father, stepmother, grandmother and sister have vanished into space and he doesn't know whether they fell into Japanese hands or not. Really the stories you hear when you ask a simple question these days.

There's a Dr. Bates, American professor of sociology at Nanking University who has stayed all through this beastly business. Just recently there has arrived in Hankow a copy of the daily letters he wrote to the Japanese embassy describing things he had himself seen or heard at first hand. I have not seen it myself yet because Dr. Kepler has had to take it away with him. I don't think I want to. It is ghastly beyond words. How that handful of foreigners in Nanking has lived through all the horrors of Japanese occupation I simply don't know. I think I would go insane under such conditions. And the Relief Committee in Shanghai has 700 tons of food to be sent into Nanking and the Japanese refuse to allow a permit. They are deliberately trying to starve the whole population to death. I think it is the most ghastly thing I have ever heard of. . . .

Lots of love
Nessie

Letter to Ethel Law from Hankow, 7 February 1938:

Dear Ethel,

. . . I am staggered when I think of the decades of reconstruction that will be necessary even after this war of destruction has ended and there seems at present no end to it. It has now very definitely entered its second phase and that is likely to last a long time. Guerilla methods are proving moderately successful and though perhaps no decisive victory can be won by guerilla warfare yet its effect on the Japanese morale is already marked. It means of course that the Japanese have to go on fighting subject to unexpected attack wherever they are weakest. Some people think that if the Chinese can keep it up long enough the Japanese will in the end find the strain of garrisoning what they already hold in China too great and will be forced to withdraw at least partially. That is what we should all like to believe but how far such a hope is based on fact and how far it is rationalisation we cannot tell.

Meantime wholesale massacre goes on unchecked, women, even if refugees, are raped by the hundred and the thousand and the most barefaced robbery in the shape of looting and removal of machinery from Chinese factories is carried on by the military command. I marvel continually at the spirit of the Chinese. Sometimes I wonder how our own Chinese secretaries manage to keep going and maintain any kind of courage in face of what is happening. They really are wonderful.

Warm greetings to the staff and committee,

Nessie

Letter home from Hankow, 13 February 1938:

My dear Mother,

I have just had your letter of Jan. 9th and hope you discovered long ago it was Hangchow and not Hankow that was so severely bombed early in January. We have never had a raid as severe as the one we had on Sept. 24th. We have them quite often, but lately they have been confining their attention to the air field and arsenal which are far away from this section of the city.

The last raid came in the afternoon and I was down in the godown. We had a marvellous view. The planes were so high that I could not see them but they were visible with glasses. Bombs were dropped the whole length of the air field and you could see plainly the row of smoke smudges marking their path. Fortunately nothing was hit on the air field although some white smoke later indicated that something went up, probably a mat shed nearby. Last time we had an alarm the planes did not come over here but visited Wuchang instead. The air field is well away from the city over there but evidently some villages were hit and villagers killed. I leaned out my window and listened to the noise of the bombs. The explosions were much louder than they are over here, but people say that it is often quite true a bomb at some distance sounds louder than one at relatively close quarters.

There is not the least likelihood of the New Zealand Association asking me to come home and if they did I would never hold up my head again. N.Z. would be forever disgraced. Western secretaries are badly needed especially in the places held, or likely to be held by the Japanese. In spite of many unpleasant incidents foreign flags are still respected a little more than the Chinese flag and if the worst occurred I would probably go and live in the Y.W.C.A. and wave a British flag over the institution.

The river is at present much too low for an attack from gun boats. Japan has already found it is not nearly as easy as they thought it would be to get round to Hankow by land. A little while ago there was an announcement in the papers by the Japanese military command stating they are not going to attack Hankow in the near future because their lines of communication would be much too easily attacked. That is true of course. If they take Hsuchow, which is the junction of the line from Tientsin to Nanking and the line that goes East and West, they might in time make their way along to Chengchow, which is on the Peiping–Hankow line and then south to Hankow; but they would only hold the line and at every point Chinese guerrillas forces could attack. That is what the 8th Route Army is doing farther north and only last night I heard that their skirmishing troops had captured five towns between Paoting and Shichiachung. Whether they can hold them remains to be seen but they captured a goodly amount of ammunition and machine guns and things. In one town, Tinghsien, the Japanese soldiers took shelter in the yamen, which is the magistrate's quarters. The Chinese surrounded the yamen and burnt it to the ground with all the Japanese in it. It sounds horrible but so often it has been the other way round. Thousands and thousands of Chinese have been burnt to death and buried alive and killed in other less humane ways.

Meantime life goes on here. According to figures in the newspaper the other day there are about 1300 foreigners in Hankow. About 400 are Russians who technically have no country. But the rest are British, American, German, French and so on. There are 195 registered Americans and I imagine at least that number of British. Most of the women have gone and there aren't many children about but there doesn't seem any likelihood of direct attack here in the immediate future. I met someone from Chengchow the other day who said that that city had not once been bombed and since every other city seemed to have suffered at one time or another they were beginning to feel left out and their feelings were hurt!

The other day I went to see the Panay film.[3] Has it been to New Zealand yet? I can hardly believe that there has been time for it to get back here, but it certainly was. It was the last film in an hour's news item of all of the war here, Shanghai, Nanking and so on. The film was excellently done and was most interesting especially the 'Panay' one but parts of the others were pretty horrible. As I said afterwards you cannot come away from news reels saying it is only a film. I don't believe all I hear about what is happening, but Dr. Kepler has letters written every day by Dr. Bates of the Nanking University staff to the Japanese Embassy describing only those things which he knew for a fact had happened on the university compound after the taking of Nanking. It is positively gruesome reading. I know Dr. Bates personally and he is not a man to exaggerate in any way. It will take centuries for the Japanese to live down the atrocities that their soldiers have committed under officers' orders.

Much love to you all,
Nessie

Letter to Eva Skinner from Hankow, 13 February 1938:

Eva dearie, I wish that letters would write themselves. There is so much I could yarn about and so little I can get on paper. We live here in stirring times and yet I feel that my letters are hopelessly dull and don't give any sort of picture of things as they really are. I really think I write a better letter when I write by hand, as my slow brain doesn't have to move so fast, but with airmail necessary for every letter I would be hopelessly overweight every letter I wrote.

I am one exhausted female today. We have had a World Peace Campaign here in Hankow with its culmination synchronising with the International Boycott Conference in London. It was well-planned and some of the processions and demonstrations were very good. The final huge effort was held out at the Chungshan Park not very far from the air field and people were no more than assembled when the air raid warning sounded. When the second alarm went they all took shelter in the dugouts and after the planes departed came out and then held their demonstrations with redoubled vigour. Think how the Japanese would have enjoyed a target of several thousands of Chinese youth.

Anyway last night the anti-aggression Dramatic Association of China put on four plays intended to depict what is happening and to stir up people to stronger resistance. The Wuhan Anti-aggression songsters sang some patriotic songs first of all. It was excellent singing and the conductor had done jolly good work with his group. The first play was the weakest and amateur of the lot; but the others were marvellously done. I thought the realism of the New York stage would take a lot of beating, but I never expected to see anything like the grim realism of last night's performance.

As I said before I feel positively exhausted today. Everything we saw on the stage is happening in this country all the time and to have it so vividly before our eyes was as much as I could bear. I leapt sky high every time anyone was shot and once when the lights went black out and the theatre was filled with the noise of bombs I really thought an air raid had overtaken us.

But the suffering of the people was worst of all. In one play a Chinese leader of volunteer troops is a prisoner and is required to disclose some information about the hiding place of his volunteers. His daughter, also a volunteer is taken and the father is afraid that under torture she may reveal the secrets. So he poisons her. The Japanese are furious and when Pa again refuses to tell anything he is shot dead. I thought the acting very good. The father at first refuses to recognise the girl and insists that his daughter is away in Shanghai at school. The girl does not understand her father's refusal to recognise her and the father sees that the Japanese do not believe him.

Another play is the story of a small farming family in Hopei. A Chinese traitor leads Japanese soldiers to the farmhouse and they shoot the old grandmother, the husband and the child and obviously have designs on the woman. I shall never forget her absolute agony of mind. She stood for a long time making practically no movement of any kind and the expression and the pose revealed everything that was in her mind. Later she pretends to be friendly to the soldiers and provides food and drink. They get drunk and sleep and she shoots the lot of them including the traitor. How's that for drama? It sounds rather like melodrama, but the Chinese do awfully good work on the stage and there's always a restraint and an artistic touch that prevents overdoing of the thing.

The last play was the most dramatic of all. It was partly symbolic. The first scene had two white-clad figures, one the spirit of International Peace and one the figure of Liberty. Between them was a map of China and over the top of the map appeared the head of a Japanese officer snarling like an animal. He came out and snarled at the two figures, tore the wings off one and blew out the torch of the other.

The next scene was the most gruesome of the whole lot. A Japanese firing squad was on one side of the stage and four Chinese prisoners, bound, on the other. The same snarling officer was in charge. He spoke not a word but continued his snarling with various degrees of ferocity. The first prisoner symbolised culture and his book which the officer pulled from his clothing was thrown to the ground and the first of the firing squad ordered to raise his gun. The second prisoner was the merchant and his abacus was spat on and thrown down and his money pocketed. The third was the artisan and his little hatchet was seized as was the sickle of the fourth – the farmer. The officer looked them over snarling all the time and then put them together and they made the Communist symbol. You should have heard him. It was terrible. The prisoners were shot, one by one and then a woman and child were dragged in. The child was bayoneted with the most appalling laughter and the woman dragged off by the officer. Later she rushes back to get her child and is dragged off again by the firing squad.

It was ghastly, positively ghastly. But it is no use being sentimental at present and no one can do anything at all to stop them. Dr. Bates's letters to the Japanese Embassy telling what he knew took place on the Nanking University Compound every day, a refugee zone by the way, are appalling reading. I don't suppose I would have gone to see the plays if I had realised what I was going to have to sit through, but there were times when my mind was completely absorbed by the artistry of the thing. Things that on a western stage could not help being crude and melodramatic and overdone were sheer tragedy and suffering and heart break. I can't see what it is in the Chinese technique that saves the situation from being crude and unrestrained. I think perhaps it is in the simplicity and naturalness of the acting, but that is not the whole of the secret.

The final scene showed China – a procession of students, soldiers, farmers, etc, all mixed up together restoring the wings to peace and the torch to liberty. One scene in it, which was set on top of the godown in Shanghai where the doomed battalion kept the Japanese off for several days, was most striking and when the Chinese girl guide arrived by boat on the river right under Japanese lines and presented a flag to the Commander the whole audience rose to its feet and cheered. Really this is an interesting country to be living in. To our way of thinking the Chinese act off the stage too, but there is a tremendous reality in their unity and nationalism these days. Behind it all is terrific suffering, but they have hope and a marvellous spirit in spite of everything. In about two years' time I'll be telling you all about this, but I often wonder what lies between then and now and how long both Japan and China can stand the strain of this war.

Dr. Kepler read a letter at tea time today copied from a Japanese paper in Shanghai and telling the story of the welcome the Nanking people gave the Japanese soldiers there and the deeds of mercy of the Japanese in giving food and medical care and kind treatment to people who had been kicked, cursed, and deprived of every human care by their own soldiers. It was such a complete reversal of the truth that I felt sick, even more sick than last night. Somehow you can stand the truth however brutal, but the self- satisfied lying of that paper article made my tummy turn over. The awful thing is the whole of Japan is being fed all the time on lies like that and they have not the faintest idea of the real situation.

There are thousands of Japanese who would be horrified and humiliated if they really knew what was happening, but they are not allowed to know. How long can a government go on fooling people like that. It seems to me there must come a time when sufficient truth leaks through to make the people suspicious of what the government is handing out to them.

Lots of love. How I long for you all and a touch of normal life at Rustat.[4]

Nessie

Letter home from Hankow, 20 February 1938:

My dear Mother,

It is a lovely sunny day today and the only fly in the ointment is that it is a lovely day for bombing. We are expecting a punitive expedition any day now because on Friday morning when we had 38 Japanese planes bombing us, only 22 reached home. As they prepared to leave Hankow Chinese planes at a terrific height caught them unprepared and in the dog-fighting that followed no less than 12 Japanese planes crashed. The Chinese lost four, but it was a thrilling fight and the tails of the Chinese are well up. The other four planes may have come down in remote spots. No one seems to know what happened to them. Mr. Frilman, who helps me in the godown saw some of the fighting from his home on the outskirts of the city and he said it was most exciting to watch. He saw two planes crash, one in flames, but learned afterwards that they were two of the Chinese planes.

We were at lunch here when it all happened and all we saw was a few of the planes making off towards east. The same day Chungking had its first raid. That I am sure is pure bravado. Of course they can do considerable damage from the air, but they can't hope to march their armies as far inland as that.

Fighting is terribly fierce at the moment both on the Peiping–Hankow line and Tientsin–Nanking (Tinspu) south of Hsuchow. We are wondering what the outcome will be. Maybe we shall all be getting out of Hankow before so very long! I had a very insistent letter from Jesse the other day telling me he thought it was time I gathered together all the Y. girls and trekked west to Chengtu.

I have just been reading the Japanese account of Friday's raid, they say 30 out of 45 Chinese planes were brought down and their own losses will be announced later. Ha! Ha!

Much love

Nessie

Letter to Eva Skinner from Hankow, 20 February 1938:

Eva dear, there doesn't seem to be a thing in the world to write about. During the week when there isn't a moment to think of letters I can think of all sorts of things I want to tell you about, but on Sundays without the stimulus of work my mind goes blank and my letters are hopelessly dull.

On Friday we had an air raid. The alarm went at 12.15 p.m. and all through lunch the bombs and shells were making an unholy din. By the time we had finished the fun was over. I repaired to the roof to see the last of the planes making off eastward. News began to leak out during the afternoon and we heard that four Chinese planes had come down and eleven Japanese. Yesterday morning's paper gave the name of the Chinese pilot in each plane that had brought down a Japanese plane and the place where it had fallen. Then yesterday a twelfth was found a little farther away from Hankow. Thirty-eight Japanese planes left their base and only 22 got back. The other four we don't know anything about. A radio report from Tokyo heard over here stated 35 out of 40 Chinese planes had crashed and Japanese losses were not yet announced.

The Chinese are most frightfully bucked of course. They really are doing much better in the air. Some people say of course that it is the Russian pilots and that may be true. Certainly there are many Russian pilots operating the planes that have been bought from Russia. One tale we heard last week was that Chinese planes had raided the Japanese airfield at Woosung near Shanghai and had found 100 Italian planes on the ground being assembled. They destroyed 40 of them. However I have not seen that report confirmed. It does look as though the intervention in Spain has been transferred to China. We have all the elements of a Communist–Fascist struggle. The difference is that this government is not in the least Communist, far from it. Only the people do appreciate the fact that Russia is the country most disposed to help them. There are quite a number of American pilots in the Chinese Air Force too. We hear about the casualties of course, because they are brought into the International hospital here.

The Japanese seem to be making terrific efforts to get Hsuchow and Chengchow, the east and west junctions of the Lunghai railway where it crosses the Tientsin–Pukow and the Peiping–Hankow lines. Chengchow had an awful bombing last week with something like 500 casualties. The hospital is very busy and I had to rush some stuff out of the godown yesterday in response to a telegram which has taken three days to get through. The stuff we packed so hurriedly for Weihwei is too late I am afraid. The Japanese seem to be in possession already. Now that Chungking has been bombed people in West

China feel much less secure. We are beginning to wonder what will happen here in Hankow.

The whole thing is a beastly, beastly business and I wish it were all over. But I do not see how China can possibly accept terms that Japan offers and Japan is certainly not going to vacate territory she occupies at present so the thing will have to be fought through somehow.

I think they must be testing new planes to-day. There is a constant droning of planes over our heads. The Training School has moved farther west so we do not have planes up as constantly as we did. Quite often though planes move out early in the morning and we know they are off on a raiding expedition somewhere. It is tantalising not to know where they are off to, but a great thrill when we see them come back again.

Another International train is going out to-morrow; at least some international carriages on the passenger train. They are full up, so is the rest of the train because the Chinese feel more secure travelling in a train that is supposed to have special protection. I had a letter yesterday from Eleanor Booth who travelled down on a similar train a few weeks ago. She said they had a very long trip because several times they had to back up into the mountains when Japanese planes came over. It was better to be where they could wait in a tunnel rather than out in the valleys. They travelled by night from Canton to Hongkong and stopped suddenly at one place because there was a report of Japanese planes. It was the most bombed and least protected spot on the whole line so they were glad when they got past it. . . .

Ever so much love, I am so longing for a letter

Nessie

Letter to Eva Skinner from Hankow, 27 February 1938:

Dear Eva, we had a series of thunderstorms last night which kept me awake . . .

The Foreign Residents Association is at present busy making preparations for provisioning the concentration camps for a month. How much wheat flour does one person eat per day? Of course this is only a precautionary measure and does not mean that the situation is any worse than it has been. Everyone is making preparations. The French Concession is putting up enormous wooden gates at every entrance to their Concession. They don't have as many troops here to defend their rights as they have in Shanghai. Crowds of people are trying to rent or buy houses in the French Concession and prices are soaring there. It will be the only comparatively safe place if the Japanese do come. I imagine that event is still a long way off, though of course it is always possible that with the river rising Japanese gun boats may make a raid up the river.

We have not had an air raid for over a week, not even an alarm. The fact twelve planes were brought down in the last raid is evidently giving the Japanese food for thought. I am enclosing a paper cutting with the Chinese and Japanese accounts of the raid in Formosa. You will see how hard it is for us to know the truth. However inside information coming from the secretary to the Minister of Finance states that four Japanese hangars and several petrol tanks were actually destroyed. The Japanese were totally unprepared for the raid; I don't suppose they will be unprepared next time. . . .

I really must get some other letters written and there goes the first supper bell. I'll let you know when we win the war!!

Nessie

Letter home from Hankow, 27 February 1938:

My dear Mother,

This afternoon I went out to tea at Mrs. Klein's. . . . I met a most interesting Australian out there, a Mr. Farmer who is, or rather was, a newspaper man and was in Shanghai all through the fighting there. Now he is doing publicity for the Chinese Government and is really a mine of information so told us all sorts of things. He has no doubt about the final outcome of the war. He doesn't think the Japanese will stand the strain, though it may of course take two or more years for them to be willing to give in. He said that to begin with the war was a life and death struggle for the Chinese but now it has become a life and death struggle for the Japanese. They dare not give up because their whole future depends on their winning. They have lost a tremendous amount already in the way of trade and markets and such and defeat would mean the loss of a very great deal more. I hope Mr. Farmer is right. He also doesn't think the Japanese will ever take Hankow. He said there were several million Chinese soldiers massed north of Hankow. They are all ready to go to the front, but it would be embarrassing to the Chinese to have more soldiers at the front than they have already so they are waiting here. It means of course that the Chinese have almost millions of reinforcements to take the place of the wounded. I hate to think of massacre on such a wholesale scale, but it is great to be reassured about the ability of the Chinese to hold their own. . . .

The other day Dr. Maxwell had a letter from a N.Z. doctor named Grey, who has been sent out to China by the fund raised in N.Z. under the Red Cross there.[5] He wrote asking if there was work for him up here as there didn't seem to be anything to do further south. Dr. Maxwell wrote telling him to come up straight away. He said in his letter there are other N.Z. doctors on their way out to China. I hope they all come up this way. Of course the International Red Cross will send them on up country to the places nearer the front I expect, but even so they may be in and out of Hankow. It will be fun to have someone who speaks my language!

Much love to you all,

Nessie

Letter home from Hankow, 6 March 1938:

My dear Mother,

. . . Dr. McClure was down from Chengchow last week. He is a Canadian doctor and the field agent for the Red Cross in Honan. He is a very jolly soul and he and I always enjoy a crack. He came down to the godown one afternoon and did a really thorough loot. It was great fun watching him at it. Then he had to get Dr. Maxwell's OK and the backchat between them was a perfect riot. In the end he succeeded in getting rather more than he had intended. But Dr. Maxwell cut him down on one or two things just to save face. I spent the best part of the next two afternoons packing the stuff he had selected. Now it is ready to ship up to Chengchow.

Most of the drug orders have been filled and I am now dealing in surgical instruments. Awful looking things most of them. I don't recognise many of them by sight yet. Two of the Community doctors, Dr. Skinner and Dr. Stevens, came down one afternoon and inspected things, especially needles. They evidently wanted to sew up someone's bowels and had lengthy discussions of various different kinds. I don't know who the unfortunate victim was. The next afternoon two Sisters came along from the Catholic hospital. They are Canossian,[6] I think that is right. Anyway they wear brown habits and black bonnets and shawls. They were tremendously interested in the godown and all its contents. People are only just beginning to wake up to the fact that we have one and that it is very interesting. I shall be very sorry to give it up at the end of the month because it really belongs to me by virtue of the fact that I have worked in it for six months. However I fear I must depart for Sian without delay once March is over.

The Japanese seem to be making a drive down towards Tungkwan between Chengchow and Sian. If they cut the line there I shall have fly to Sian and fly out when it is time to leave. The only other way out of Sian is five days by bus to Chengtu and I draw the line at that. My personal problem at the moment is what to do with my few possessions. With the prospect of having to fly out of Sian even if I take the train in I can only take a few things with me. If I leave them in Hankow and Hankow is taken then I will not be able to get back to them and if I send them on up to Chengtu and then don't get through to Chengtu but come back to Hankow I won't have them either. I certainly don't want the expense of having to provide another winter wardrobe when I have two in the country already!

It is impossible to plan in times like these but even if I lose everything I possess up here it will not be anywhere near what so many hundreds of people have lost in this country. The burning and looting have been appalling and foreigners as well as Chinese have been left with only what they stood up in or what they were able to bring out in a handbag.

We have had no air raids here for just over two weeks though we had an alarm this morning. I am writing this with my fingers crossed because I feel that this is only a temporary lull. T.V. Soong, who was for so long Minister of Finance has just been appointed Chairman of the Aeronautical Commission and many people think that the air force will now be much better organised and the Chinese planes will do much more in the way of attacking Japanese air fields and concentration points and so on. It should be a great help because the Chinese army has suffered very seriously from attack by Japanese planes during land attacks.

Much love to you all and don't worry. There really is no need.

Nessie

Shared letter of 20 March 1938 from Hankow:

We have had a perfectly grand display of fireworks this week. After being left alone for about three weeks the Japanese could bear themselves no longer and with a full moon along they came.

Monday began it. We had a warning signal about 5.30 but an hour later the all-clear sounded and I watched eleven of our pursuit planes come down on the field. Then I went to dinner and the second warning must have sounded just as I arrived about 7.5 p.m. but I did not hear it. Some five or ten minutes later all the windows of the room shook as though we were in a severe earthquake, but I did not hear any explosions or guns and that was that. People who had a better view than I, (I was dining on the first floor of an apartment building) said that a direct hit had been scored on the air field and a fire started. I wished I had been at my fifth floor window.

The next evening I went to a movie at 6.p.m. and about 6.45 the fact that the air raid warning had gone up was flashed on the screen in English and Chinese. We came home as we preferred not to have to wait in the theatre for an hour or so. The urgent alarm went later and before long when the moon was well up, the droning of the planes could be heard louder and louder. They dropped flares to light the city and immediately Hankow's new big search lights bought from Germany were sweeping the sky to the south east. In a few moments they spotted the planes flying very high in the direction of the airfield. The lights followed the planes all the way and it was fascinating to watch the little silver birds travelling steadily through the air. As soon as the search lights picked up the planes, tracer bullets, machine guns and anti-aircraft guns burst into action and there was a grand hullabaloo. Then the bombs came down, ever so many of them in quick succession. I couldn't count them. The planes flew on without apparently a scratch, but big fires were soon blazing on the air field.

After the planes had been gone for about ten or fifteen minutes there was a huge explosion out there and another fire started. Evidently one fire was oil because it had the deep red flame and heavy black smoke oil has. We groaned because China can so ill afford to have any of her planes or oil destroyed. Still the all clear did not sound and it was just beginning to dawn on us that there might be a second call when we heard in the distance the sound of planes again. They came from the same direction and dropped their flares and were picked up by the brilliant search lights in just about the same place. The sky seemed to be filled with red and yellow lights and the long beams of the searchlights moving with the planes and the most awful racket and then the bombs came down on the airfield again.

The fires started in the first visit were a good target for the second gang and they scored direct hits and there was another huge fire. Then they went on their way, the lights following them and guns in different parts of the city coming into action as they moved on. It was the neatest piece of work you could wish to see from the Japanese point of view, most spectacular from the point of view of 'neutral observers', but not nearly so good from the Chinese point of view. However, I imagine the damage done was a mere bagatelle compared with the total destruction in China during these last eight months. The papers told us, the next day, that a plane had been destroyed and a petrol tank, but I have heard unofficially that eight planes were lost. Of course the whole city was in total darkness all the time except for the brilliant moonlight, so supper was a late meal. The all-clear did not sound until a quarter to nine.

On Wednesday I went out to supper at a Chinese restaurant knowing that the raid if it came would be at least half an hour because of the moon rising later. Sure enough I had not been home long when the warning sounded. The night was brilliantly clear and I took up my stand again at my fifth floor window and waited. Some of our planes took off as soon as the warning went but of course I could not see in what direction they went. We listened to the sound of planes for some time but I didn't know whether they were Japanese or our own. However one by one the searchlights flashed on and there were the planes coming from the north west this time. Soon they were dropping bombs on the airfield and the city guns were banging away. I could see the bombs picked up as points of silver by the searchlight as they left the planes. Then the planes turned and made a bee line for this building with the lights following them. I knew of course that they had dropped all their bombs, but believe me it is not so hot when they come straight at you. I retired from the window. Then I went out on the roof at the back of the fifth floor and watched them fly on down river with guns still banging and searchlights still in action. Some say that there was dog-fighting in the air but I did not see it. The Chinese planes do not engage them over the city for obvious reasons and we do not see the fighting.

Thursday night was not so clear and we were not visited. However the next night, though it was again not very clear, we were disturbed by the shrieking and blaring of the sirens and hooters about 3.45 a.m. The street lights went out immediately and no sooner had the hooters stopped than they started up again with the urgent alarm. Two Chinese pursuits went up and flew in circles over the city under the clouds. They showed lights on their wings, one red and one white so that they could not be mistaken. I thought it seemed a very good way of telling the enemy where Hankow was but the Japanese planes fly high and could not have seen them through the clouds. After about an hour I saw the landing signals on the air field and then a minute or so later the all-clear went.

When the planes do not come I am always consumed with curiosity as to where they do go. The urgent alarm means that they are within thirty miles of Hankow. I heard a rumour that they went to Siaokan north of Hankow on the railway. There is an air field there too. The person who told me said that there was considerable fighting in the air but there has not been a whisper in the newspapers so it is either not true or else the Chinese came off worst in it. If the Japanese planes had been brought down I think we should have heard. How's that for a week? I have sometimes thought that I would like to change my room because the light is not very good, but I couldn't bear to have a window on any other side of the building.

Meantime Chinese planes have not been inactive, and there have been various raids on Japanese air fields and concentration points in China. As a matter of fact the Chinese have been more than holding their own this last week and Chiang Kai-Shek's strategy is beginning to tell. The Japanese came right down to Tungkwan at least to Fengliutu on the other side of the Yellow River and it looked as though they might cross the river. But wherever they go they hold only a thin line along the railway or highway and the Chinese troops began to press in from both sides and hold them in a neat sandwich making it difficult for them to advance or retreat. There seems to have been a shift of Japanese troops away from that vicinity though there is still news of fighting.

The Japanese are having a busy time shifting troops. They brought them away from the Tsin-Pu fronts to concentrate in southern Shansi and now their garrisons are losing ground in southern Shantung. Today's paper said that the Japanese have decided that Hankow must be the next objective. Without Hankow they cannot accomplish what they want to do. That sounds interesting to us of course. When the river begins to rise they may quite possibly try to come up but I still think it would be very risky unless they can make an attack by land as well. There are already gun emplacements built on the outskirts of Hankow so that guns can be trained on to the river. However I shall probably have to rush the Branch Office up to Szechuan before that happens. . . .

[no signature]

Letter to Eva Skinner from Hankow, 20 March 1938:

I had your letter of February 24 last week dearie and right welcome it was. The second of two New Zealand doctors arrived in Hankow yesterday morning at an early hour. The first a Dr. Grey I did not meet because he was in the city only a few hours. Dr. McClure was down for a few days and whisked him up north and he is now in Loyang in a mission hospital there. Dr. Tremewan has gone on today, left at 7.a.m. and does not yet know which hospital he will be sent to. Dr.Grey wants him in Loyang, but there may be other more urgent calls.

I composed myself on my bed for slumber after lunch and after reading for a time was interdisturbed by the howl of the air raid alarm. It was a grand old whizzbanger when it came about half an hour later. I did not see the planes. When they fly so high they are very hard to pick up in a blue sky. Someone who did see them said that they came in two long lines and one line went on to the airfield here and one over to the Wuchang side. They dropped a terrific number of the bombs on the airfield but when the smoke of the bombs cleared away there were no fires. But over on the other side they got a dump of petrol; a direct hit. It was down river some distance from the Wuchang railway station and I feel injured because I did not know there was a dump there and yet the Japanese knew all about it. I heard later that the petrol had just arrived. It's perfectly amazing how quickly the Japanese pick up news of that kind. China has of course hundreds of petrol dumps all over the country, so that to lose one is not so frightfully serious, but when you think of the difficulty of getting stuff up the railway and that apart from the difficult roads from Russia it is her only source of supply, you can't help groaning when you see the black smoke rising after a raid. . . .

Lots of love. I think of you often, though it is quite impossible to fit 'Rustat' in with this stormy situation. Nessie.

This is my last week with the Red Cross. I hate giving it up but I simply must be free to visit other Associations if necessary.

Letter to Eva Skinner from Hankow, 3 April 1938:

> Well dearie, here is another Sunday bobbing along. The way the weeks fly is perfectly amazing. It rained last night and early this morning so we are not expecting a raid to-day. We have not had even a warning since last Sunday. The Japanese have been so busy elsewhere that they have not had time to give Wuhan a thought. These last two weeks or so the battle has been going very much in favour of the Chinese and we are positively breathless with excitement at times, though fearing to rejoice too soon. The Japanese have very definitely had to withdraw on several fronts and have great difficulty getting reinforcements through because of the way the Chinese guerillas are hampering them and cutting communications behind them. It is hopeless trying to make out where the armies are. There are very few regular lines but miles and miles of territory seem to be overrun with bands of soldiers from both sides fighting wherever they get a glimpse of each other. In some cases large groups of Japanese have been completely surrounded by Chinese and food supplies have had to be dropped from aeroplanes. On one occasion at least the food fell in the wrong camp and the Chinese benefited. Of course it is still a long, long way to the end of the war but one can't help being glad that the Chinese counter offensive is proving successful.
>
> I have now cut the cables and am no longer anything to do with the Red Cross. Officially my job ended on the 31st but I carried on till yesterday afternoon and still have one or two things to hand over to my successor. However I am not going down to the godown again unless a major crisis occurs.
>
> I had planned to go to Changsha to-night, but have not yet been able to get my Chinese travel visa. It is quite a process these days. I had to go to the British Consulate to get the necessary form which has to be stamped as seen and approved by the consul. As a matter of fact the man I saw stamped a blank form and didn't even ask where I was going. Then I had to get my photo taken because the Chinese Police headquarters require three. It is an awful thing and I am <u>not</u> sending any copies home. The police headquarters is quite a long way away in the Chinese city and I have to trek over there again to-morrow to pick up my passport.
>
> I thought I would go Tuesday night, but Madame Chiang Kai-Shek is addressing the Wuhan Missionary Fellowship on Wednesday afternoon, a very significant event so I have decided to stay over for that. Wednesday I shall most certainly start unless I hear from Cheng Tsui Hsiang that she is coming down from Sian. If she comes down I shall have to postpone my trip till next week.
>
> It was really terribly funny last Tuesday. Dr. and Mrs. Maxwell gave a farewell party for me to which all the big wigs from the Executive of the Red Cross came.

Word had gone forth that I was resigning from the Red Cross because I was leaving Hankow. They of course could see no other reason why I should resign. By the time the Mayor had made a farewell speech and about twenty people had severally and respectively asked me where I was going and when, and given me their good wishes I realised that to save my face I would have to get out of the city for at least a week or so. It really became quite a joke and I could hardly bear it. I was most relieved that I had the Changsha trip planned. It would have been most embarrassing otherwise. . . .

Ever so much love,
Nessie

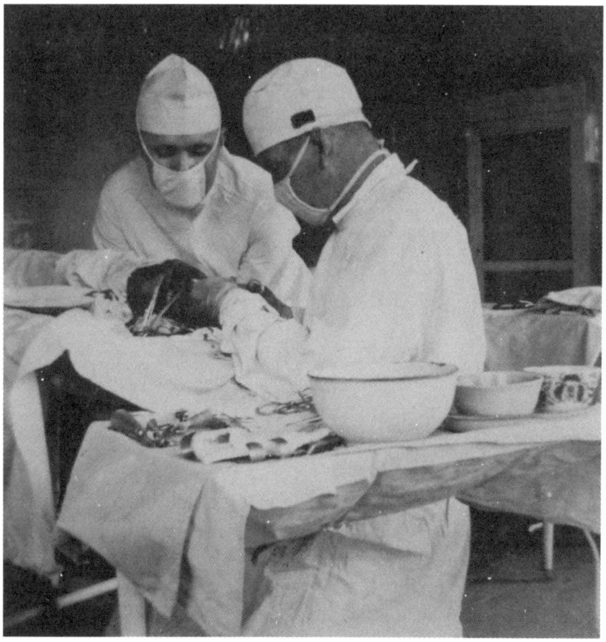

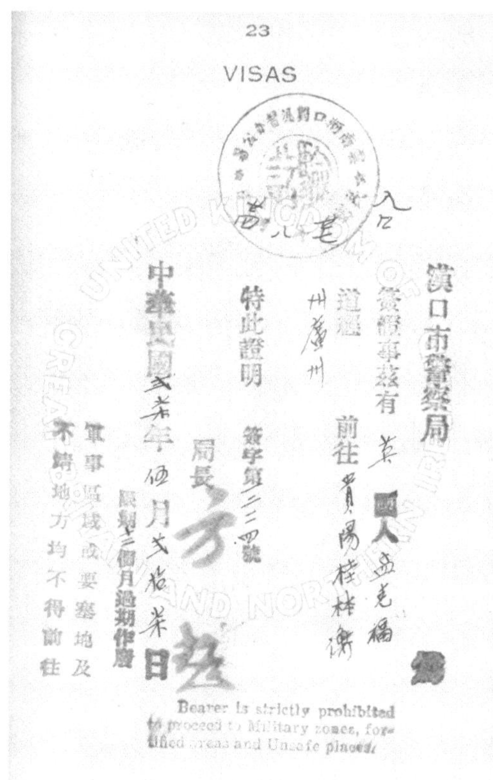

Top: One of the doctors sent to China by the New Zealand Red Cross, Dr Robert Grey of Auckland (on right), operating in Chengchow with equipment from the Hankow godown. April 1938. Gillian Pope, Dr Grey's daughter

Right: Visa for travel in China. Note at bottom: 'Bearer is strictly prohibited to proceed to Military zones, fortified areas and Unsafe places.' 1938. Moncrieff family collection

6
After the Godown
April–July 1938

Nessie returned to full-time YWCA work as the National Committee's city coordinator for the Central China cities of Hankow and Wuchang and further afield Changsha, Shenchow, Sian and Kweiyang. She remained based in Hankow, increasingly under threat as Japanese forces advanced up the Yangtze. Between April and July 1938 she undertook trips to Changsha to see the work of the Association there and to Ichang to explore the possibility of starting a new Association. She continued to use 'As from: Miss Nell Elliott, Church Guest House, . . .' as her address.

Letter home, handwritten from Changsha, 10 April 1938:

> My dear Mother,
>
> I am torn between writing letters & watching the turtles disport themselves on some tree trunks that are lying in the water alongside me. There were eight up at the same time just now but I scared them away by moving my chair further into the sun. I am in Changsha for a change & am staying with Winifred Galbraith who lives in the I Fang School.[1] You wouldn't recognise the school as such because it is in lovely old temple grounds that used to house elderly scholars in their declining years. She has a large room far removed from the school buildings & a partition divides it into bedroom & study. My own suite is a detached two room pavilion – bed & bath – not far from hers. The only other inhabitants are spiders, flat & grey & about two & a half inches across. Dora [younger sister] would not like them.
>
> I left Hankow on Wednesday evening & arrived here the next morning at 8.30 a.m. The train was clean & comfortable & up to time. I travelled third class which was hard & public, but I had a sleeper & one of the men I was travelling with lent me his sleeping pad, likewise wash basin. It is so long since I had a night trip on a Chinese train that I had forgotten what to take with me. Winifred met me & escorted me here & since then I have been busily interviewing secretaries & finding out all about their work. The first day was frightfully hot & muggy and I

sighed for more summer clothes, but a thunderstorm that night cleared things up a bit & yesterday I was shivering in a coat.

Yesterday Winifred was free so she took me for a stunning walk in the hills. We came down a very steep path to the Hunan University near the river bank. It is a lovely spot for a university – quite remote from the city with hills all round & great space for playing fields. Further out we could see the new buildings that Tsinghua University put up. They moved down from Peiping & spent one term here & have now gone on to Yunnan, as it looked for a time as though Changsha might be attacked. The Japanese could not possibly get to Yunnan so the university is safe up there.

Changsha is so different from Hankow, or at any rate from the part of Hankow I live in. It is thoroughly Chinese and has little narrow paved streets lined with very small shops. The wares nearly all seem to be made in the open doorways & I feel I could almost make wooden buckets and tubs myself now.

There was a Chinese victory last week. I am not very sure what happened because there is no foreign newspaper down here, but several thousand Japanese seem to have been surrounded & wiped out. Supplies were dropped down from aeroplanes, but they fell behind the Chinese lines by mistake. It is the first decisive victory the Chinese have had & they celebrated here with firecrackers till we thought we were suffering a major bombardment. However there still seems to be stacks of fireworks left in the shops.

The day I left Hankow Madame Chiang Kai-Shek addressed the Missionary Fellowship meeting. It was a great occasion and the members turned out in full force – over a hundred strong I should say. The meeting was held in the Lutheran Home & there was only just enough room with overflow into the dining room & the hall. I had not seen Mme before. She is very gracious & most distinguished looking. Her English is excellent with hardly a trace of accent. I was especially intrigued with the 'wings' she was wearing. She was Chairman of the Aeronautical Commission & is still a member of it. So she wears the badge done in platinum & diamonds. . . .

Lots of love to you all,
Nessie

Letter to Eva Skinner, handwritten from Changsha, 11 April 1938:

Well dearie, I am in Changsha . . . Winfred took me for a most perfect walk on Saturday . . . There are grand views all the way of the river & nestling in a valley is the Hunan University. You could not imagine a more perfect setting. It was so peaceful & so beautiful. Then yesterday afternoon Japanese planes came & bombed the University setting the whole library block on fire, destroying one corner of the dormitories killing several students & hitting a small cottage killing about a dozen people inside. They also did considerable damage to the new Tsinghua Univ. buildings a little further on. What purpose could they have in destroying university buildings like that. For one thing you'd think they'd see it as the extravagance it is. All that petrol for 30 planes not to mention bombs of $1000 per piece & then destroy nothing of any military importance whatsoever. Casualties are over 100 . . .

Lots of love
Nessie

Letter to Eva Skinner from Hankow, 20 April 1938:

Eva dear, I don't know how I am going to get down all the news. Such lots of things have happened since I wrote last. . . .

I had a very nice Easter. We began at the Y.W.C.A. with a service at 7.30 in the garden, which is very lovely. At the end of the service there was an Easter play with the garden as setting. It could have been most effective, but the production needed a good deal of tidying round the edges. Winifred and I left the group consuming oil cakes and pao tzu[2] and went off to the foreign communion service at 9.a.m. It was a small group and half of them belonged to other denominations, which added a good deal to it. I suppose with a very small foreign group like the one in Changsha you do feel closely bound together. . . .

At 4.30 p.m. we went to the ordinary foreign service, or rather I should say English service, and from there I went direct to the train. We had had air raid warnings on Friday and Saturday evenings as the moon was brilliant and I knew the Japanese planes would be out again on Sunday. However I had to get back. Sure enough at 1.30 a.m. we pulled up with a jerk and all the train lights went out. Then we backed slowly into a cutting for greater protection and waited. The moon was perfect and it seemed awful that such beauty should be spoiled by bombs. Some of the passengers went off into the fields, but the only preparations I made was to put on my shoes. I had not taken off any of my clothes. It is the eeriest feeling waiting for planes to come when there is no protection and you know a train is always an objective. However after a wait of two and a half hours, word came Wuchang had been bombed and the engine whistled a warning to people in the fields to come back. I watched several women with very small babies come back on to the train. Poor souls. It must be awful to know you cannot protect your babies.

We were very late of course getting into Wuchang station, but doing the last part of the trip by daylight gave me the opportunity of seeing country that I could not otherwise see. It was beautiful country too, but spoiled by bomb holes every here and there. There were quite a number at the approach to a bridge at Yenning. They were pretty close but none had touched the bridge. Then when we were nearly in Wuchang we passed the aerodrome and barracks and the end of one building had completely disappeared. I presume that was the result of the bombing the night before. However life was going on as usual and hundreds of soldiers were out drilling. I got into the Lutheran at 11.30 and headed for the bath. The trains on the Canton–Hankow line are very clean and comfortable, but one doesn't feel exactly fresh after sleeping in one's clothes. . . .

Pearl had been busy with arrangements for Madame Chiang Kai-Shek's broadcast to the U.S.A. Convention and we were invited to lunch with Madame on Tuesday. There was hardly time to get all the kick we might have out of anticipation, but the event itself was most enjoyable. Madame is delightful and she has a very good foreign cook. She and the Generalissimo had talked over plans and arranged their movements so that she could be back in Hankow for the broadcast which is on the 28th at 7.45 a.m. I suppose that would be about midday N.Z. We have not done any publicity as yet but will begin this week. The only difficulty is the Japanese do much interference with Chinese broadcasts. We could not hear the Generalissimo's Easter message on account of interference though the Hankow station had been perfectly clear up till then. They are both up at the front at the moment.

I think I told you about the celebrations while I was in Changsha due to the Chinese victory at Taierchuang. The Japanese could not get their reinforcements there quickly enough and finally had to withdraw.[3] However in the last two weeks they have been piling up their forces in Southern Shantung and there is very fierce fighting going on round Lini and Yihsien. It is a matter more of face than military importance with the Japanese now and they are making another desperate attempt to get through to Hsuchow. Everyone seems to think that a good deal depends on this offensive. If the Japanese win there may be serious consequences to this part but if the Chinese win again there may never be another major battle. The Chinese are certainly massed round Hsuchow to receive them and everyone is busy hoping that the Japanese get it in the neck. They have taken divisions from Shansi and from Tientsin to reinforce southern Shantung and the Chinese guerilla forces are making hay while the sun shines and the Japanese garrisons are weak. Some think that it does not matter much what happens in southern Shantung because the trouble that is brewing between Nanking and Shanghai is so much more important. There has been a good deal of fighting there recently and evidently the Chinese are piling troops into that section. . . .

Much love – Nessie

Letter home from Hankow, 26 April 1938:

My dear Mother,

. . . Pearl is making plans to leave Hankow very soon. She has not heard definitely from Shanghai about her furlough, but she feels that she is needed at Fushan so she plans to leave here some time in May. I don't know what I shall do without her. It has been such fun having a companion in my exile here.

We have heard recently of a proposed conference of general secretaries in Hongkong about the middle of July. I shall be required to attend. The thought of leaving Hankow makes me quite excited. Of course I do want to come back after the conference. I should hate like anything to go to Shanghai or anywhere else in occupied China, but it will be fun to see Hongkong again. The only fly in the ointment is that it will be cruelly hot travelling in July. The trip is supposed to take 44 hours but thanks to Japanese attention it has sometimes taken five days. It somewhat depends on the moon. You do not travel in China at the full moon if you can help. There are always air raids. Last full moon Hankow had a series of raids that lasted from 11.p.m. to 5.a.m. one night and another series that lasted three hours the next night. I missed them through being in Changsha, but the second night I was on my way back on the train and it was eerie to stop in the middle of the night and then back into a cutting for greater protection. We stayed there for two and a half hours until things were pronounced clear. Two Chinese in my compartment slept through it and did not know that we had stopped at all. They snored gently most of the time and I was fooled over and over again thinking I heard droning of planes in the distance. . . .

Pearl had a great thrill for me when I got back. We have been trying to arrange for Madame Chiang Kai-Shek to broadcast to the National Convention of the Y.W.C.A. in the U.S.A. and she wanted to see us. They waited till I got back from Changsha and then Pearl and I were invited to lunch with her in her home. Can you imagine the thrill? The only thing was that we did not have long enough to enjoy the anticipation. It was all over so soon. However, Madame is very eager to broadcast as it is to be a national hook-up, so everything is arranged for 7.45 till 8.a.m. on Thursday next. Pearl and I are to go to the broadcasting station to act as a sort of reception committee and Colonel Huang, who is a big wig of some kind in the Government, is sending his car for us.

There are two things that may happen to spoil it. The Japanese have made a fine art of interference and when they get going it is impossible to hear anything. Also, if they feel like it they may stage a raid on the broadcasting station. Madame is absolutely fearless, but her advisors may not be willing for her to expose herself as a target for Japanese bombs. Pearl and I are very excited as you can imagine.

Another excitement when I got back from Changsha was being introduced to the new British Ambassador, Sir Archibald Clark Kerr. I went to a reception given by Mr. Simms Lee and his wife. He is vicar of St. Johns here. It was to farewell the Bishop [Bishop Logan Roots] who was leaving for America the next morning. All the good and great were there including the Ambassadors of the U.S.A. and Great Britain. Mr. Moss, the Consul General here in Hankow introduced me and I was all comeoverish at the honour.

The next evening I went to a dinner party at the Crawford Brown's to meet a New Zealander who is a foreign press correspondent here. His name is Rex Warren. It was quite fun to see another New Zealander. There were two other interesting men present. One was Tommy Chow, a representative of Reuters, who has quite a reputation as a journalist. The other was a Mr. Ma, who was First secretary at the Chinese Embassy in Tokyo right up to the time that it withdrew from Japan. He had some interesting things to say about Japan and the war situation generally. . . .

Much love to you all,
Nessie

General letter from Hankow, 30 April 1938:

The outstanding event of this week was the broadcast given by Madame Chiang Kai-Shek to the National Convention of the YWCA of the USA. I think the suggestion originated in Shanghai. A broadcast from China by Madame, introduced by Mrs. J. H. Sun, our National President, was the thing they hoped for. The international situation made it impossible to have such an introduction but the Hankow Branch Office took the matter up and discovered that it would be technically possible to arrange a broadcast from Hankow, but that arrangements would have to be made from the American end. With Japanese censorship of telegrams in Shanghai it was difficult to get word to the National Committee and it was our sixth attempt, a naval radio through the American consulate that finally got through. Time was getting very short and cables began to fly back and forth. Shanghai was not able to count on getting a message through to New York and had to send it down to Hongkong for transmission. Meantime Madame had been approached and had consented and we were getting very perturbed lest word would not get through in time.

At last a cable came suggesting April 21st, but arrangements were not yet definite! Finally a New York cable direct to us in Hankow stated that all arrangements had been made through the Columbia Broadcasting Co. for Thursday morning 28th April, Hankow time 7.45 a.m. This was 7.45 p.m. the evening before by New York time. The cable came just as we were setting off to have lunch with Madame and talk over the speech. It was grand to have such definite word. When the cable had suggested the 21st Madame had talked things over with the Generalissimo and arranged their visit to the Shantung front so that she would not have to leave Hankow before the 21st. Then when the later date the 28th was fixed plans had to be arranged again and an earlier visit planned. We had a feeling that the whole war was being arranged so that the broadcast could be given! . . .

At last the day arrived and at 7.15 a.m. we set out for the broadcast station. . . . Madame was accompanied by Mr. Donald, the Australian Adviser who seems to act as an aide to Madame, and one plain clothes guard. There were a great many plain clothes men at the station but they were quite unobtrusive. Madame was looking even more attractive than usual I thought. She had had a busy time with her speech. I believe the one she gave was the fifth effort. It certainly gave evidence of a great deal of thought.

In one room we could hear Madame from Hankow station and across the hall our ear phones gave her voice coming back from Manila and from San Francisco. The latter was even clearer than the former so we were pretty sure that the 3000 Y.W.C.A. delegates in Columbus, Ohio were enjoying good reception. That evening cables came back from Columbus to the YWCA and to Madame saying that it had been a thrilling experience. It was an exclusive broadcast over the whole American network so that many more than the delegates to the Convention were listening, though the speech was directed to the Convention. It seemed quite impossible that Madame's low clear voice should be reaching such an audience so many thousands of miles away. After all our doubts and uncertainties and questioning about air raids and Japanese interference and so on, it was such a thrill to have the broadcast so successful that we went round with broad smiles on our faces all day and found it hard to concentrate on our work.[4]

The air raid that we had been afraid of came next day. It was the birthday of the Emperor and everyone felt that there would be military 'celebrations'. For that reason more planes than usual were at the air field here and even before the sirens shrieked their warning about 2.25 p.m. the first Chinese planes were off the ground. From our first floor (English count) office we saw 40 rising up and up until we could no longer see them in the blue of the cloudless sky. The droning of the planes always gives me a peculiar feeling and it is so loud and insistent when there are so many planes. Soon it increased in volume as 39 Japanese planes arrived. Then the explosion of bombs and the barking of anti-aircraft guns interrupted it. The droning went on and on but we could see nothing from our office as the windows were on the wrong side. We could however see smoke rising from the direction of the arsenal. Those who were up on the rooftops reported later a most thrilling series of dogfights. The Chinese planes have greater manoeuvrability than the Japanese and prove more skilful fighters on the whole.

At one point we heard the awful howl of a plane crashing and again and again the sound of power dives as they attacked. Later, we watched the planes come down to the air field again, but as they circled round and were lost behind the high buildings and reappeared again we were not sure of the count. Reports later said that of the 39 Japanese planes only 15 returned. Three Chinese crews left their planes by parachute, one made a forced landing and four others had not returned by 6.p.m. It is hoped they made forced landings elsewhere but of course it is possible that they crashed somewhere. Japanese radio reports last night said that 51 Chinese planes had been brought down. That is possibly the total number that went up and we saw the majority of them return with our own eyes so there must be something wrong with the count somewhere!! The city of Hanyang suffered a good deal. Only one bomb hit the arsenal, but all the others did considerable damage to life and property. . . .[5]

Affectionately,
Nessie

Letter home from Ichang, 8 May 1938:

My dear Mother,

I don't seem to write to you twice running from the same place these days. Here I am in Ichang just at the beginning of the famous Yang Tze Gorges and only four days sailing from Chungking. I could get to Chengtu in six days from here by boat and bus and in about six hours if I took to the air. It just seems too bad that I can't go on up and see Jesse and Vee. However, there is neither time nor money just now. I had a letter from Cora [Deng] last Monday saying that she expected to leave Chungking about the middle of last week. It takes only two days for her to come down and me four days to get from Hankow to Ichang so I made enquiries straight away and found there was a boat leaving for Ichang on Tuesday evening. I knew I would have to make this trip before so very long so my work was all up to date and I was able to get away without much of a rush.

Tuesday afternoon there was a garden party to farewell Mr. and Mrs. Moss [the British Consul-General] who are going on furlough and I was glad that I could attend that. It was held out in the Jardine Estate Garden. That is a sort of garden suburb. There are some lovely houses out there with beautiful gardens and a lot of the foreign community people live there when times are normal. Just now a number of the houses are vacant. The garden covers acres and acres and there are grand stretches of green lawn. All the foreign community and a fair number of Chinese, officials and such, were out there and it was quite good fun. It is much nearer the air field than where we live in the city but there were no alarms while we were there.

I came up on Butterfield and Swire's 'Changsha' which is not a bad tub as river boats go.[6] There were only three other passengers in first class. One was a B.& S. captain coming up to join an Upper Yang Tze river boat and there was a young English doctor coming out to join H.M.S. 'Gannet,' the local gun boat. It is about two by four and I think Dr. Owen was a little staggered when he saw it. If a doctor serves with the navy he gets a thousand pounds when he leaves and that starts him nicely in a practice, so many young doctors join up for the sole sake of the money. The trouble is they go rusty with so little work to do. Dr. Owen was very relieved to know there are two mission hospitals here and they would probably be glad of help with their wounded soldiers. He cheered up immensely. Yesterday I paid some calls on foreigners and was able to tell the doctors at Rankine Memorial Hospital about him.

The river trip from Hankow to Ichang is not very exciting except for the last six hours or so the river winds and winds and you seem to be going round the same old corner over and over again. Even when the river is moderately straight for a few yards the channel zigzags over it. I wouldn't mind a dollar for every turn of the ship's wheel. The country is flat nearly all the way and very dull. We left Hankow at 10.p.m. and sailed all that night, but the nights afterwards we had to anchor at dark as navigation is impossible.

The third night a squall came up, probably the tail end of a typhoon they were enjoying at Hongkong, and we dragged anchor. I was wakened by a most persistent swishing of water that had not been noticeable when I went to bed and behold it was the waves breaking against the river bank. Our stern was pressed hard against the mud bank. There were vivid flashes of lightning that lit up the whole place almost like daylight and I could see just how we were fixed. A seaman was busy taking soundings and the Chief Officer was clad in mackintosh and beret getting very wet as he supervised operations. I think something must have pulled us off, as of course we could not turn the propeller in that mud. We gradually glided into midstream and all was well. No one mentioned it the next day and I was the only passenger who had been aware of what had happened. My first thought was 'Hurrah! here's a week's holiday while we wait for the river to rise high enough to float us off,' but alas there was no difficulty.

We anchored at 7.30 a.m. on Saturday morning and Deaconess Reibe sent me a chit to say stay on board and she would call for me. I didn't know anyone up here of course but Miss Dexter of the American Church Mission in Hankow had given me Deaconess Reibe's name and I had sent her an air mail letter as soon as I knew I was coming, asking her if she would find me a place to stay. She is the only foreigner in the Mission here and she lives with the Clergyman and his wife, Mr. and Mrs. Nelson Liu.

The compound is large and beautiful. It is like a vast park rather overgrown in spots but with lovely trees and birds that seem to sing all day long. There are various and sundry buildings, most of them in a state of disrepair, but several are quite habitable and I am living in a small house all to myself. I have a huge living room with a desk and easy chairs and so on and a large bed room with a bathroom attached. Deaconess Reibe comes over here to sleep so that I will have company. And I go over to the Lius for my meals. They eat Chinese food, but it is very nice indeed. In Changsha I hated the Chinese food, both at the school and at the YWCA, but here, cooked in small quantities and well planned, I like it very much. . . .

Much love to you all
Nessie

Letter to Eva Skinner from Ichang, 8 May 1938:

Well dearie, here I am in another place. Join the YWCA if you want to see the world. Ichang is not far from the entrance to the first of the Yang Tze Gorges and I am dying to go up river now that I have got as far as this. However there is no time and no money so here I stay until I go back to Hankow.

Ichang is a beautiful place. There are lots of hills round about and folk say that there is grand hiking on the other side of the river. There is one hill that rises straight out of the water and it is called the pyramid for an obvious reason. I think there is probably a wonderful view from the top on a clear day. I hope there is a chance for a walk or so before I go back.

I am staying in a huge compound which feels like parkland. It is a bit overgrown in spots but full of lovely trees and the birds sing all day long. They are new ones to me and have very interesting notes. This is an American Church Mission Compound. I haven't quite discovered how many people there are living in it but there are no foreigners except for Deaconess Reibe. It would really be a stunning place if I were here permanently. It would be fun fixing it up. At present there are no coverings of any kind on the floor and no curtains as it is not in general use. But there are loads of windows which are all screened and verandahs all round. It might be cold in winter, but if I were here doing YWCA work I would like nothing better than to live here. The Lius are awfully friendly and he is quite a brilliant man, educated in America and carrying responsibility for all the work done here. There is another house in this compound formerly occupied by a foreign family in the Mission but now rented in normal times to business people. It has a most attractive and dignified 'colonial' porch covered at present with a perfect riot of honeysuckle. Unfortunately most of these houses are very old but I'd love to live here all the same.

Do you remember writing to me when I was struggling with the hostel in Peiping and telling me about a Miss Moore from Central China who knew that the hostel was doomed to failure because I had been in China such a short time? Well I met her here yesterday. She is a retired member of the Scottish Mission here but is still working in the city, busy with a variety of deeds.

My job at the moment is to find out if Ichang wants a YWCA. The Scottish missionaries quite obviously don't. They haven't the foggiest idea what a YWCA is all about. The people who will really decide whether they want a YWCA or not are the Chinese women. They are a much more up and coming bunch than the Scottish would lead one to believe. There are two young Canadians on the hospital staff, Dr. and Mrs. Brown. She was most encouraging and thought there was a lot a YWCA could do here, but agreed that raising funds to support might be very difficult at the moment when so much money is being raised for relief work of one kind or another.

Cora Deng is coming down river to help with this survey but she is late. She may be delayed by the fact that about 16,000 Szechuan troops are coming down the river at the moment and all available craft is needed for them. We passed one boat load as we came up a day or two ago. I can't do much but call on foreigners until Cora comes as my Chinese is not up to the strain of conversing with wives of officials and so on. I hope she comes soon as she has to be in Hankow by the 17th at the latest and that does not give us much time if we want to call a meeting of women or do anything like that.

The trip up river was quite fun. There were only four passengers in the foreign class so I could be conversational when I wanted to be. The scenery is very dull.

Mr. Liu has a radio but that is the only way of getting any news here. The papers come at least four days late. Last night the Hankow and Changsha stations were very difficult to get as there was much static. However we did hear that the Japanese are trying another way to get to Hsuchow. They are endeavouring to land at Haichow, which is the eastern terminal of the Lunghai Line. They have been unsuccessful at Taierchwang again and I hope the Chinese manage to hold them at Haichow. It was being developed as a port by the Chinese Government, but I think the harbour works were blown up by the Chinese when the Japanese showed signs of wanting to use it as a landing place some months ago.

Gosh! this is an awful war. I wish it would end, but it won't till the Japanese will agree to reasonable terms and they won't do that for months, if not years to come. Everyone says that if the Chinese continue to have the success they are having at present the whole Japanese adventure will become too expensive and will have to be dropped. I wish it would hurry up and prove too expensive.

I am wondering about getting back to Hankow. It will be full moon again and there are bound to be Japanese planes at large. For that reason I would vastly prefer to travel on a British boat. Not that it makes a great deal of difference, but I always feel that there would be less panic and more organisation on a British boat if anything unpleasant occurred. I must find out about buses. They run when the weather is decent and take only ten or twelve hours to get through. Rather crowded and unpleasant hours I would imagine, but I would like to see what it is like. However that is a week or more ahead and I cannot make any plans until Cora arrives. . . .

Much love –

Nessie

Letter home on board the *SS Changsha*, en route from Ichang to Hankow, 15 May 1938:

My dear Mother,

Every time someone tells me I have to go off on a trip I inwardly protest but I am afraid that the day is soon coming when I will protest if I am not sent off on a trip. While I was in Ichang a telegram came from Shanghai asking me how soon I could leave for Kweiyang and Kweilin to make a survey of those two cities. I had thought that I would not be travelling again until I went down to Hongkong in July, but now it seems as though the whole of June will be spent on the road and what a road! It will be terrifically hot and laundry will be difficult and buses will be stifling but everyone says that the scenery down that way is marvellous and that I am very lucky to get a chance to see it. . . .

It is amazing how one can get about the country even when there is a war on. I don't relish the prospect of Chinese inns on the way. Rather too bed buggy I am afraid but I shall buy up a good supply of Flit and take plenty of oiled cloth. If you put it under your mattress the bugs don't reach you as they hate the smell of it. I shall have to purchase a mosquito net and some more sheets and towels before I set out. I have no idea whether or not I shall be sent back to Hankow afterwards so will have to take everything I possess with me. I think China Travel can send what I don't need on the trip straight to Hongkong. It will take weeks to get there, but so will I.

I am on the boat now on my way to Hankow. There has been an air raid or so down there in the last few days. This is a British boat and we have the Union Jack painted all over us but that does not stop the Japanese from trying to get to us if they feel like it. Kweiyang and Kweilin have not been bothered by the Japanese so I shall probably have a rest from their attentions for a while.

I am the only woman passenger on this trip and my fellow passengers are all men off a French gun boat at Ichang. They eat first and I have exclusive meals with the captain and first officer. Last night we had an awful time with mosquitos. We have to anchor at night and the place was swarming with them. The door from the servery on to the deck was open and though the saloon was screened every time the stewards came in with the food several hundred mosquitos came in with them. I had a georgette dress on and they bit my shoulders through it not to mention ankles. I was in misery in no time and it took a good hour before I felt comfortable again. However, the captain ordered the boys to put up a mosquito net over my bed so I wasn't bothered in the night.

I really had a very good time at Ichang. Mr. and Mrs. Liu and Deaconess Reibe went out of their way to do all sorts of nice things for me. I planned to leave on Thursday evening, but when I came on board I found the 'Changsha' was not sailing till Friday evening. That gave me another day in Ichang. When I was leaving the night before I gave Deaconess Reibe a cheque for the 'warphans' they are going to have on their compound. When she demurred I told her it was my birthday[7] and that I would like to give someone a present. I wouldn't have told her if I had known the boat was not leaving. Anyway, next afternoon there was a resplendent birthday cake made by Deaconess Reibe with lighted candles. The five Liu children were at the party and helped me blow out the candles. Then that evening they had special feast dishes prepared for supper and I felt quite embarrassed and wished I had not said anything. . . .

One day Deaconess Reibe took time off and we went for a lovely all day picnic up to the Three Friends Cave. It is a beautiful spot. We took ricshas for about two and a half miles up the river, then ferried across and walked through fruit orchards, plum and orange and crab apple. Then along the river beach till we reached a small stream coming down a very narrow little glen with very high overhanging cliffs on either side. It was terribly hot by that time so we found a shady spot and had lunch. Then we strolled up the valley. There are swimming pools in various spots and an ice factory and an incense factory further up. On the way back we climbed out of the valley to the cave which is rather smelly and unpleasant and has the inevitable temple at the entrance. From the top of the ridge you have a wonderful view looking right up to the first of the Yang Tze gorges. I did want to go up through it but that is an all day trip and you have to leave about 5.a.m. I was glad to see it though and I feel I know what a small one looks like. The mountains on either side are very much higher as you go further in. There are lovely hikes around Ichang and I would like to spend a holiday there some time but in April and May rather than in the heat of the summer. . . .

Coming back from the Three Friends Cave we took a small Chinese boat and came down the Yang Tze. It took over an hour and four steamers from Chungking passed us on the way. It had been such fun on the way up to Ichang watching the Chinese sampans pitching and tossing in the wash of the steamer and we had a sample of it ourselves. It was not nearly as bad as it looked. We had stopped at a tea house and had our coffee flask filled up with hot water so we had a grand picnic tea on the sampan. The coffee was rather weak but we were so terribly thirsty that anything would have tasted good. . . .

Love to you all,

Nessie

Letter to Eva Skinner from Hankow, 22 May 1938:

Dearie I think there have been three letters from you since I last wrote . . . This morning I read two mimeographed letters that the National Christian Council in Shanghai has had put together. They were written by American men who have stayed in Nanking. I was very nearly physically sick. How they can stand it all and remain sane and normal I do not know. To live in the midst of hideous suffering like that week after week and be able to do very little to help must be perfectly terrible. And all of it suffering that is caused by perfectly hideous beastliness. It will take centuries for the Japanese army to regain its reputation for being a well-disciplined army actuated by loyalty to the emperor and the old chivalric samurai traditions. And the appalling thought is that this sort of thing is going on all over the place wherever the Japanese army is in occupation. I hate to think of Hsuchow at this very minute and in all the villages around where wholesale massacre and rape are going on.

Dr. McClure is down again from Chengchow. He has been through all the awful bombing up there. There was one terrible day when the three mission compounds with their hospitals were the only objective. Everyone spent all day in the dugouts and the destruction and casualties were appalling.

I expect you have heard of the Chinese planes that flew over Japan and dropped leaflets, several tons of them. It is perfectly marvellous to think the Chinese had those cities entirely at their mercy for several hours and did not drop a single bomb. The Japanese were entirely unprepared and not one plane took off in pursuit. Of course they are trying to pretend that it didn't happen, but it did and I think the restraint of the Chinese was typical of the finest there is in this nation. I don't suppose the Japanese will take any more notice of the leaflets than the Chinese do of those the Japanese drop, but those who do any thinking at all must be impressed by the fact the Chinese could have dropped bombs and didn't. The planes came back to Hankow and there was a marvellous welcome accorded to them on the air field here. We have been expecting a return compliment ever since, but with bombs instead of leaflets. But the Japanese had such a bad time on the Mikado's birthday that we haven't had even an alarm since.

Mr. Farmer of the Chinese Government Publicity told me the other day that Miss Iris Wilkinson, the New Zealand journalist, is missing. They are very worried about her. He said they absolutely refused to give her a permit but she went on several 'tear bats' (his own phrase) and they had to give her one. Now they haven't heard of her for days and don't know whether she has got mixed up in the retreat from Hsuchow or not. I think she was crazy to go near the front lines at such a critical time, especially as she is lame. Even if she was not afraid for herself she should have considered the Chinese who accompanied her. They, if caught, would be killed for certain but she might have got away alright. I must try to see Mr. Farmer tomorrow and see if they have had any news yet.

Dr. McClure took prayers this morning and I was very most impressed by some of the things he said. He spoke of the way the way Chinese doctors and nurses in the hospitals had lost all concern for their own lives and how tribulations of this kind had deepened their spiritual life. He said we belong to a fellowship that has abandoned all concern of that kind. If we have a future good, but if we have not that is also good. He is one of the bravest and most resourceful men I have ever met. He is a very able surgeon, a member of the Royal College of Surgeons and an expert on radium and X-ray besides. He goes through the Japanese lines when necessary and got back to his old compound in Huaiking, made himself known to the Japanese and had dinner with them. He told us an amusing tale yesterday of a Japanese officer of very high rank saying 'You know these Chinese make things very difficult for us. We have defeated them many times and yet they are still fighting.' Isn't that killing? I wish he would write a book about his experiences. They would be intensely interesting reading.[8] He told us of a nurse in one hospital where the Japanese were in occupation. The village where her people lived had been burned and all the villagers and livestock machine gunned. All her family had been killed in that way. She dressed herself as a boy and went on nursing in the hospital and attended to the Japanese wounded and not one of them discovered that she was a girl. At that time no woman of whatever age was safe from the Japanese. Dr. McClure said that he had seen her in the hospital and when she came into the chapel and took her place among the women he was completely flummoxed. This is a heart-breaking cruel business, but the spirit of some of the Chinese is just marvellous. . . .

Ever and ever so much love. It would be marvellous to see you but I have not the faintest desire to leave China at this time. Now that Hsuchow has fallen we may get it in the neck here in a few months' time. I hope I will be able to stand up to it without too much jittering.

Nessie

Letter to Eva Skinner from Hankow, 5 June 1938:

> Well dearie here I am still in Hankow when I thought I would surely be in Kweilin. On Monday afternoon we had a meeting of the Advisory Committee to the Branch Office. When it was reported I was going off for four to five weeks there was a general protest. They were told earlier that if there was any trouble here I could stay through it and help if help were possible. No one knows of course what is going to happen but the Japanese occupation of Hofei has brought the war perceptibly nearer and the attempt to bomb the boom at Kiukiang the other day makes it appear that the Japanese are serious in their idea of making a drive on Hankow. I rather pooh-poohed their protests because I don't really think that anything is going to happen in the immediate future, but they were very serious so we sent off a telegram to Shanghai the next morning. There was no reply for several days and we were unsure if it was censored or not so on Friday afternoon I got Mr. Hansen to arrange for a longer telegram to be sent by the American Naval Radio. We had an answer yesterday afternoon and Cora is off today, seeing various members of the Advisory Committee. I think she will go in my place and I shall be very glad to have her out of the way in case anything really does happen.
>
> When the telegram came saying that Miss Liu would not get to Hongkong till the 4th or the 5th I decided that I would have my tonsils out immediately and made an appointment with Dr. Miller for Tuesday at 10. [She had chronic follicular tonsillitis.] He did not turn up until nearly twelve and it was 12.30 before he called me in to the surgery. By then we were in the middle of an air raid so I can proudly boast that I had my tonsils out in the middle of an air raid. It is a most unpleasant operation and I was glad that Dr. Miller is the famous surgeon he is. I was a bit wuzzy and you should have seen his tiny nurse who had to stand on tiptoe to get her arm anywhere near my waist supporting me to the lift. I just had to laugh, tonsils or no tonsils.
>
> On Thursday I worked in my room and on Friday I went to the office and to Dr. Miller to have the gap painted. At the same time I got a prescription for my other complaint [worms] and am at present on an exclusive diet of carbon tetrachloride and castor oil. Coming at the end of four days of almost starvation I am not enjoying it. Indeed yesterday I thought I would pass out completely. Thank goodness tomorrow is the last day. Tomorrow I have the gap painted again and also the third injection for typhoid and cholera. After that I hope my troubles will be over for another year. I weighed myself the other day and find that I have lost twenty-three pounds [10kg] since this time last year. I am almost elegantly slim.

Eva, it is possible, even though not probable, that by the time you get this the fighting may be much nearer Hankow. I expect now to stay through everything though I can't say I am looking forward to it. The Foreign Residents Committee has plans in hand for the concentration of all foreigners during the take over and about six weeks ago I paid my $30 for a month's food in a concentration camp. The food is all bought and ready. I imagine if it comes to the serious bombardment of Hankow I shall have a boring time sitting in the Shell building with nothing to occupy my time. This building is to be the point of concentration I think, but probably only for American citizens. If I can possibly wangle it I will stay here. The worst thing will be that there will be no possibility of getting letters in or out for some considerable time. You may not hear from me for weeks and weeks except through cables saying that all foreigners are safe. That is what happened in the case of Nanking.

This sounds a bit like making my will but I thought I would tell you what is likely to happen. I have put my name down as willing to do any kind of work so I may be Red Crossing again or even washing chopsticks in a hospital. I don't think that during the bombardment I can be of any real use to the YWCA but I can live there as soon as possible afterwards and keep the property from being seized by Japanese military. On this side the YWCA is only a block from the Lutheran Home, but I do not think I shall be able to give much help to Wuchang. Even though the members of the Advisory Committee were so strong in their protest that I should not go away, I do not think that they have any very definite plan in mind whereby I can help them. The worst feature of the situation will be that we will know that the most awful things are happening around us even though perhaps some of us do not see much of it. Sometimes I can just not believe that it is possible that the things that happened in Nanking and elsewhere will surely happen here if the Japanese come in. It is all too fantastic and terrible and so remote from the ordinary decencies of human life.

Well this is not much of a letter. By next week I may have more cheerful news to relay. The most desperate fighting is going on near Kaifeng. The Japanese are determined to break through and the Chinese are equally determined to hold them. Every day or so we hear rumours that Kaifeng and Chengchow have fallen but they are not yet true. Ever so much love – Nessie

Letter to Ethel Law from Hankow, 6 June 1938:

Dear Ethel,

. . . I don't know whether I have ever told you of the plans made here by the Foreign Residents Association for the concentration of foreigners in case of attack on Hankow. We are registered under three heads. 1) those who want to go on board a boat and steam up river to a place of safety till the bombardment is over; 2) those who want to stay on their own premises as long as possible and then go to a point of concentration and 3) those who want to stay in their own premises whatever happens. I have registered under 2) saying at the same time I may have to remain on YWCA property if required. I've been required to pay $30.00 as my share of a month's provisions for a concentration camp. All this was done several weeks ago and was not an indication of any immediate danger but merely necessary precautions sponsored by the consuls. The situation is still much the same though the fighting has come a little nearer. Should Hankow ever be taken there will be no possibility of being able to get word out to you for some time. There will probably be consular advice to say that all foreigners are safe and that will be all till communications are re-established. The National office in Shanghai may be able to get more detailed word from the consulate in Shanghai. I don't know.

It seems unnecessary to be writing all this, but in case anything should happen I thought you would like to know. I have not written this to my Mother as I thought it might alarm her unduly and there is no cause for alarm.

With all good wishes to the staff and committee.

Yours, with love,

Nessie

Letter to Eva Skinner from Hankow, 12 June 1938:

Well dearie I came upstairs after tea determined to write letters then I sat down and darned stockings, a much needed occupation . . .

There really isn't any news. I am still feeling limp and exhausted after the week I gave myself last week and I don't seem able to snap out of it. The 'Born tired' feeling is very hard to live with. On Tuesday we had another Advisory Committee meeting and they decided it was time for our Branch office to move up the river away from the Japanese advance but of course they don't want me to go with it. We have decided that Chen Ya-Chun is to go up, taking the Chinese files and the duplicator with her and I am to keep the English files and the bank account here till things really tune up. Meantime there is no work for me to do here if the Branch office goes. Neither of the local Associations [Hankow and Wuchang] want me to do anything more than just sit about in case of trouble. Anything more boring than being left without a job I can't imagine. On Thursday I went to a meeting of the Hankow YWCA Board of Directors. They are all planning to get out of Hankow as soon as possible, and probably all the secretaries should go too. They want to hand all the responsibility over to me as soon as things look bad. I don't know what I can do about it. I won't go and live at the Association unless there is another foreigner to live there with me so I think the best thing to do is to persuade all the hostel guests to go. They are mostly refugeeing from other places and ought to move on. The rest are in government offices and I suppose will be evacuated by their departments before the trouble begins. . . .[9]

I feel terribly concerned about the situation and rather resent the Chinese attitude of getting well out of the situation and leaving it all to the foreigner. This being the only foreigner is simply awful. It was all right when Pearl was here and we could talk things over and make decisions together. The International Red Cross has set up a sub-committee to discuss the possibility of organizing a Safety Zone for Chinese. If the YWCA were in the Safety Zone it would not be quite so bad. But even so it would be more than a one-man job keeping the Japanese soldiers out of the building and try to protect the girls. I don't think I could do it by myself.

The Wuchang YWCA also wants me to take some responsibility for their building, but if there is fighting in this section there will be no possibility of getting back and forth across the river. It's a pity because the YWCA owns its own building in Wuchang and it would be well worth trying to keep the Japanese army out of it.

The Japanese are not likely to arrive in this part of the country for several months so I am getting fussed about things long before I need. It is probably because I am not feeling well. I wish I could take my holiday this month before anything happens, but the Advisory Committee would not hear of my going to Kweilin and Kweiyang on business so I can hardly hope to go anywhere on holiday. I would like to get out of it all for a few weeks.

We have had almost two weeks of cloudy weather with rain which is particularly fortunate in view of the threat to bomb Hankow indiscriminately. The results of their bombing in Canton have been simply ghastly. Hundreds of people have been killed and some bombs have fallen over a mile from anything approaching the military objective. A friend arrived here last week from Hongkong and her story of getting through Canton on the way was hair-raising.

Several times we have heard that Japanese planes have headed for Hankow, but have had to turn back on account of the bad weather. It is a full moon now and we are extremely glad that it is still raining. There was a glorious sunset last night and I was sure today would be fine, but it has been pouring steadily. It's a crazy world in which we welcome long spells of wet weather. . . .

The river is coming up very quickly and some days freshets coming down the Han have made that river impassable. It is so funny to look towards the Bund and see almost the whole of the steamers above the level of the road. Not so long ago only the tops of the funnels were visible. Japanese gun boats are active further down below Nanking and troops are being landed. The other afternoon I watched planes going out in formation on business bent and was not surprised to read the next day that the gunboats had been bombed and one sunk.

All the wounded soldiers are being moved out of Hankow to leave the hospitals empty for those who will be wounded when the fighting begins in the mountains about a hundred miles north of us. We hear that there are already forty divisions of fresh Chinese troops placed in the hills ready for the Japanese when they come down across the Honan plains. The refugees are also being moved out. There are about 40,000 in these three cities. There is one special boat that does nothing but move refugees out at government expense further south. It goes up river, which is a south-westerly direction and then across the lake and up the Siang river and to Changsha. It is almost impossible to get a berth on the train these days; everything is booked up till the end of the month, and the boats going up river are just as heavily booked. Two planes are running every day to Hongkong instead of one because there are so many people trying to get out.

On Tuesday there is to be a meeting of all British residents to discuss concentration plans. I am jolly glad to know the Lutheran Home is a point of concentration for missionaries. I will not have to move out at all unless I go to the YWCA which is only a block from here. I got my registration and identification card for emergency food supplies the other day. I had to pay $30.00 towards my share of a month's food supplies last month. All the food is already bought and stored at the concentration points. Really sometimes I wonder if I am living in a real world or just indulging in a dream.

Well this is a gloomy letter. Take its gloom with a pinch of salt. I'll be on top of things in a day or two, but oh my dear, I wish I wasn't quite so much alone.

Lots and lots of love. I do hope there are some letters on the way. – Nessie

Letter home from Hankow, 19 June 1938:

My dear Mother,

. . . I have had a busy week seeing people off. Last evening Cora [Deng] started out for Changsha and the trip to Kweiling and Kweiyang that I should have taken but did not. We did not go across the river, but saw her off at the railway ferry on this side. Today Wang Hsiu-King left for Hongkong. . . . She has been up in Chengtu for four months and is just returned to Shanghai. I hated the thought of her travelling alone all the way through that section that they are constantly bombing and it was a great relief to find one other passenger in her compartment was a YWCA member from Chefoo. They knew each other quite well and will be able to help each other when they get to Canton. We went all the way over to the railway station with her. The ferry was jambed with soldiers and there were army horses everywhere. The station platform on the other side of the river was simply crowded with soldiers and there were troop trains in the station with soldiers everywhere, even sitting on top of the coal truck. I made Wang Hsiu-King promise to telegraph me from Canton and from Hongkong. Canton is an awful place to go through at present. Several people who have come up recently have said it was pretty much like their idea of hell. I do hope she does not have any hair-raising experiences. She has never been in an air raid because while the fighting was going on at Shanghai, she was in Chefoo and since then she has been in Chengtu where they have not yet had any raids. I hope her first experience, if she has one, is not too terrifying.

Today we heard rumours of a clash between Japanese and French troops in the French concession of Shanghai. I can hardly wait to see tomorrow's newspaper. The French have been very careful not to let Japanese troops in to their concession at all and on one occasion put motor trucks across the road where the Japanese were trying to force an entrance. This time they say that machine guns were brought into action and there were several casualties. I do hope it is only a rumour.

The breaking of the Yellow River dykes[10] near Chengchow has solved our immediate problem here. There will be no chance of a Japanese drive till the dykes are mended or the river subsides. As July is the worst month for floods there is not likely to be much improvement. However, the Japanese may cut the railway to the south and come in from that direction. They are still trying to land down river from here, but don't seem to be having much success according to the reports we get. People are going up to Kuling for the summer holidays and the consuls don't seem to be making any protests, so I suppose all is well for the time being.

I went to a meeting of British residents last Tuesday afternoon called by the consul general. The Foreign Residents Association is making arrangements for another international train to go through to Hongkong. It is to leave next week, I think. They say it will probably be the last of its kind. I can't get away as early as that, but I am supposed to be going to the Hongkong conferences next month and have written for sleepers for the 15th of July for four of us. I wonder what it will feel like to be in a really safe place again. I am supposed to come back here if the situation gets worse. But if the Association decided to send me to another part of China I don't know what will happen here. . . .

Miss Wang, the General Secretary of the Wuchang YWCA, brought me over $1000 in bank notes today to look after for them and use in an emergency if need be. I have put it in the safe downstairs and if I go away they will have to look after it themselves. I think it is a bit early to make preparations of that kind but they feel happier when the money is in a safe place. What they are afraid of if there is real danger here is that the banks will not open and they will be stuck for funds. It is just as well to have some money against the day. I carry round more cash myself than I care to have, but having been stuck once at Kuling, I am hoping to be better prepared next time.

Yesterday morning I went to breakfast with Miss Couch and Miss Dexter. I have a standing invitation from them for Sunday morning breakfast and I really enjoy it. They live in the Bishop's house now since he left. Just at present they have a New Zealander there, a Mr. Shepherd from Dunedin. He works in the New Life Movement which is the pet hobby of the Generalissimo and Madame Chiang.[11] It has gone to his head rather and he is inclined to think he is the whole works. . . .

Much love to you all,
Nessie

Letter to Eva Skinner from Hankow, 27 June 1938:

Well dearie, there is not so much to write about at the moment. We look eagerly at the news each day and our spirits go up or down in accordance. Most people think that the Japanese will not be here for a month or so. These last few days the Chinese have been using their air force to advantage and according to the reports we have had they have done most effective work down river. The Japanese are trying hard to get at the boom in the river below Kiukiang but so far they have been held by Chinese forces. Equipment in the way of new planes and tanks and so on is pouring in here and being conveyed down the river. Meantime people are calmly going to Kuling for the summer. I hope they don't get marooned during the Japanese occupation of Kiukiang. An international train goes out tomorrow morning with over three hundred foreigners on board. It will go straight through to Kowloon and that is the one reason that makes me wish that I was travelling on it. The Japanese have been notified about it and it has a 'qualified' guarantee of safety. I shall go down on the 15th and will have a busy time dodging bombs on the way and in Canton while I am waiting for the boat. The full moon is on the 12th so we are bound to meet something on the line. I hope it isn't too exciting.

Chen Ya-Chun [the office secretary] has just come back into the office with bad news. According to her the Japanese have already got through the boom in the river. Ouch!!! That is pretty bad. I wonder what will happen now. There isn't much that can happen but the Chinese will break the dykes here and flood all this area before they let the Japanese come in. What a life we lead. This continual jerking from a feeling of quasi-security to a state of fearing the worst is <u>very</u> hard on the system. . . .

Ever and ever so much love – Nessie

Letter to Eva Skinner, handwritten from Hankow, 3 July 1938:

> You're getting a letter by hand for a change dear, because all the afternoon sun is pouring in to my room & my desk in the window is an impossible spot. So I'm out on the 5th floor porch which is cooler; but there are several people out here so I don't like to wield my typewriter.
>
> I have read Bertram's 'Crisis in China' just recently & am vastly intrigued. It is superficial of course & he has simply relayed the opinions of the Chinese group he hunted with; but it is very interesting isn't it? It is supposed to be the only account of the Sian incident that gives Chang Hsueh-liang's side of the story. It's hard to believe in the whitewashed Chang he presents & the deeds of the Tungpei forces in this war have not been such as to put them on a pedestal exactly. I met Agnes Smedley in the street yesterday & felt for an absurd moment that our acquaintance was on quite a different footing since I had read his account of her. Personally I'd hate to be published to that extent. She is a very interesting figure & the influence of Bishop Roots has had a mellowing effect on her as well as on several others of the communist group. People are still moving away from Hankow. There is still no immediate danger, but people are moving away as fast as boats & trains can take them. The Japanese are making a very determined effort to get up river. Planes from here have been making night raids on their concentration points, even though it is over a week till the full moon. We hear them come back about 3.a.m. The weather has been fine these last few days so we may have a clear full moon. A poor look out for Hankow & Wuchang.
>
> Ever so much love to you all. With luck only one more letter from Hankow.
>
> Nessie

Letter to Eva Skinner from Hangkow, 13 July 1938:

> Eva dear this is my last chance to get a letter out on the boat that leaves Hongkong on the 15th, so I'm doing this in office time. As a matter of fact it doesn't matter whose time I use these last two days. There is so much in the way of odds and ends to attend to at the last minute and I have not even an office secretary to help me at present. Chen Ya-Chun has gone off to Changsha for a few days to look at their work down there and I am left with the pieces. I have been racking my brain to think if I have left everyone with plenty of money in case anything happens. The July salaries are all looked after and one reason why I am so infernally hot is because I have been running round getting bank drafts and money orders to send all over the countryside. I am hanging onto the office till the end of this month at any rate, though I am clearing everything out of it except for the hired desk and chairs.

This office is in the ex-British concession and at present enormous concrete posts are being made for terrific gates at all the entrances. It is costing $10,000 and there are rumours that the Chinese Government has given the concession back to the British. I don't know whether it's true or not, but I wouldn't be surprised. If it is true I think we should hang on to this office at all costs because we could have people living here in comparative safety if the worst came to the worst. We are only just inside the gates, but it would be fun to look down from our balcony and see the Japanese not being allowed to come through.

Yesterday we had a ghastly air raid. It wasn't on this side of the river at all but Wuching was simply strafed. The planes were so high that they couldn't get their objective which, with a flight of imagination, people think was the military academy near the railway station. One bomb hit the roof of the Provincial Hospital and went through three floors. The only patients were obstetric and ever so many of them were killed. St. Hilda's School belonging to the American Church Mission was hit though no one was killed. Boone Compound got one just outside the wall which did a good deal of damage. The Christian Missionary Auxiliary had a ring of bombs around it. There are about two hundred dead and four hundred injured. I suppose this is the first of a series like Canton had. It came at lunchtime and we tried to keep the conversation going but the thought of what was happening to other people was too much for us and we got more and more silent as the bombs came down. Really it will be a rest to be in Hongkong for a bit though it is the knowledge of all the suffering that wears one down and that goes on and on and on. I hate this war and there seems to be months if not years still ahead of us. . . .

I leave on Friday the 15th. Our friends the enemy have been bombing Canton and the railway again so it looks as though we may have a thrilling trip especially as the moon is full at present. I loathe air raid alarms when I am travelling. You feel so helpless.

Ever so much love – Nessie

7
Travels
July–October 1938

On 15 July 1938 Nessie set out for Hong Kong in order to attend a YWCA staff conference. From there she went to Chengdu to spend time with her cousin Jesse and his family, travelling via French Indochina and Yunnan. She arrived back in Hankow on 24 September, departing again almost immediately for Hong Kong, which she reached on 11 October.

Letter to Eva Skinner from Hong Kong, 24 July 1938:

> Well, my dear, I can hardly believe yet that I am in Hongkong. I cabled to Ethel Law when I arrived because they had asked me to keep them informed of my movements and I hope you heard, but perhaps you didn't. I don't recommend travel on Chinese railways at the moment. It is just a shade too exciting.
>
> We were supposed to leave at 2.20 p.m. on Friday the 15th and when an air raid warning went at about 10.15, I congratulated myself that it had not come two hours later. However I discovered our train had not yet come in from Canton and it was not likely to pull out before 8.p.m. Two of the Chinese girls and I started out for the station on the 7 o'clock launch and reached the station at 7.30. The Lutheran Mission baggage man was waiting there with our baggage and the news that the train was not yet in, but was expected about 8.p.m. We were put off hour by hour all night and at 6.a.m. the train was still not in. I had pushed some suitcases together end to end and managed about an hour's sleep in snatches. It was bright moonlight and we expected a raid momentarily but fortunately none came.
>
> About nine o'clock the train came in and the baggage man telephoned the Lutheran Home to send us over some breakfast. I have never tasted such good food! Just as the train was almost made up in the yards the air raid warning went. The station was alive with troops and crowded with piles of ammunition, guns, tanks, trucks, etc. and I felt sure that the Japanese would know about it all. We didn't know what to do. Most people made for the ferry and went back to

Hankow. But the second alarm came right on the heels of the first and the planes were over our heads before the ferry started. I saw us with a direct hit mid-stream so decided to chance things on the Wuchang side.

The only foreigners catching the train were two C.I.M. [China Inland Mission] families from Lanchow, each with two small children. We dashed along a piece of half submerged railway right down at the edge of the river and I have never leapt so nimbly from sleeper to sleeper. A coolie was hired to carry one of the children so I had his bamboo pole and rope. We sheltered under a mat roof that would have knocked us silly if it had come down, but was not strong enough to protect us if anything heavy landed in our direction. It had housed horses and was not very clean, but I lay with my face in the mud and was quite happy.

The Hankow airfield and the Hanyang arsenal were bombed heavily. There were over a hundred bombs altogether I should think. We could trace the course of the planes by the coming into action of guns in different parts of the cities and when the station gun started barking over our heads we thought we were in for it. However they passed over and we could hear the noise of the planes and distant dog fighting and then that gradually faded out too. We waited for the all-clear and then went back to the station.

The sleepers were a bit harder to manoeuvre going back. When the first alarm went trains had moved out of the station one after another. First a long train of tanks and guns and motor trucks, then a long train of all the best rolling stock, really good carriages that they are not using at present. Then our own train followed. Where they went to I don't know but they probably hid in the long grass further up the line. It was 12.45 p.m. when we finally pulled out.

Our progress was painfully slow because hundreds of military trains were on the lines and every last troop train had right of way. Troops and supplies were being rushed to the front down the river near Kiukiang. I went to bed about 9.p.m. but was wakened shortly after 10 with the news that the air raid alarm had been given. We backed out of the station and waited in a cutting. The moon was not really bright enough for a raid and it was cloudy where we were so I didn't get off the train but sat on the train step and enjoyed the beauty of the night.

Next morning we had gone hardly any distance at all but during the morning arrived at Yochow; ordinarily seven hours down the line, but we had taken about 19 hours. We stopped there four hours while ever so many trains passed us and finally the passenger train which had left two hours after us caught up. That evening about 6.p.m. we reached Changsha and the other members of our party joined us. One was travelling second class, but so many people got in through the windows that she could not get to her reservation and had to sleep on the bench in one of our first class compartments all the way down.

We should have been in Hengyang early next morning, but when we woke up we were precisely one station down the Changsha line and the air raid warning had come through. Presently the urgent signal was received and we were all ordered out of the train. There was a hill on one side of us and a ditch on the other so the prospects for hiding were not good. We clambered up the hill and found a spot that looked a good place to lie down in and waited for the worst. It didn't come and presently people began to wash themselves and their clothes in the ditch. The train was packed, of course, with refugees travelling on top of the first three tenders. Then the engine whistled and we all scrambled back. The only way the carboy could keep our first class moderately empty was to keep the doors firmly locked. I didn't like the feeling of being locked in, but the doors seemed to open when we really needed to get off so it wasn't so bad. Water was a problem. At various stations down the line they fill up the tanks, but when the train takes three and four times the time it should, the tanks are empty long before we reach the watering place. There were hours when we had no water for washing or drinking and the heat was terrific.

A second air raid alarm came that morning and we thought two before 8.a.m. was a bit thick. About 4.p.m. we got into Hengyang which is the junction of the new line that is going to connect Central China with Yunnan. Once we had passed the junction of the line that goes off to Nanchang we had made much better time because the military trains were all going that way.

We waited for hours at midnight at a station in the mountains because it is necessary to do the last run by night because that is the section they bomb most often. Early in the morning we started again, but stopped at Lochang right on the Honan-Kwantung border.

Shortly after twelve (it was Tuesday afternoon by this time) we pulled out of Lochang and down the most wonderful valley. The scenery for hours and hours was perfectly magnificent and the only thing that spoiled the trip was the fact that every station down the line had been bombed. The ruins were grim and in so many cases half the village had suffered too. In the stations we could still smell the peculiar smell of charred wood on which water has been thrown – from the bombings of that day. I was glad when darkness came because the moon was well on the wane and we had no more to fear.

At 2.30 a.m. on Wednesday the car boy called us and about 3.30 a.m. we pulled into what was once the Canton terminal station. I never saw anything so gruesome in my life. I think it gave me the creeps more than anything else on the whole trip. We had passed the wrecks of locomotives and rolling stock and the repair sheds had been badly bombed, but of course all the tracks had been repaired so we came through alright. I was all for getting off the station as soon as possible. I couldn't bear the sight of it. While we were waiting for a taxi the telephone rang somewhere in the building and I thought how typical of China carrying on in the midst of ruins.

We went straight to the Taikoo wharf, but had to wait on the pavement till 6.a.m. I was sorry for the C.I.M. people and their little babies, the youngest was seven months. Think of a journey like that with children. I travelled saloon on the boat and had a marvellous bath. It was a British boat and plentifully be-flagged. We pulled out early to the tune of the air raid alarm and had a wonderfully peaceful trip down the river to Hongkong. With health inspection, etc. it was 3.p.m. before we landed. Five days on a journey that should have taken two and a half and not an uninterrupted night in the whole time. I found that Miss Hancock is on the staff of this school where we are holding our conference and she piloted me to a large breezy room far from the madding crowd where I had a good rest.

Chen Chi-li came down two days later and had a much more exciting trip than we had. Her train had to stop seven times for alarms and spent nearly the whole of one day in tunnels. They drew into Pan Shih only to find that the signal had come so they pulled up the line again into a tunnel. When they got back to Pan Shih they found that the place had been bombed. Lochang was bombed that day too, the place where we had waited in what we thought was safety when we came down. Since then the Japanese have announced their intention of bombing all trains except those that carry third party nationals. That means no train will be even as safe as ours was. Even if you get out of the train and hide under the trees they machine gun the trees. I do not like the thought of the return journey. It is frightfully exciting while it lasts, but I have had quite a reaction since I arrived. However I do not yet know what National will want me to do. If things go as I want them to do I will fly from here to Szechuan, have my holiday there and then go down river to Hankow. I do not know whether the Japanese will allow me time to do that. They may want to take Hankow earlier. They are not making very rapid progress at present, but they have been rushing reinforcements to their positions at Matang, Pentseh and Hukow so I don't know what will happen. . . .

Ever and ever so much love – Nessie

I hope the war is over long before I have to leave China.

Letter to Eva Skinner from Hong Kong, 14 August 1938:

Well dearie, I am afraid that I am writing very unsatisfactory letters these days, but it is hot and I am tired and the least thing seems an effort. This is rank ingratitude when I get such nice long newsy letters from you. I had an air mail written on July 14th and was very glad to have it.

'Y.W.C.A. Spring Staff Meeting'. Nessie third right, back row. 1938. Skinner family collection

Our staff conference ended on Wednesday and I came over here to the Guest House to stay on Thursday. It is very nice and restful though a little harder to reach from town than St. Stephen's where we had the conferences. However, my boat to Haiphong leaves on Tuesday and I am beginning to get moderately excited at the prospect of another trip. I wrote yesterday to Mr. Hansen to ask him to book me a seat from Hankow to Kowloon on September 29th.[1] I don't know of course whether trains will still be running then, but I will write to him again from Chengtu and find out if he advises travelling down by rail at that time.

This morning I went down to Blake Pier to meet Dr. Anderson and Eleanor who have come down from Chengtu by the route I am taking up. They are staying here at the Guest House and it is fun to see them again. He has been appointed to the CMS [Church Missionary Society] office in London to head up the medical work of their mission. They are disconsolate at having to leave China but a stern sense of duty prevails. Eleanor really looks younger than she did five years ago. I wonder how she does it.

Another person I met unexpectedly was Dr. Kathleen Pih. Do you remember her at Otago Medical School? She has been with the Presbyterian mission near Canton[2] and has been through all the bombings that were so near to the compound. Now she is marrying a very nice Chinese lad who is on the staff of St. John's University in Shanghai and they are going up there early next month. I shall enjoy seeing something of them when I am up there.

I had to fight the Staff for permission to go back to Hankow, but they will not permit me to stay there through the Japanese Occupation. I think they are right when I view the situation objectively, but it will be hard to come away. They want me in Shanghai for a few months and I loathe and despise the thought of it, but short of resigning I see no way out of it. I am quite seriously thinking of scouting round here to see what the chances would be of some educational work in Hongkong in say two years' time. I hate this constantly moving on in the YWCA here and am dying to be left in peace for a few years. I really am concerned lest I lose the ability to stick to one job in one place. Maybe I have lost it already. I ought at least to try myself out in something more permanent. I am not happy over the results of our conferences and am conscious of a dead weight of disapproval on the part of some the staff where I am concerned. We are certainly hard on each other in this organisation and it is difficult for me to give of my best when I am so conscious of criticism. Please don't mention this to anyone as I may feel vastly improved after the holiday I'm taking. . . .

Ever so much love,

Nessie

Letter to Eva Skinner, handwritten on board *SS Kwangtung* en route from Hong Kong to Hanoi, 19 August 1938:

Dear Eva,

. . . I am sitting on the S.S. 'Kwangtung' off Hoihow, a port on Hainan Island, & it has been & still is thundering & lightning at a great old bat. We have been anchored here for over 24 hours & a lot of cargo has been taken off on to great Chinese junks which hoist sails made of pieces of matting all sewn together & sail off to land as soon as they are full. We have not been ashore as it means staying ashore for seven hours & as there is nothing to see beyond a small Chinese city no one thought it was worth it. One passenger, a missionary, left the ship here & the rest, five in all are going on to Haiphong. One is Japanese. He sits at a table by himself & spends most of his time in his cabin. No one speaks to him. He may be thankful that the Chinese stewards do not put poison in his soup.

We left Hongkong on the 17th at 10.a.m. & had not gone far before we sighted two Japanese cruisers lurking on either side of an island at the mouth of the river. Then a few hours later we passed a Japanese aircraft carrier. Its planes have been carrying out daily raids on the railway and I wished I had the power to sink it.

At 12 o'clock yesterday an alarm sounded & the special police on board & all the officers suddenly began to dash about with ugly looking guns & revolvers. I got all excited but it was only 'pirate practice' which is carried out on every trip up or down this coast. It is really preferable to the ordinary boat drill because the passengers don't have to participate.

These four days at sea are proving an ideal rest. I have written a few letters that I didn't have time to finish in Hgkg, have read a book & done nothing else but eat & sleep. We reach Haiphong on Sunday and I am going straight on to Hanoi. The express train leaves on Tuesday and I think I shall wait for that & go straight through. You can take three days travelling only by daylight & staying at small hotels by night. I don't think that would be much fun by myself. I hope to get a plane from Kunming to Chengtu on the 26th. It takes just three hours. I do hope there's a seat to spare that day. . . .

[no ending]

Letter home, handwritten on board the *SS Kwangtung* en route from Hong Kong to Hanoi, 20 August 1938:

My dear Mother,

I regret to mention that the good ship S.S. 'Kwangtung' is pitching fit to bust & the general effect on me is extreme sleepiness. I don't know how far I am likely to get with this letter. We left Hongkong a long, long time ago, the 17th to be exact & most of the time we have been sitting in Chinese ports unloading cargo on to big clumsy looking junks. On the 18th we reached Hoihow a port on Hainan Is. and sat away far out & beyond the sand bar for over 24 hours. Then about 8.p.m. yesterday we set out for Pakhoi which we reached about 8.30 this morning. It wasn't quite so far to land this time so we went ashore in the customs launch & wandered up & down the streets.

We came back again in a sailing junk & had an adventurous time. I lost my hat overboard & we turned around & picked it up with a grand flourish. It is my one & only so I was glad to see it again though as it is in white felt it is looking somewhat the worse for wear.

The ship holds very few passengers. One got off at Hoihow & the rest go on to Haiphong which we reach tomorrow morning. Two are going on up to Yunnanfu so I hope to have someone to travel with all the way. They are a very nice young married couple. He Scotch & she American. They have been in the Philippine Islands for some years, but the firm has now sent them to Hgkg & this is a business trip.

Did I tell you that I saw Dr Kathleen Pih married in Hongkong last Monday? Mr. McNeur married them & it was fun to see some New Zealanders for a change. Paddy Jansen asked after you all. Kathleen married a very nice lad who is on the staff of St. John's University in Shanghai, Dr Francis Chang. Science of some description is his line. It will be fun to see something of them when I get back to Shanghai.

I expect to reach Chengtu on the 26th, but I do not know yet whether I can get a seat on the plane that day. It's a three hours' flight over wonderful mountains. Yunnaufu is about 6000 feet above sea level & Chengtu about 2000 so it will be something of a come down. I do hope it's fine so that I can see the mountains of Tibet & everything else there is to be seen. . . .

I must stop and pack up. The captain has threatened to get us into Haiphong before breakfast tomorrow morning, but we say we're going to have breakfast at his expense whatever happens.

Much love to everyone – Nessie

Letter home from Chengtu, 27 August 1938:

My dear Mother,

I can hardly believe it myself but here I am actually staying with Jesse & Vee in Chengtu. I arrived yesterday & you can imagine the thrill it was. But I'd better begin where I left off in my last letter if I can remember where that was. Information about the train from Hanoi to Yunnanfu was so contradictory that

I decided to go up to Hanoi at mid-day on Tuesday. I found there was a train leaving that evening so I visited the Chinese Consulate to see that my passport was in order, sent a telegram to Yunnanfu, bought a book for the journey & then went to the Railway Hotel to wait for my supper & the train. The train was Pullman style so I couldn't even take my dress off. There were two French passengers & one Scot & the rest were Chinese.

We were wakened next morning at 5.30 a.m. and bundled out on to a station labelled Pho-Moi where our passports were collected & we had breakfast – coffee & a roll. Our train – a slow one because there was a bad slip on the line & the Michelin[3] was not running – pulled out at 6.22 and we started to climb. At Lao-kay we crossed a river into China & at the border were visited by Customs etc. I had my doubts about the provisions I was bringing in for Jesse, but was asked no questions so didn't mention them.

We climbed steadily all day through magnificent scenery alongside a river almost red in colour. It was pouring with rain but as we climbed higher the weather improved. It must be the most beautiful railway route in the world. I don't see how anything could be more beautiful & it is a most amazing piece of engineering. There are about 170 tunnels on the line & ever so many bridges.

We were stopped inside a tunnel for the landslide. The engine was out but I was in a rear carriage. There was no light worth mentioning & we had had no warning so we groped for our belongings & got out. The coolies had made for the baggage van and I thought I would have to carry my own stuff, but once down from the carriage with water from the tunnel roof dripping all over me I found the coolies & struggled through the mud (you should have seen my white shoes!!)[4] across a bridge which seemed to have been weakened by the slip & into the other train. Then we went on climbing. We came back on our tracks & could see way beneath us the landslide & two trains waiting one on each side.

We ended up at a place called Kai Yuen about 8.p.m., about 4000 feet above sea level & the hotel full to the brim. I had discovered an American third class passenger by that time – Mrs. Wallden & we shared a room in the Railway Hospital which evidently takes guests. Meals had been very scrappy out of my lunch basket so we were relieved to find it was not too late for dinner. We both slept well & were dead to the world when the boy called us next morning at 5.30.a.m. By 6 we were along at the hotel for coffee & rolls (two this time after our starved conditions the day before).

We left at 7.12. I think it must be like the rail-cars that run on the Wairarapa line. I switched to first class because there is only 1st & 3rd and the seats were very comfortable. In fact the Michelin was extremely comfortable altogether. We continued to climb up through narrow river gorges & upland plains; the scenery changing constantly all the time.

We arrived at Kunming about 1.p.m., once more in a starved condition, and I helped Mrs. Wallden find a hotel & then set out to find Dr. Watson at the C.M.S. Hospital. I knew Kunming pretty well by the time I found it. They had not had my letter explaining myself but only my telegram & didn't know whether I was one or a party of six. However I found that Mr. & Mrs. Evans of the English Methodist Mission were expecting me so I went over & had a very fine welcome & lunch! You should have seen me tuck it away. Mr. Evans took me to the Eurasia Office & I found there was a plane leaving next day at 1.30 p.m. I had been told at one tourist office in Haiphong that the service had been suspended between Kunming and Chengtu & had wondered all the way up if I would get through. I had to have a guarantor before I could get a ticket & Mr. Evans obliged with his Mission chop[5] & when I folded my ticket into my purse I was so excited, both at the thrill of my first flight & at the thought of actually seeing the Chengtu folk.

Promptly at 1.30 next day the plane took off with me inside feeling a bit apprehensive at leaving terra firma so far behind or rather below. Yunnanfu is 6500 above sea level so we had a good start. If I tried for a life-time I could never do justice to that trip. It was positively thrilling to see mountains & rivers from so high above & the mountains are wonderful. For over two hours we flew above the grandest & most rugged you could imagine.

We followed more or less the course of the Upper Yang Tze, & could see it, a muddy stream far below between the high cliffs. We flew over little patches of rice high up on the tops of mountains & razor blade ridges that I'm sure no one could ever walk along. On our right & left were much higher ranges with cotton wool clouds lying on them. For about twenty minutes everything but a high peak or so was blotted out by cloud & we flew in sunshine over a floor of cloud. Then everything seemed to melt into a blue haze which looked like a lake stretching for miles & miles & it gradually resolved itself into the Szechuan plain. We had been flying at 9500 feet most of the way. It took us about three quarters of an hour to cross the plain & the last 20 minutes we were gradually coming down. Then there was Chengtu, a huddle of grey roofs below us & soon we were flying over, or almost over, the University campus, then right across the city & out to the air field the other side. The whole trip was perfect. I wasn't the least bit air sick & most of the way it was absolutely steady like travelling in a car. The trip took exactly 3 hours. It's a month by chair & eight days by bus.

We landed a fair distance from the bus & had to wait till the coolies brought the luggage over. But at last we set off for the city. Jesse was in the doorway of the Eurasia Office when we arrived & were we pleased to see each other again after sixteen years.[6] He had his bicycle & I piled into a richsa and off we started. Ruth Weiss whom I had known in Shanghai met us on the way & wasn't long before we arrived. Robert & Douglas[7] were at the gate & gave the signal for the fire-crackers to be set off & Vee was half way down the path.

It was the grandest arrival you can imagine & we were all frightfully thrilled & excited. . . .

Ever so much love to you all,
Nessie

In a shared letter typed later, Nessie wrote:

> I was wondering whether I would enjoy air travel and was provided with smelling salts and a small bottle of brandy in case the altitude made things uncomfortable. There were various formalities to go through on the airfield. The military police had to look at my passport, upside down incidentally, but my effort to turn it right side up was not acceptable. When the officer saw the photo and then took a long look at me I thought I was going to be turned back because of the lack of any similarity between me and my photo but I passed.'[8]

Letter home, handwritten on board the *SS Wanliu*, en route from Chungking to Ichang, 19 September 1938:

My dear Mother,

I am on board the 'Wanliu' at Chungking waiting to go down river to Ichang. The river is too high at present so it will be the day after tomorrow at earliest before we move. I am beginning to be a little perturbed about my booking on the railway from Hankow because we may be held up here indefinitely. However I can always save a day or so by flying from Ichang to Hankow & I am now badly bitten by the flying bug.

But to go back. On Thursday evening word came that the plane from Chengtu to Chungking had been delayed by a day & would not leave till Saturday. Great rejoicing in the Moncrieff family. On Saturday Jesse went into town with me at 1.p.m. and after waiting an hour or so we heard that the plane was late. We sat in the stuffy bus for a long time & just before 4 o'clock were told that the plane would not go till next morning. It was an awful waste of an afternoon, but I didn't mind having another evening with the family & Virginia was not planning to change the sheets on my bed till she knew for certain that I had gone!

The next morning the Company's car was sent out to the campus for us at 7.30 and we had a great send-off with crackers that sounded like big guns. I hated leaving because goodness knows when I shall ever see them again. However I was very glad that Jesse could come as far as the air field. It was 9.20 when we finally took off & Jesse waved me off the field. I'm simply bursting to come home & give you all the news about Jesse & Vee & the children. I can hardly believe that I have spent three weeks with them. Chengtu has always seemed like one of the most remote places on the face of the earth & now it isn't any longer. It is such fun to know them & they were awfully good to me. It's grand to have family that I know in China & they couldn't have given me a grander welcome if I had been Jesse's sister.

The trip by plane to Chungking was not nearly as grand or exciting as the one from Kunming had been. I suppose one's first flight is always the most thrilling. We flew much lower because there were no very high mountains & we were only 1500 to 2000 feet above the plain. It was clear most of the way & we could see the bus road winding over the hills below us & all the paddy fields & farm houses & little toy villages. It takes just an hour & ten minutes to reach Chungking. The air field is some miles down river from the city & we had a good view as we flew over.

I had met two of the passengers on the plane before & one, a Mr. McCurdie who had accompanied the school children up to Chengtu on the truck a few days before made it his business to look after me. We made a perfect landing, but unfortunately in a shower of rain. We hurried across the fields to the river where a Chinese row-boat took us out to a hydroplane that was waiting for us.[9] The big plane had been full – 14 passengers; but we all managed to get in plus luggage & mails though I thought we should never rise out of the water. The river winds a great deal, but we were high enough to cut a few corners. I thought we were going to cut a hole in a few hillsides on the way but we didn't. We landed in the water near the winter airfield which is an island when the river is low but completely submerged during high water. Then another Chinese boat ferried us to the shore & we climbed up flights of steps to the bus waiting on the road above.

At the company's office I met Mr. Drumwright, a member of the American Embassy whom I had met in Hankow. He was just leaving for the air field to fly to Chengtu where he is going to stay with Mr. & Mrs. Phelps who live two houses from Jesse & Vee. I scribbled a message on a card & gave it to him to deliver that night. I know they would be glad to have it.

Then Mr. McCurdie called a richsa and I set out for the Canadian Mission Agency where I was to stay. Mr. Jones, the manager, had already bought my ticket on the 'Wanliu' which was due to leave this morning. It did not come in till about 6.p.m. yesterday afternoon & as soon as we saw it coming Mr. Jones hustled me off so that I could get across the river before dark. The Chinese row boats go back & forth across the river all day long. The current is very swift at present & carries them downstream a long way. We hit the bank ever so far down & were poled slowly up close to the shore working our way out round junks that were tied up & ducking our heads as we passed under the ropes and gang planks of Butterfield and Swire's hulks.[10]

Of course I discovered as soon as I came on board that we would not be sailing this morning, but I have stayed on board all day to-day as it has poured with rain & I have no rain coat, umbrella or shoes other than summer ones. It has really been quite cold to-day & I am beginning to think longingly of my winter clothes in Hankow. I am impatient to get there now I have started & do not like the delay.

The Captain is going to find out if there is any other boat going down before the 'Wanliu'. Some of the bigger ones can manage the rapids in high water even when the 'Wanliu' can't. I would prefer to sail under the Union Jack even though a flag is not much protection these days. The Chinese boats carry troops down river so they won't do, & I think the French boat is laid up at present.

One of the officers on board came up on the 'Changsha' as a passenger on the same trip as when I went to Ichang. They have all been very nice & lent me books as I have as I have none of my own. I am the only passenger so far. There's nothing like using the 'Wanliu' as a hotel; but I wish it would move on. . . .

Much love, Nessie

Letter home, handwritten on board the *SS Changsha* en route from Ichang to Hankow, 24 September 1938:

My dear Mother,

Here I am on the last lap of the journey back to Hankow & beginning to wonder how I will get out to Hongkong. I think I wrote to you last while I was waiting for the water to get low enough for the 'Wanliu' to leave Chungking. We sailed finally on Wednesday morning at 6.30. There were two other passengers on board – both Hankow men, one returning from a business trip to Chungking & the other returning from a holiday spent with his wife in Hongkong. He intended to be away from Hankow a week, but the plane service was suspended & he finally decided to return via Indo-China.

We didn't have much cargo when we left Chungking & went rolling down to Wanhsien. There has to be a special pilot on board all the way & my goodness when you see the water you realise he's needed. The captain lent me 'Glimpses of the Yang Tzu Gorges' by Captain Plant[11] & I was glad to have it though as the account is written from Ichang up to Chungking it's a bit difficult to spot things. Jesse gave me a copy of it [when Nessie was in Peiping] & it may still be on my bookcase somewhere. If you are interested, look it up because it does give a good idea of what the Gorges are like. I was thrilled with the first part, but lower down it simply takes your breath away.

Of course it is impossible to navigate after dark so you have to tie up at night. The first evening we reached Wanhsien & tied up at a hulk quite close to where the C.N.A.C. [China National Aviation Corporation] planes come down. It was pouring with rain so there was no encouragement to take a stroll. We had to fill up the ship's tanks with wood oil for Hankow & that was done through a pipe from the storage tank up the bank so there was nothing to watch.

The next morning was rather dull, but about mid-day a sampan loaded with tins of petrol tied up at the C.N.A.C. raft so we knew a plane would be in before so very long. The one from Ichang came first. It flew over us & came back because the hydroplanes have to land with the stream. It made a perfect landing & was soon tied up to the buoy a little way from the raft. It was the Commodore which holds twelve passengers. I was interested to find the petrol tanks are in the wings. It was quite interesting seeing them filled. The passengers came out on top to stretch their legs, but it wasn't long before the caps were all screwed on again & the empty tins in the sampan & the pilots once more in the cockpit & off they went downstream because they can't get the necessary speed against the current. Hydroplanes take a long time to rise off the water & they climb slowly but soon it was overhead again & flying off to the west.

About an hour later the Dolphin – a six seater – came in from Chungking. She is a faster plane & did not need to refuel. Mail bags were taken off & passengers climbed in, & off she went. At 2.30 p.m. we moved on ourselves & about 6.30 tied up at Kweifu just at the entrance to the first gorge. We dropped anchors at the stern & at the bows in about 80 feet of water. Usually the B&S ships anchor east of the town but the pilot said there were bandits about so we stayed west near the police headquarters. There were soon half a dozen or so boats round us selling fruit for which Kweifu is noted

Next morning we were away again at 6.30 & we had to be up early to see the Wind-Box Gorge. It was magnificent. The cliffs tower up either side. I am longing to see the Gorge in winter now because with the water 50 to 80 feet lower the cliffs must look even grander. Of course there isn't much danger from the submerged rocks when the water is so high, but the higher it is the more dangerous the eddies & rapids & whirlpools are. You never saw such boiling, seething water. Junks can't do the trip at all when the water is high & the 'Wanliu' had all it could do to get through. The river was at the maximum height that the 'Wanliu' can manage.

We reached Ichang about 1.p.m. and the whole morning was most interesting & exciting. I crossed my fingers once or twice, but the pilot was an old hand at the game. Once or twice the Chief Officer came back & told us what to look out for. He pointed out the little streams that mark the boundary between Szechuan & Hupeh provinces & the village where Captain Plant lived. He built a house looking right down to the Lampshine Gorge & there is a memorial to him standing near it above the signal station.

I should have spent the morning on the observation deck above the bridge, but I have no warm clothing with me & it was very chilly. I simply had to retire to my bunk from time to time & roll in a blanket to thaw out. Thank goodness I have some winter garments in Hankow. Cotton dresses & wide scanties are decidedly unfashionable. The cold weather has come very suddenly this year.

In Ichang the 'Wanliu' brought up alongside the 'Changsha' which we rejoiced to see was flying the Blue Peter.[12] After lunch we crawled down into the bowels of the boat & and out on the lighter in between & then onto the 'Changsha'. I wanted to go ashore & see Deaconess Reibe & the Lius, but we were anchored away below the town & the river was a raging torrent. I hated the thought of risking my life in a sampan, especially on the way back. Moreover it was raining off & on & I have no umbrella or rain coat & my white shoes are very well ventilated. So I stayed put & spent a long afternoon pacing the deck. I have nothing to read & have not dug deep enough to get any sewing out so there's not much to do.

We sailed at 6.30 this morning & should be into Hankow early Monday morning, but it rather depends on how long we have to spend unloading cargo at Shasi. I shall be very glad to arrive in Hankow. . . .

Ever so much love to you all,

Nessie

Letter home from Hankow, 6 October 1938:

My dear Mother

. . . The great excitement of last week was an air raid here. We had an alarm the week before, but the planes were chased off before they got here. Friday was a very cloudy day and the planes were not spotted till they were well inland. Consequently the warning was very short. This section of the city is near enough to the French Concession and the Japanese Concession to be more or less safe. The Japanese are such rotten marksmen though that there is always a chance of a stray bomb. I think the bombers get nervous and the shaking of their hands releases the bombs before they mean them to go! Anyway they are jolly good at hitting hospitals and refugee camps and residential districts and leaving the points of military importance alone.

Everyone thinks they were aiming at the Arsenal in Hanyang, but the worst damage done was in a congested Chinese area where about 200 people were killed and many more injured. The Methodist Hospital, quite near where the bomb fell, and the Union Hospital were frightfully busy afterwards with wounded. A whole section of buildings collapsed and a lot of people were hurt. The electric wires were brought down and they had to perform major operations by candle light. Dr. Maxwell had to go along to the hospital at 2.a.m. to take his turn at the operating table. The doctors were working in shifts. Dr. M. said most of the injured were women, because the men had not yet come home from work.

I saw in the paper, yesterday I think it was, that the British war department had almost perfected a device which would keep fighting on the land and render bombers practically useless. All power to them! War is bad enough on land, goodness only knows, but when hundreds of women and children and non-combatants are mown down, it's just the limit. The planes were only above us 10–15 minutes and they did all that damage. Dr. M. says he thinks that the British are working on a detonator shell which explodes into very small fragments in the air. The force of the explosion can destroy any plane that is nearby and the shell doesn't necessarily have to hit the plane. It seems awful to be inventing such destructive things, but bombers are very much worse.

Mrs. Maxwell and I were at the Methodist hospital and had just left on our way home when the alarm sounded. We didn't hear it because of the noise in the street, but we saw all the shopkeepers putting up their wooden shutters and all the people in the street running. We kept on because I had a hunch it would be just as well to be out of the area. We were stopped about six times by the police and ordered off the streets and I thought we would never reach the Customs House which is on the edge of the foreign business section. The second alarm went before we got there which meant that the planes had arrived. We tumbled into the basement door and shared a corridor with all the Customs employees and commissioners and their wives and sundry fire hoses and so on. We had been in only a few minutes when there was a most terrific explosion which simply shook the building. Everyone got down on the floor with great rapidity. I thought the building must surely have been hit, but actually the bomb dropped almost a mile away on the very street we had come along fifteen minutes before and quite near the Methodist Hospital, so my hunch was right after all.

Pearl had a very unpleasant experience. She had been over here in Hankow and was on the ferry going back when the alarm sounded. The ferry instead of going to its usual berth up river went straight across the river and landed everyone just about opposite the Customs House on the Wuchang side. Pearl wanted to walk on but the police stopped her and made her take shelter. She was just beside a large cotton mill and anchored out in the stream in front of her was the Chinese navy, one diminutive gun-boat. Two bombs fell almost immediately in front of her in the river and it seemed as though they were aiming at the cotton mill. She could see the planes nose-diving to drop their bombs in Hanyang and Hankow too. The 'all clear' sounded about 5.45. just about an hour and a quarter after the first alarm had sounded.

The Chinese Police Department really does a very good job on preparation for air raids. It helps a lot to have even a few minutes warning, and we usually have as long as half an hour. No one is allowed on the streets and if the police see you standing at a window they come in and order you away. If it is at night the electric current is turned off at the power house and you are not allowed to light a candle or even smoke a cigarette. Nanking has bomb proof dug-outs, but up here that isn't possible yet. The river is still in flood and is fifteen feet higher than this time last year. If you dig two feet you reach water, so nothing can be done until the river subsides. Some people think that the bombs that fell in the river were intended for the dykes by the Custom House. If they were broken Hankow would be inundated. What good would that do the Japanese I don't know, but it might of course flood the airfield and that would keep the Chinese planes tied up.

They say while the Japanese planes were here, all the Chinese planes that were not bombers flew in circles over the foreign residential areas and the French and Japanese concessions. The Japs. would hardly attack planes flying over their own concessions. And all this time the Chinese police have been guarding the Japanese concession and there has been no confiscation or incendiarism.

Well, this seems to be a very warlike letter. By the time you get this the war may be over. I hope so, but I don't want the Japanese to have a 'walk-over' victory. It would be the limit if they did because they would be so darned pleased with themselves and such brutal savages.

I was glad to see that a crowd of two hundred people had gathered outside the Japanese Embassy in London and shouted at them to stop their murderous ways in China. It is a relief to know that people in Great Britain are taking as much notice as that. If only the League of Nations or some other international conference of the powers that be would decide to boycott Japan or close the Panama and Suez canals to her shipping or apply sanctions that would make them have to sit up and take notice. Something ought to be done because Japan has broken all international laws and even common decency by bombing refugees and non-combatants and hospitals as she has done. Today's paper contains an account of the bombing of Nanking yesterday and in all the stromash[13] no soldiers were wounded, only civilians.

We were talking at lunch about the possibility of opening the big Japanese Hospital in their concession here as a hospital for wounded refugees and civilians. I suggested painting a Japanese flag on the roof. Dr. M. said that he would like there to be enough Japanese prisoners so that there could be a prison camp alongside every hospital and then he would notify the Japanese Govt. that the camps were there and that if they bombed hospitals they would be liable to kill their own men. He thinks that is the only way to make the Japanese stop bombing hospitals. . . .

Much love to you all,
Nessie

Shared letter from Hankow, October 1938:

Dear Friends,

Some of you have had a lengthy account of my trip from Hongkong through Indo-China and Yunnan to Chengtu. I did not write up the trip down river to Hankow though it certainly was not without interest. Partly because it was difficult to settle down to write in Hankow when my attention was focussed on trying to find a way to get out of the city. I had expected it to be difficult, much more difficult than in July, though it was not exactly easy then.

I arrived in Hankow on September 24th and learned that the through express which runs to Hongkong twice a week had left the day before. However that evening the passengers were back in Hankow with a story of the train having been bombed and machine-gunned by Japanese planes. No bombs had hit the train, but two had landed neatly one on each side of the engine and some of the planes had returned and raked the train from end to end with machine gun fire. No windows were left intact and those who had remained on or near the train were killed. The majority of the passengers who were hiding among some trees at a little distance or in the long grass escaped.

On Tuesday the 25th the train left again and on Friday at 2.a.m. reached Changsha, a journey which ordinarily takes twelve hours. From that point better time was made and the train arrived at its destination on Sunday morning, a week after the original start from Wuchang. However further bombing of the section between Wuchang and Yochow had done more damage to the bridges at Shenling and Ting Tzu Chia and no train left on the 27th. The passengers who had booked on that train left on September 30th and all other passengers were correspondingly delayed. It became more and more difficult to get reservations.

It seemed likely that some passenger trains from Canton were being turned round at Changsha. There might be a possibility of getting a reservation on such a train. However there are several ways out of Changsha. The main road runs south to Hengyang and then on to Canton, but at Hengyang another road runs south-west to Kweilin and Wuchow. The new railway from Hengyang to Kweilin is now open to passenger trains and from Kweilin on there is a bus service taking three days to Wuchow or one can take a native boat for two days down the Kwei River to Wuchow. From there on British boats run to Hongkong. Several of the big foreign firms have their own fleet of trucks bringing up goods from the south and returning empty. The river is very high this year and the river steamer 'Kutwo', one of the largest and swiftest on the river, was still running. It was due to leave Hankow on October 1st.

In the end I decided to try my luck at Changsha and was fortunate in securing the last berth on the 'Kutwo'. It had a full passenger list with several Class A passengers having only camp cot accommodation. The third and fourth classes were packed with Chinese refugees. There must have been over a thousand in those two classes alone. . . .

We steamed up the Yang Tzu and next morning reached Chengling which is at the entrance to Tungting Lake. There we picked up a lighter and towed it alongside. It proved a great boon to the passengers on the lower decks for when the sun passed to the west they were able to enjoy a comparatively cool trip. Soon we passed the old city of Yochow and were in the broad waters of the lake. We kept close to the east shore and had the blue hills of Hunan in sight all the way. In the afternoon we entered the Siang River which is very lovely. We dropped the lighter as we came to a very narrow section of the river and there was a sudden return of all the passengers on to the ship. Along the river bank are many kilns in which giant earthen water jars were being made.

After dinner we could see the lights of Changsha in the distance, but it was 10.30 before we were tied up alongside Jardine's hulk. I had not intended to go ashore that night but a YWCA servant was down to meet me and climbed over the side of the ship calling to me that it was he who had seen me off to Hankow in April. Even after his arrival there was a long wait as the coolies were all employed carrying off baggage for the Chinese passengers on the lower decks. I had five pieces of luggage, a camp stretcher, a bedding roll, two suitcases and a commodious lunch basket with all the left-over-and-won't–go-into-anything-else impedimenta. You should have seen the coolie with his two pieces of baggage swung on each end of his shoulder pole making his way down the steep stairway from deck to deck in a crowd of jostling people impatient of delay. However the baggage did not fall into the river and I was soon being pulled along quiet streets to the YWCA. I roused Miss Galbraith and she told me that because hostel beds were short I was to live at Yale-in-China.[14] She nobly put on a garment or so and got out her bicycle to escort me there.

My first choice in the way of travel south was still train, so next morning I made the first of several visits to the railway station. Passenger trains to Canton were very crowded and it was difficult to get on them.

Each time I went to the station I met Mr. Wenger, who seemed to get quite different information from mine. It sounded pretty hopeless. He was also exploring the possibility of trucks, which was my second choice. Finally I called on Anderson Meyer and Co and found they had a truck leaving on Saturday the 8th and would let me travel on it. I would have to travel on the back of the truck because they already had passengers who would occupy the front seat. I was taken to see the truck, a new four-ton International on its first trip from Canton. It had a green canvas cover which did not allow much view as there were only five peep holes, two on each side and one at the back. However I would have to sit on my bedding roll on the floor of the truck so would not be able to see anything anyway.

At 1.45 p.m. on Saturday I arrived at the office with a bunch of bananas in one hand and a loaf of bread in the other. Mr. Wenger was ahead of me. He had bought a light wicker chair, not very comfortable, but the best the city had to offer. Coolies were busy with last minute preparations. An oil drum was being secured with ropes so that it would not roll round the truck and flatten the passenger. I climbed up. The driver, the man in charge of the truck, Mr. Wenger and a Chinese passenger, Mr. Chu, in front and I occupying the chair of state at the back. I could see out through an opening over the driver's head, but had to stoop down and forward to do so, not a very comfortable position but the only way to see anything.

About fifteen miles south of Changsha I recognised the place where I had sat on the hillside during air raids on the way down in July. It was a relief to reach the ferry at Siangtan and get out and stretch my legs. The Chinese ferries are primitive, but wonderfully efficient. The ferry itself is a lighter towed by a steam launch. The trucks run up planks about two feet wide on to a hulk tied to the shore. From that they run on to similar planks on to the lighter. A ferry had just pulled out so we had to wait for the next. It was a beautiful place in hot, hot, sunshine. It was something of an effort for me to get on to the truck again without a step of any kind. Another inch and it would not have been possible. By the third day I was so tired that I had lost my spring and could not manage it, but by that time there were empty benzine tins for a step.

As we neared the bus station just outside Hengyang we passed a long line of military trucks lined up at the side of the road. In one spot they were lined up on both sides of the road and we had a long wait while they moved slowly out of the way. One was being towed and that complicated matters. We had passed dozens and dozens of trucks and busses on the way, most of them on the road, but some of them in the ditch.

Hunan roads are good and we had averaged about thirty miles an hour even allowing for the time lost on the ferry. Four and a half hours on the back of a truck going at that speed had been something of a joy ride. There was no monotony for our numerous pieces of baggage had done a constant dance around the truck, one of my suitcases going so far as to climb on to the bunch of bananas, quite a feat but not so good for the bananas.

We went to a Chinese restaurant for our supper and a noisier and more crowded restaurant it has never been my lot to eat in. It was dimly lit which was just as well, though one could guess at the dirt one could not see. Unbeknown to the Presbyterian Mission Mr. Wenger and I had planned to stay there that night but the driver was anxious to cross the river so he could make an early start next morning and not have to wait his turn at the ferry. So we climbed on to the truck again and crossed to the east side of the river.

We drew up at an inn not far from the railway station. The inn had two floors and was built in the form of a rectangle with a central court. At one end was the entrance and there were rooms on the other three sides on both floors opening into the court which was covered with a glass roof. Each room had a window opening into the court but there were no outside windows. Unfortunately there was only one room vacant. It was large, had a bed and a table and looked moderately clean. We picked our way round and over the many people sleeping in the court and climbed some rickety stairs lit by a feeble kerosene lamp. The men decided that I should have the room and after trying one other inn in the neighbourhood without success they decided to sleep on the truck.

Before I had time to move my things off the truck the air raid alarm sounded and I decided to take no chance in that inn. It looked gimcrack enough to come down without any encouragement at all. It was full moon, the full moon festival in fact, but the clouds were heavy and there was, I thought, insufficient light for a raid. All the people waiting on the station for a train streamed past us up the road to the river bank, engines whistled as they pulled trains and spare rolling stock away from the station, the fire crackers that had been popping all round us were silenced and soon we had the street to ourselves except for a few soldiers on guard and the inn servants who were standing in the doorway. The driver of our truck was stretched out in the cab, Mr. Wenger had my stretcher and the other two men had spread their bedding on the floor of the truck. I sat on the step. The urgent alarm soon sounded, but for a long time nothing happened.

Every now and again there were rifle shots in the distance which were, I suppose signals of some kind back and forth across the river. Suddenly there was shouting in loud and angry voices and rifle shots all round me. Soldiers came running from all directions and soon there were about thirty battering at the door of the building next to the inn. One soldier had been up a tree on the other side of a pond and had seen lights in this building. A conversation was conducted through the closed door loud and angry on both sides and finally the soldiers were allowed to enter. They had not cleared the matter up to their satisfaction when the sound of planes was heard in the distance.

I had climbed on to the truck during the fuss with the soldiers, but green canvas did not seem very adequate protection against shrapnel so as soon as the anti-aircraft guns came into action I shot off the truck and got under it in company with the two Chinese men. Mr. Wenger and the driver kept their seats and their dignity.

The street we were in ended at the river bank and across the river we could see three huge searchlights focussing on the planes. Fortunately for us the airfield and not the station was the objective though the former was close enough for us to feel that we might be hit. Bombs come down in such quick succession that it is impossible to count the explosions but it sounded like forty or fifty. Hengyang is well supplied with anti-aircraft and some of the guns were very close to us. I could see tracer bullets from guns across the river and the flash of a gun near us preceding every explosion. The searchlight followed the planes in their course and seemed to be focussing immediately above our heads. However they moved on slowly and the sounds of the planes gradually faded till they were out of earshot. I got out from under and sat on the step again.

The next excitement was seeing the red glow from the fire on the airfield. Evidently a petrol dump had been hit. It was about 12.30 when the all-clear sounded and I went up to my room. The amah who brought me water to wash in asked me if I was afraid. 'Scared to death,' I said. 'I got under the bed,' she said. 'What did you do?' 'I got under the truck,' I said and we both laughed.

I washed off the day's dust and the grease I had collected under the truck and was just surveying my bed and wondering if any one spot would be less hard than any other when the air raid alarm sounded again and the servant came in to put out the light. I felt my way downstairs and reached the door. There the doorman tried to stop me. I had on a dark dress with a flowered design and he told me that no one was allowed outside in a flowered dress during an air raid. I said, 'What utter nonsense' in forcible English. 'What's that?' he said, but I took my place once more on the step. That was one of the many occasions when I simply didn't understand Chinese!!

I sat on the step of the truck again. The sky was clear and the moon brilliant. At 1 o'clock the urgent alarm went and at 1.10 the planes arrived and the whole performance was repeated. I retiring under the truck once more. The sound of the planes had all but faded when a soldier came along. He was so surprised to see a foreigner under the truck that he pointed his rifle right at me. 'Where are you from?' he asked. 'From off the truck,' I said. That seemed to satisfy him and he went on.

The soldiers had rounded up about fifteen people after the first raid and escorted them to the police station so I was a little nervous lest they thought I had anything to do with the lights showing in the building next door. Presently people began to move back from the river to the station but were sent back to the river by soldiers who said that another urgent message had just come through. I groaned. Even a moonlight night is meant for sleeping and I couldn't bear the thought of a third again. I went upstairs and called the boy to light my lamp. I took off my shoes and lay down. This is called 'undressing' in a Chinese inn! It had never been my misfortune to meet anything quite as uncomfortable as that bed. It was too short and I was afraid to stretch diagonally in case I extended over the edge of the oiled cloth which is a fair protection against livestock. I had not had to endure it more than a few minutes when the air raid sounded the alarm again. Down I went to my step and watched the people passing along the road to the river for the third time. . . .

There was no urgent alarm this time and at 2.30 the all clear sounded and I went back again to my room. We were to be on the road at 6.a.m. and I hoped to sleep, but the night had been too exciting and the bed was too hard. I managed about half an hour and woke by 5.50. It didn't take long to put on my shoes and roll up my bedding.

Everyone was a little late rising and it was 7.a.m. before we were on the road again. . . . I travelled in the back again but, after we had stopped at a little wayside teahouse, Mr. Wenger changed places with me. It was certainly easier going in front though the back of the seat stopped just at the middle of my back and my spine seemed to ride uneasily on the edge. I was bruised at the end of the day all down my left side from my forehead to my knee.

About 2.30 p.m. we stopped for lunch at Pan Shih. I remembered it from the trip down in July. Then a whole section of the village against the mountain had been destroyed by bombs. The houses were a blackened ruin and the trees on the hillside were scorched. To my surprise we lunched in a teahouse that had been built on the ruins of the old one and business was very much as usual. The trees were still scorched and dead but there were few other evidences of the bombing.

Most of the morning the road had led through beautiful undulating country but after Pan Shih we began to climb in earnest. About 3.p.m. we reached the summit after a terrific climb up a narrow winding mountain road. This summit marked the boundary between the two provinces. In many places the road is too narrow for trucks to pass and we had to wait several times on corners at which two trucks from opposite directions had arrived at the same moment. There were so many trucks on the road that it was not long before several were held up each way. All the drivers get out and have a conference on the subject. Then there is sudden agreement, 'hao la, hao la, hao la'[15] they all chorus and all begin to wave their arms, shouting directions to the driver whose truck is to move first. There are literally hundreds of narrow little wooden bridges on the road, the railings of which have nearly all been damaged by trucks that were not careful enough in their approach. In many places a concrete bridge is in the course of construction. Some are finished; some are waiting for the approaches to be built up. There must be thousands of coolies at work on the road in one place and another. Our driver was very careful on corners and bridges, but I don't think he once changed gears without the most hideous screeching.

We had two other ranges to cross before we saw away and below us on the plain the city of Lochang. We should have stopped there for the night, but the moon was very bright and Lochang is one of the most frequently bombed places in North Kwantung. We passed through just after sunset exclaiming at the wrecked station buildings and rattled on to Hsiao Kwan about thirty miles further south. The road was not very good so it was rough riding after dark and I was not sorry when we arrived, at 8.p.m. or thereabouts. Hsiao Kwan is a large city but it is packed with people and it was not easy to find accommodation. Our driver seemed to know all the ropes and found us rooms at last in a most unprepossessing inn. On the second floor there was a double row of little cubicles. One man slept on the truck but all the rest of us found rooms for the magnificent sum of 60 cents each (about five pence at the present rate of exchange) I filled my Flit can and lent it to everyone so we were smelling like a Flit factory before we were through. I scored several bites during the night but I think they were all mosquitoes. We could get water for a wash and I achieved a sponge bath at which one becomes an adept in China even when the wash basin is very small. The inn was terribly noisy and by the time we had supper, washed and settled ourselves it was almost 11.30. There was not much chance of sleep as guests kept arriving all through the night and no one in a Chinese inn thinks of walking or speaking quietly. I did however sleep through one air raid alarm and was wakened by the other guests returning noisily to their rooms.

We were up at 5.30 because the driver wanted an early start to allow for probable air-raid hold-ups during the day. The road follows the railway fairly closely though it is not always in sight. It is frequently the objective of the raids so nothing is allowed to move on the road during alarms. We left our inn and turned the corner to pass along a street that had been heavily bombed and was lined with ruins. I had imagined that the inn was a long way from the railway but we were within a block or so and the statement that Hsiao Kwan is not bombed is hardly factual. Evidently it was the bridge over the river and the railway that the planes had tried to get. Both seemed intact and we sped across the bridge and onto one of the roughest stretches of the road of the whole trip. I was in the back again and got the full effect.

After three hours we stopped at a bus station for breakfast. Mine consisted of grape nuts and klim followed by baked beans (cold) on cream crackers, but the others had a Chinese meal. The truck had ruined our thermos flasks one by one and thirst became a problem as the day wore on. We did not stop for another meal that day, but when the Customs officers were examining us, Mr. Wenger and I shared a tin of tomato juice. About mid-day we passed the time of day with the drivers of some trucks travelling north. They had been held up further south by air raid signals when a section of the railway had been bombed. The Japanese must have taken the afternoon off for we did not have a single stop for raids that day.

By 7.p.m. we had pulled up at the New Asia Hotel in Canton, stiff and tired and thirsty – especially thirsty – but very satisfied that we had arrived safely and very grateful to Anderson Meyer and Co. The scenery was magnificent all the way and it was great good fortune to have a chance to do the trip by road. Another time I shall arrange to have a few more springs underneath. Did I mention that the distance covered was <u>600</u> miles. Two days and a half was not bad going, considering the roads, the bridges and the amount of traffic.

From the New Asia Hotel I shot round the corner to the Butterfield and Swire wharf to see if I could go straight on board the 'Fatshen'. I was given a berth and was told I could sleep on board, but the steward omitted to tell me that I could not bring my luggage with me. I dashed back to the truck to collect the five pieces which had to be put together in the dark because we had been using the stretcher on the truck to soften the journey. I piled it on to two ricshas and got it as far as the wharf, only to be stopped by customs officials who asked if I had a purser's permit to ship freight after 6.p.m. and it was too late to get a permit. Customs officers don't work after 6.p.m. The effort involved in getting two more ricshas and shipping it back to the New Asia seemed more than I could manage so I explained that I had had three days on a truck and had not had my clothes off all that time and must have a bath, etc., etc., etc. They relented and as a special favour condescended to look inside my suitcases and let me pass. Was I thankful!

But there was yet another crisis when the steward told me firmly that there was no one on duty and I could not have a bath till the morning. No bath. The day had been terribly hot and Canton was plain awful. It would have served them right if I had slept on their sheets dirt and dust and all. But I trotted out my tale again and he said he would speak to the chief steward. Then I fell on to the carafe of water and drank six glasses straight off, leaving only the most meagre allowance

> possible for cleaning my teeth. Supper consisted of a glass of klim and a whole tin of pineapple which I didn't enjoy as much as I might have because I couldn't help thinking of the pineapple famine in Chengtu and how far even a small tin can be made to go there.
>
> The cabin was very hot but I slept soundly till 6.a.m. when the coolies on the wharf began to move about and the Customs began to function. Even after that I lay and gloated over the comfort of a bed and all the luxuries of a British steamer. At 3.p.m. we were alongside in Hongkong and it did not take long to reach the Church Guest House in a taxi.
>
> That afternoon came the news of the landing of the Japanese at Bias Bay[16] and Thursday's boat was the last one to come down the river before the boom was thrown across at Bocca Tigris[17] forts. I had come down just in time and I have not heard whether the train, which presumably left Hankow on the Thursday before and which I might have travelled on, ever did get through to Kowloon.
>
> Three days on the P&O 'Ranchi', with the temperature dropping considerably each day and a nasty head wind which did not encourage anything but choosing the safest chair and the fluffiest book, brought me to Shanghai. A positive bodyguard of secretaries escorted me from the Customs Jetty to the office where in between times, I still reflect on the adventures of travel in the interior. If you don't believe me come and try it.

Before this letter reached New Zealand, YWCA members were able to read in November's issue of *The New Zealand Girl*:

> We are so truly thankful to be able to report the following cable which arrived in the National Office on October 11 from Hong Kong: ARRIVED SAFELY – MONCRIEFF.[18]

On 25 October 1938 Japanese army forces entered Hankow. The following day Wuchang was occupied, and the next day, Hanyang. Six days later, on 2 November, Japan withdrew from the League of Nations.

8
Back in Shanghai
October–December 1938

Nessie arrived back in Shanghai on 17 October 1938, and resumed her duties with the national committee of the YWCA. The majority of letters in this chapter are on the headed paper of AGNES M.MONCRIEFF, 133 YUEN MING YUEN ROAD SHANGHAI, CHINA, which was the address of the national office.

Letter home from Shanghai, 30 October 1938.

My dear Mother,

I didn't get a letter written to you last week-end. I had my boxes delivered from the YWCA storeroom and had a disgusting week-end unpacking. I am so tired of cleaners, and tailors that don't come and seeing piles of clothing and things round my room. On Thursday my hamper of woollens came from cold storage and thank goodness they don't need anything done to them. I am so much thinner that everything has to be altered; even my silk pyjamas nearly fell off when I tried them on. . . .

Shanghai has been very moist for the last few days. It quite spoilt the fireworks planned by the Japanese to celebrate the fall of Hankow. We sent a naval radio through the American Consulate to Hankow to find out where the YWCA secretaries are and Mr. Hansen, to whom I sent it, added that all friends at the Lutheran Mission were safe. Wasn't it decent of him to add that? I have been thinking of them so much this last week or so. It must be a difficult experience to go through and I left there so recently that I feel that I belong with them all.

Much love to you all,
Nessie

Letter to Eva Skinner from Shanghai, 1 November 1938:

Dearie, I am developing into a very bad correspondent but please blame Shanghai. This is a hectic city and there never seems to be time for anything, not even time for work. As soon as I start there are bound to be interruptions. I shall have to bring work home in the evenings. I tell them that it is nine tenths consultations and one tenth work and that is about right. Of course in the Branch Office in Hankow I often longed for a little consultation, but I could get lots more work done. Here there seems to be someone putting something on your desk or calling you in for a consultation every minute of the day . . .

This morning my job was to take Miss Amaron and Miss Adams round the devastated areas. When I first came back Talitha [Gerlach] said to me, 'I suppose you want to see the devastated areas.' I explained that they were the last thing I wanted to see as I had seen plenty in the centre of China. However it is all part of one's education and I was told to escort the visitors this morning. Mr. Smith, the Activities Secretary of the Navy YMCA, took us in his car. He has evidently taken dozens of groups round because he was able to tell us where the trenches were and all that sort of thing. It is all a gruesome wreck, acres and acres of it and of course we did not see the whole of the picture. We saw Chapei and the big Commercial College that was the headquarters of the Chinese military. It was a beautiful set of buildings with touches of old Chinese architecture and you should just see the ruin. It all just about ruined my day. It is horrid to see Japanese soldiers policing everywhere.

The only Chinese we saw were the police employed by the puppet government, two or three farmers back on the land, and one family that had returned to its home in Chapei and was living in a sort of island in the midst of desolation. I don't know where they get their food supply. All the section out beyond Chapei where we were this morning was under cultivation yielding two or three crops a year, and now there are precisely three little patches that are being cultivated. Shanghai's food supply is coming from much further afield. We saw one farmer wheeling his vegetables into the market. They say that with taxes and squeeze and so on the Japanese don't leave much for a living for the farmers.

We were back in time for Mrs. Huang's address and then most of the staff went off down to the Customs Jetty to see her and Miss Amaron off. After office hours this afternoon I went to a Missionary Fellowship and heard Ronald Rees speak on Christian work in Central China. He spoke very well and it was interesting to see the clear picture he gave but it was a bit too clear in parts. I found myself back in Hankow with all the wounded and the refugees and the air raid victims. I wish I could be back in Central China. In spite of the suffering and the dangers it is the real China and this is not, not by a long chalk.

However there are some nice things about Shanghai and one of them is the Municipal orchestra concerts on Sunday afternoons. I have been both Sundays and have a ticket for next Sunday. They are very crowded and you have to buy your ticket a week in advance. Last Sunday I had quite a giddy day. I went out to the Columbia Club to lunch with Suzanne Adlam and then went to Jeanne van Hengel's to hear Captain Carlson speak on his trip through Shensi and Hopeh observing the work of the Eighth Route Army (ex-communist). I knew some of the things he talked about, but it was most interesting to hear an American Embassy Military Intelligence man talking the way he did. He is going to Washington to resign as he wants to be absolutely free to write and say what he likes about the guerillas and partisans in that section and he can't as long as he hold his official position. . . .

Very much love

– Nessie

Letter to Eva Skinner from Shanghai, 16 November 1938:

Dearie . . . I have a radio. At least I had it for a week but it is now back at the shop having some minor repairs. It is second hand and I paid the equivalent of three pounds for it. It is short wave but we haven't an aerial here so I can't get short wave stations except Hongkong which I have heard in the distance several times with news relayed from London. Heard Big Ben. I was fiddling with the short wave the other evening and suddenly heard a weather report talking about the Tasman Sea. I pricked up my ears and sure enough it was Melbourne, but I think it must have been relayed from somewhere because I am sure I could not get so distant a station without an aerial. There are several stations in Shanghai and they give good musical programmes. It is mostly records of course but I like working against a background of Mozart or Chopin or Gilbert and Sullivan.

Maud Russell and Ruth Packard [American foreign secretaries] left for the interior this morning. Maud is going to Kweiyang and Ruth to Chengtu. Kweiyang won't allow permits to foreigners to reside in the province so I do not know what Maud will do. She may have to go on elsewhere, but she is headed for Kweiyang and will remain as long as possible. They went off on a little coastal boat which calls at Swato, Hongkong, Pakhoi and then Haiphong. I hope the seas are smooth. Ruth came down on it from Tientsin and had a pretty bad trip. . . .

I have indulged in a sort of reaction since I came to Shanghai and feel terribly exhausted most of the time. I tootled off to the doctor the other day and my reaction to her knee taps nearly knocked her out of the room, so I suppose the trouble is nervous. I am taking some dope and feel a bit better, but some days my mind doesn't seem to function at all and I fumble mentally and physically and am useless and depressed. I think the worst is over. I hope so anyway. I hate feeling as tired as this.

Much love to you.

– Nessie

Letter home, handwritten from Shanghai, 23 November 1938:

My dear Mother,

Here it's Wednesday already and I haven't written a letter to you this week at all. There are so many meetings & conferences & such that I seem to have no time to myself at all. I wish I could live nearer my job. It would save so much time. Yesterday & today I represented the YWCA at the National Christian Council for Religion Education Conference. I'm heartily bored & will be glad when it is over. They are discussing problems that are quite different to ours and I don't feel that I have anything to add to the discussions.

Last week I figured in the newspaper in connection with police court proceedings. I had my bag snatched on the way home. The thief dashed down a murky side alley & I after him. Fortunately a plain-clothes policeman saw the dash & also gave chase. There have been various bag-snatching incidents in the locality & fifteen plain clothes men have been placed round about. I didn't know he was a policeman & when I caught up he had caught the thief & the bag, I grabbed what I thought was the bag & found myself clutching the muzzle of a loaded revolver. I didn't waste much time in letting go.

Then there was a grand procession to the police station – policeman with thief, bag & revolver ahead, I next & then the whole of Shanghai following on to see what would happen. It was ages before I got out of the clutches of the police, but I refused to go to court next morning so they kept my bag as evidence; the detective kindly allowing me to take my keys & some small change for tram fares. It was some time before I could get my bag back as it was kept locked in a safe & I could only call in the early morning or in the evening hours when the detective in charge of the case was off duty. I existed over the week-end on a borrowed $5.00. . . .

Much love to you all,
Nessie

Letter home from Shanghai, 21 December 1938:

My dear Mother,

I didn't write last Sunday or the Sunday before so must try and get a few lines off by the mail tomorrow. I have been feeling very tired since I came back to Shanghai and have had a touch of my old 1927 heart which alarmed me. I toddled off to the doctor and she is building me up with vitamins. You should see the array of bottles and such. I expect to go back to work after the New Year. It has been great to have some time to myself and I have slept day and night with great diligence. I am really feeling a lot better and go out walking every day. I have been out to supper twice, but I avoid large and noisy gatherings and above all meetings. Even though I go all the way down town to the Bank I pass by the office as though it didn't exist.

Stella Purchas and Margaret North have been in Shanghai. In fact Stella still is. Her school has moved from Hangchow to Ningpo and she doesn't know yet whether she is to go to Ningpo or not. Meantime I see a fair amount of her and when we have nothing better to do we mosey round doing a bit of window shopping in Yates Rd. and that area.

I am trying to get a few mild Christmas presents ready, but haven't got very far yet. People are being awfully kind inviting me to parties and for weekends and so on, but I stick to the hostel. I don't mind going out, but I like to come back to my own bed and my radio and really relax. Last Saturday evening I went to supper at the Bernard Reads and they took me out to 'Snow White'.[1] I went in trepidation because I had not been out except for short walks. However all was well and I felt better for the excitement. . . .

Much love to you all,
Nessie

Five months previously, in a letter to Eva, Nessie had mentioned that she'd been feeling miserable with what seemed to be the same sort of heart problems she'd had in 1928 while in Dunedin and would try to find a specialist when she was in Hong Kong. Originally Nessie had been expected to go to China in 1929 but ill health the previous year had necessitated a delay:

> Miss Moncrieff would be so eminently suited for work in China. It would be better to wait a year until Miss Moncrieff was restored to full health. Sympathy was expressed for Miss Moncrieff in thus having her plans frustrated.[2]

Letter home, handwritten from Shanghai, 27 December 1938:

My dear Mother

I am going back to work next week & don't want to in the least. It's been fun having time off and I've enjoyed the walking & the outings that I would have had to turn down if I had been working. I had stacks of invitations for Christmas including two for the whole week-end, but I didn't accept those partly because it's more restful at the Hostel & partly because of the string of bottles that I seem to live with. Remembering which to take when is as good as a course of Pellmans.[3]

The doctor said last Friday that I am lots better & so I am. I still get tired easily, but I recover much more quickly. I've a horrid fear that I'm putting on weight. I should be with all the N.Z. butter & milk I am consuming. Anchor brand milk powder is obtainable here. It's made in Hamilton, $2.25 a pound (about 1/10). A pound doesn't last very long though.

On Saturday evening I went to an awfully nice Christmas party that Dr. & Mrs. Bernard Read gave. There were several people that I knew including two teachers in the Municipal schools here who had been at the American School in Kuling the summer I was there. It was 8.15 p.m. dinner so we didn't get up from the table till after 10. p.m. Turkey & Christmas pudding & all the etceteras even to brandy on the pudding. Then after the men came into the drawing room we played games. I managed to avoid the consolation prizes so feel I did pretty well. There were presents for all the guests. In fact it was a most perjinct[4] party in every detail. It was 1.30 a.m. when I got home.

On Christmas Day I went to lunch at the Hawkings. They have a wonderful home at the Limit which is on the Hungjao Rd opposite the aerodrome where the incident happened which precipitated the Shanghai war last year. Both Chinese & Japanese forces were through their grounds during the fighting, but very little damage was done. I had not met the Hawkings before but Mrs. Hawkings & two of the daughters are at Kerikeri at present with her parents who are the Littles who practically started Kerikeri. It was quite a big lunch party with several young naval officers who had just come down from Hankow. They didn't know many of the people up there that I knew, but I enjoyed hearing the general news of what was happening up there. The Limit is of course in Japanese occupied territory now & you have to pass through the Japanese barrier to get out. All the people who live there have to have special passes. It makes me mad to see the way the Chinese have to take off their hats & bow to the Japanese sentries as they present their passes. . . .

Much love to you all,
Nessie

Letter to Eva Skinner from Shanghai, 29 December 1938.

Well Dearie,

. . . Christmas has come and gone & it is almost 1939. I enjoyed Christmas & really I did a good deal considering. . . .

I am going to see the doctor again tomorrow and I think I am going to suggest to her that I take another month off. I'm heaps better, but get tired very easily & my mind simply refuses to work. It seems much more sensible to take another month now rather than have to take three later on & go through all the miseries of two weeks all over again. If I do take another month off I am considering going down to Hongkong to get right out of the Shanghai atmosphere for a bit.

You can't imagine how I've pined for N.Z. and specially N.Z. sunshine these last weeks. I suppose one always wants home when one is off colour. There were

From left: Margaret North of Nelson, Church Missionary Society (CMS) nurse at CMS Guangji Hospital, Hangchow; Dr Phyllis Haddow of Auckland, then acting superintendent at the CMS Guangji Hospital; Agnes (Nessie) Moncrieff of Wellington, foreign secretary for the YWCA of New Zealand in China; and Stella Purchas of Christchurch, then a CMS teacher in Hangchow. 1939. Moncreiff family collection

days when I would gladly have stepped on any old ship that would take me – barring one nationality – but those days are over and one day soon I'll be interested in my work again. At the moment I have no desire to go back to the office, though I know my absence is giving the others extra work. Complete paralysis of conscience! . . .

Lots & lots of love – Nessie

9

Sojourn in Hong Kong

January–February 1939

Over the months of January and February 1939, Nessie was in Hong Kong, recuperating and taking leave. She stayed at the address she had consistently used when based in Hankow, the Church Guest House, 50 Kennedy Road.[1]

Letter home from Hong Kong, 12 January 1939.

> My dear Mother,
>
> There is an airmail out tomorrow so I'm trying to get some N.Z. letters written today. I've forgotten when I wrote to you last and can't remember whether I told you that I had decided to come down to Hongkong for a holiday. I don't think the holiday was an absolute necessity because I went back to work part time in the office last week and felt pretty good, but it seemed a sensible thing to do so here I am. Shanghai was frightfully cold and we had snow the night before I left so I was glad to leave.
>
> I had to give up my room in the International Hostel and the packing was awful. I said I was glad the Japanese had looted my possessions, but I wish I could have decided what they could take. Everything except for two suit cases is stored at 133 Yuen Ming Yuen Rd [national headquarters of the YWCA of China] and when I go back I will have to look for a room. Shanghai is crowded and it is not easy to find anything comfortable at the price I can pay. There are 4,000,000 people living in an area of 8 square miles so you can see how tightly packed we are. Hongkong is crowded too but you can't pack people as closely on hills as you can on the flat so there is more of a sense of space. . . .
>
> I came down on Butterfield and Swire's S.S. 'Soochow', a small coastal boat which takes six passengers. It is about $60 cheaper than anything else which is why I travelled on it. Fortunately the sea was smooth all the way and though we nearly perished with cold the first day, the temperature rose by leaps and bounds as we came south. We called at Swato but I did not go ashore. I sat on deck in gorgeous sunshine and purred all day.

The drum major and a sergeant from the Seaforth Highlanders, the wife of an American Navy N.C.O., a Portuguese sea captain and I were the passengers and at Swato we picked up a Chinese. In the Chinese class there were a good many travelling, but we did not see them except when they came on the foredeck for medical inspections at Swatow and at Hongkong. The Highland lads were great fun and had a good time introducing Mrs. Wagner to Highland ways and idioms. I acted as a sort of umpire and we had a riotous time. The saloon was immediately underneath the bridge and I wondered sometimes if the Captain could hear well enough to navigate above the din we made.

Mr. Wagner is on a gunboat stationed in Swatow so there was great excitement when we passed it on the way up the harbour. He came aboard after we docked and Mrs. W. and he spent most of the day ashore. His boat is coming down to Hongkong in a day or two which explains Mrs. W.'s trip down. The American authorities don't allow navy wives to live in Swatow. I suppose because it may be attacked by the Japanese any time. We had air raid signals while we were in port and I felt at home again. . . .

Hongkong is very warlike. We passed a submarine as we came in and hoped it would submerge for our benefit but it didn't. There is an aeroplane carrier and a number of destroyers and gun boats in the harbour and big gun practice seems to go on most of the time not to mention aeroplane practice flights over our heads night and day. The harbour is lovely though and so are the hills and I'm going to walk every day and really get to know some of the long walks I've heard about. . . .

Much love to you all,

Nessie

Letter to Eva Skinner from Hong Kong, 15 January 1939:

Well dearie, here goes for a gossip. I intended to go to Church this morning but cut it pretty close and then 3 pairs of stockings in a row had holes in them so it seemed a clear indication that I should sit down and darn stockings. . . .

Hongkong has a funny climate in winter. The sun is lovely and as long as you keep moving it is very warm. But as soon as the sun sets it is very chill and you really need woollies. This house is very cold and the small fire in the drawing room grate hardly makes any impression. I sit over the fire and think about the bath I have to take before I go to bed. There are several bathrooms, one to each room in fact, but there is no plumbing so to speak. We have a tin tub that requires one's legs to be tied in knots and one bucket of water. It requires a special technique and is very chilly whichever way you do it.

I do like Hongkong so much better than Shanghai and there are the most stunning walks all over the hills. Kennedy Rd. itself is level and Bowen Rd., a few hundred feet above it, is level too so there are elegant walks without too much climbing. I can lie in bed and watch everyone pass along Bowen Road through the top of my window. Yesterday morning an elderly fat Chinese in his long gown came along, hung his umbrella on the railings and proceeded to do his daily dozen. Of course Bowen Rd. is not a motor road and there is not a great deal of traffic but can you imagine an Anglo-Saxon being quite so unconscious to all and sundry. When his breathing exercises were over he touched his toes with great difficulty several times, picked up his umbrella again and continued his walk. . . .

We had air raid signals just as we were finishing lunch just to remind us that we are still in Chinese territory. There is a Japanese military plane which runs from Canton to Formosa with mail and military passengers every day and the signals have to sound if it comes too near Swato. No one turns a hair and there was no clearing of the streets as there used to be in Hankow.

I am reading Edgar Snow's 'Red Star Over China'.[2] I should have read it at least a year ago but it is very expensive so I waited till I could borrow someone else's copy. It is a thrilling tale and most illuminating if you want to understand the present situation. Everyone has been very upset at Wang Ching-Wei's desertion of the government, but I think it is good riddance. There are several men high up in government circles who are only lukewarm about this resistance of Japan and the sooner they get out the better. I think it has been very hard for the Generalissimo to manage them and they have objected to the united front policy and been very jealous of the Eighth Route Army people. There is more news of the war down here and we hear much more of the awful bombings in the interior. It is always so much worse to read about them than go through them. They sound much worse on paper somehow, although goodness knows they are terrible in fact. Kweilin is being bombed frightfully and a great deal of damage has been done to American Mission property. I think it is awful the way the Japanese make a beeline for hospitals. Raid after raid in Hankow did no damage of anything of military importance, but simply blew to bits street after street of residential quarters. . . .

Lots and lots of love,

Nessie

Letter home from Hong Kong, 23 January 1939:

My dear Mother,

. . . Nothing much is happening down here. The weather has been cloudy the last few days and Hongkong is not so wonderful when the sun is not shining. I practically live in the open air as I much prefer my own room to the sitting room down stairs. I have invested in some silk and wool shirts and the first day I wore one it was like a N.Z. summer day and I nearly boiled. However, I have been glad of them since. People come and go in this Guest house and you never know what sort of a menagerie to expect when you go downstairs. The latest arrival is Mr. Shepherd, a New Zealander who is a secretary in the Generalissimo and Madame's New Life Movement. I knew him up in Hankow and don't like him very much. He is rather a skite and to hear him talk you would think he is the whole works. He says he has just flown in from Kweilin, the place which is being bombed so heavily at present. He says about half of the city is still standing and the people run to the caves every time the air raid signals go. What a life! I would give anything to be back in the interior as far as interest and interesting work is concerned. But when I think of the incessant bombing I think I will wait a little longer. It certainly does get on your G-string. . . .

Much love to you all,

Nessie

Letter to Eva Skinner, handwritten from Hong Kong, 29 January 1939:

Well dearie, It doesn't seem any time at all since I wrote but it must be a week & there's an Imperial Airways mail out tomorrow. I am up on the roof, which is flat, enjoying the view while I pretend to write. Next Sunday I should be arriving in Shanghai, but I'm toying with the idea of taking another week or so off. I'm oodles better & at times feel on top of the world, but there are still spells of dizziness that are very distressing & sometimes the chatter of a roomful of people nearly drives me crazy. I've come to the conclusion that I am a typical 'case' out of a psychotherapy text book, but that doesn't tell me what to do about it. . . .

I had two glorious days last week on the other side of the Island. On Wednesday I went to Stanley & climbed a military road beyond St. Stephen's College & lay & baked in the sun with my knitting & a book. Then I lunched at the College with an Australian teacher there & lazed in the sun on a balcony till it was time to come home. Thursday was much more strenuous. I walked miles & miles & as most of it was on asphalt roads which are wonderful for motors, but no good for pedestrians, I raised a muscle or so & nearly wore my shoes off my feet . . .

Much love. It's great to think I'll be packing up in a year's time. Heighho for Rustat.

Nessie

Letter home from Hong Kong, 6 February 1939:

My dear Mother

This is one of the most perfect days we have had. Not a cloud in the sky since early dawn and I almost have sunstroke sitting here in my bedroom with the sun pouring in through the French windows. Yesterday afternoon I went to sleep in the sun which was shining on my bed and woke up all cold after it had disappeared. Then I went up on the roof which gets it for another hour longer. I don't think a day has gone by without my going out for a walk somewhere. Yesterday it was only into town in the morning to post letters, match wool and reserve seats for 'Sixty Glorious Years'.[3] But it is about a mile if not more to town so I get plenty of walking even when I don't go further afield.

On Friday I watched the P&O 'Ranpura' pulling out for Shanghai and gurgled for joy because I was not on board. I should have been but Tsai Kwei wants me to do some calls with her in connection with a financial campaign down here and I very gladly stayed, telling her that we would make the calls on cloudy days so that my tramps would not be interfered with.

On Wednesday I went over to Stanley again and enjoyed myself on the rocks until lunch time. Miss Griffin and I lunched with Mr. and Mrs. Asche. He is acting principal of St. Stephen's Boys' College and hails from Melbourne. After lunch Mrs. Asche took me for a walk up a hill near-by. It was a fairly steep pull up, but coming down was a sheer precipice and I thought a sure sign of recovery that I was able to do it. I did do some of it sitting down, though on the whole it was easier going when I managed to keep on my feet. I don't think I've ever done such a steep descent.

On Thursday Mrs. Helde and I had another long tramp. We didn't get started till the 3. p.m. bus but we went over to the Wangneichong Gap and then walked to Tam Reservoir and up to the top where we had some sandwiches and along a contour path till we struck an asphalt path and got back to the reservoir. It was late by that time so we went for our lives down a path to Ty Tam Tuk Reservoir and on to the motor road which brought us to Stanley. We were trying to get the 6.45 bus and as the headlights came up the hill we hailed it and it turned out to be a military lorry. The soldier in charge was most encouraging so we got in and came back to town at such a terrific speed. There wasn't much to hold on going round the corners and I have never come so quickly on downgrades in my life. However we got here and in time for dinner which we had hardly expected to do. The soldier said he supposed we had never ridden in a lorry before but I mentioned I had one other experience, just a little matter of 600 miles. . . .

Lots of love to you all,

Nessie

When in Hankow Nessie had become an avid filmgoer: 'Pearl and I have become movie fans by way of recreation. It is a rest to enter another world for a while.[4]

Letter to Eva Skinner, Hong Kong, 21 February 1939:

> Hello dearie what does it feel like to be home from your wanderings once more? Danny [American YWCA foreign secretary][5] used to tell the story of our cook's return to Peking, after she had taken him on a camping trip through Shansi. He had managed the cooking in odd places very well; but the expression of real joy as he spread the silver out in its rightful drawer & the sigh of satisfaction told her more clearly than words what he really felt about it all. . . .
>
> I'm due down at the YWCA any time now, but as there's an 'Airways' out tomorrow I thought I'd scribble a line & post on the way. I'm due back in Shanghai – overdue in fact, but have a lunch engagement with a Board member tomorrow that I want to keep. Then I'll take the first steamer north. It will depend on cost of the ticket. I may have to take a little coastal boat & toss to & fro for four days. There's nothing larger till the middle of next week I fear. This has been a lovely holiday in many ways, but I want to get back & see if I can really stand up to the job again.
>
> We have endured Chinese New Year since I wrote last. New Year's Day was last Sunday and I have never in my life heard anything like the fire crackers. It's not allowed in China proper because of waste of money etc., but this is the one time in the year when crackers can be set off without a permit in Hongkong & the whole population goes at it for hours on end. From the hill here we look down on the roofs of Wanchai, a very crowded Chinese section & except for a few hours at night we had an incessant and insistent – very insistent – roar, bang & splutter for 48 hours. It didn't let up even for a moment. I felt crazy by Sunday afternoon & went away out on the hills by myself, lay me down on some rocks & slept. It was the only chance of rest. I attended Church most assiduously to get out of the noise & walked in directions where there are no inhabitants. Life is liveable again, though there are still crackers going off in most directions. Noise is the most important thing to scare evil spirits away so we didn't have any displays of lovely coloured lights or anything like that. . . .
>
> I expect you have read in the papers news of the bombing of Hongkong. It was away out on the borders of the New Territories, out of earshot of the city; but the nerve of the Japanese to bomb a train two miles within the borders of British territory. A few years ago it would have been an act of war. Now there is an apology impending & that is all. Everyone is wondering if it was meant to try out what Britain would do. I should have thought that the Munich Conference was good & sufficient indication of what the British would do. Meantime a few more people have been killed or injured in this disgusting war. . . .
>
> Ever so much love – Nessie

'Danny and I on the railing, Mary Ochiltree on the step.' Taken at Hsai Po Ko Shih, Peiping, in Nessie's first term. She is beside the pole. Danny was a foreign secretary for the American YWCA, Mary Ochiltree a teacher at the Peking American School. 1933. ATL PA1-o-1191-26-1

Letter to Eva Skinner, handwritten on board *SS Canton*, en route from Hong Kong to Shanghai, 5 March 1939:

> Well my dear . . . Grey skies & a grey sea & temperature falling as we go farther north. Shanghai tomorrow morning at 9.30, but it should have been this afternoon only we had fog for eighteen hours & had to go dead slow. It's rumoured we'll be in the river tonight so I suppose the seas will soon be turning a dirty yellow. We're pitching a lot this afternoon though I can't see why. There doesn't seem to be much in the way of a swell. . . .
>
> In the library on board I found a copy of Philip Gibbs's 'Ordeal in England'. That is interesting too, but too journalistic. I was interested in Miss Bentham's comment on a book she had just read – forgotten what the book was – but she said that it was such a relief to read something by a historian after so much by journalists. I've come to the conclusion I should have studied history at College. I'm too old now for my mind to retain all the facts, but I'm going to read some all the same. I'm making a list of books I want to read. A pity they are all so expensive. The S.M.C. [Shanghai Municipal Council][6] Library in Shanghai is very limited, but I may find some of them there. I've come to the conclusion that folk are reading too much economics & not enough history. That may be quite a wrong conclusion, but I feel it is true of Americans in particular. We need the perspective of history to show us the value (or otherwise) of our economic analyses.
>
> You're having to endure all this because I'm thrilled to death to be reading again without giving myself a headache & the jitters. It's wonderful to be in possession of what I call my mental faculties once more. I've been reading psychology too & am beginning to understand what's been the matter with me. There's not much mental energy to spare yet, but at least I can do a day's work again. . . .
>
> This ship is the latest and up-to-datest that the P&O has on this run and she really is a beauty. Comfort personified – even in second class though another six inches on the length of the bed would make a great difference. . . .
>
> Ever so much love – Nessie

10

Return to Shanghai

March–May 1939

Nessie returned to Shanghai and the national YWCA office on 6 March 1939.

Letter home, handwritten while on board the *SS Canton*, en route from Hong Kong to Shanghai, 5 March 1939:

> My dear Mother,
>
> We're anchored in Fairy Flats[1] on the Yang Tzu Estuary & are due in to-morrow morning at 9.30. If we hadn't had so much fog on Friday & Saturday we'd have been in to-day because this is the newest ship on the run – on her second trip – and she does 21 knots when necessary.
>
> I hated leaving Hongkong. It is a lovely place and I am going to miss the hills & the sea & the long walks. Shanghai is horrible in comparison. Still I'm glad to be getting back to work and it's grand to be feeling well enough to work again.
>
> My next stunt will be to look for a place to live. I am going to stay with Talitha Gerlach for a little while. She & Lil Haass usually share an apartment, but Lil is up in the interior at present. Their apartment is right downtown on the 9th floor of Wayfoong House. It's very small & I think my room is the living room too. There's a porch, but it will be too cold to use at this time of the year. One thing I like is that it is only ten minutes' walk from the office. It's grand not to have the long bus trip and to be able to get home in the lunch hour. I wish I could find a place near the office for a permanent place, but there'll be no such luck. I may have to go away out to Frenchtown which will take me about an hour to get in in the mornings. . . .
>
> My clothes are all packed & stored in Shanghai except for the few things I have with me and they all need cleaning. I'm going to have to go to bed for the first few days I'm afraid.
>
> Much love,
>
> Nessie

Letter home from Shanghai, 12 March 1939:

My dear Mother,

Here I am back in the dirty old city of Shanghai with my fingernails black and my face a murky hue. It is impossible to keep clean for longer than half an hour.

The 'Canton' was late in getting in owing to fog in the estuary and it was 5.30 before the tender tied up at the Customs Jetty. Kao Jen-Ying and Talitha arrived on the scene just as I was hunting round for my suitcases.

I am living in the apartment with Talitha and sleeping in Lil's bed while she is away. Of course I must move out as soon as possible, but the problem is where to find a place to live. There is literally nothing at my price of the kind of thing I want. Stella Purchas is here and we are trying to find a place together. Yesterday afternoon we had our first experience of house hunting. It wasn't very encouraging. We put our names down on the books of two agencies neither of which had a solitary apartment or flat at the moment. Then we called at two or three places that we had seen advertised, but they were either undesirable or too expensive or too far out or a combination of all three. We rather enjoyed the afternoon in spite of the discouragement and found out a good deal about bus and train routes in the French Concession. That is really the nicest part of Shanghai to live in, but transport over to this part of the city is very difficult. It takes at least 50 minutes to come in from one of the places we looked at. I found at the International Branch hostel, where I was before, that I spent such a terrible amount of time in buses that there wasn't any time left for anything. We'll persevere but I may have to descend to a none too reputable boarding house if Lil arrives suddenly on her doorstep.

This place is very nice. It is right down town. Just a block from the river and 15 minutes' walk from the office. It is on the ninth floor so that we have a view of the river, somewhat interrupted by the Hongkong and Shanghai Bank and the Customs House. Last night there were some shots fired just after 11.30 quite near here and I am wondering if there will be anything about them in to-morrow's paper.

It is great fun being back at the office. Most of last week I spent reading correspondence and circular letters and so on to try and catch up on my job. It was really interesting to see how much had come into the office while I had been away. There are only four of us here at the moment; everyone else is in the interior.

Much love to you all,
Nessie

Letter home from Shanghai, 19 March 1939:

> My dear Mother,
>
> The sun is streaming into my office window and I am almost too warm which is surprising considering the bleak wind there is outside. I don't often spend Sunday afternoons in the office but the President of the Malayan Y.W.C.A. came on the Empress of Japan this afternoon and I am waiting for Talitha to arrive and then we are going to take her for a tour of the devastated areas, then to the annual meeting of the Shanghai Y.W.C.A. and then to a Chinese supper.
>
> At that point Talitha arrived and as she had a taxi waiting downstairs I had to pack up in a great hurry. . . .
>
> We went round the devastated areas yesterday afternoon and saw parts of them that I had not seen when we went round before. That part of the city is certainly a mess. It is just unbelievable that such a vast area should have been so utterly ruined. The most interesting thing in the annual meeting of the Shanghai Association was a movie film showing the life of industrial girls in Shanghai. It has been made specially to send abroad for Cora Deng to show during her travels in America and I am hoping it will be sent to New Zealand to be shown at the Centennial Exhibition.[2] The NZ YWCA has written asking for exhibits of one kind and another and for movie films and a committee has been set up to plan something.
>
> After the Annual Meeting we went to the King Kong restaurant and had a perfectly enormous feed. Much too much food had been ordered, but it is a good Chinese custom to have what you can't eat sent to your home, so today at lunchtime three other staff members came over and we ate the remains. There was more than enough and I think the cook had a fair meal after we had gone.
>
> Shanghai is full of refugees from Austria and Germany. They are most anxious to learn English so I am taking on a few by way of recreation. Tonight I had the first lesson. A Dr. Rosenberg, from Munich I think, who is going to start practicing here. He is going into partnership with a dental surgeon who is also going to come and talk English two hours a week. It's going to be lots of fun. I had hoped to have beginners, but these two men have studied English for some years but they need help in putting their sentences together in English. Dr. R. needs help in putting sentences in English order instead of in German and in idiom, or as he calls it 'eyediom'. . . .
>
> Much love to you all,
>
> Nessie

Shanghai was filling with Jewish refugees as, unlike America and Britain, China had no visa restrictions. Between 1933 and 1941 Shanghai accepted around 18,000 Jewish refugees fleeing the Holocaust in Europe.

Letter to Eva Skinner, Shanghai, 28 March 1939:

> Dearie, it is ages since I last wrote. . . .
>
> One reason I have not written is that I have been house hunting, a gruesome pastime in this city. There are now 6,000 refugee Jews from Germany and Austria in this city and societies of one kind and another are going hard to find them places to live and actually keeping hundreds of them while they look for work. Really and truly I don't know what I would do if I had been treated as they have been. It must be awful to look into a future that is without hope.
>
> My contribution to the situation is infinitesimal, but I am talking English for two hours with a doctor and a dental surgeon. They are opening an office in Museum Rd. I think the doctor has relatives in America and has a chance of getting in on a quota in two years' time. Meantime he wants to improve his English so that he can practice. He had a large practice in Germany and I think must have managed to get a little money out before the blow fell. He is very hard up nevertheless.
>
> To get back to house hunting. Stella Purchas and I decided that we would like a small apartment together. After days of looking at impossibilities, we have found an attic which is cute but not much else. I think it will be hideously hot in summer, but that is some months off yet. We have two rooms. Stella has the smaller one and I the larger, but mine is the living room too. Not that we do much living because we are out all day, but we have our meals in mine. Downstairs there is a large bathroom which is our kitchen too. You should see the bath chin-chinning with the electric cooker. I managed to borrow some furniture from the YWCA and we have essentials, but I badly need a bookcase, for my books are at present ranged along the top of the wardrobe. The stairs are so narrow we could not get any large pieces furniture up to our room so we had wardrobes built in and are now trying to decide on colour schemes before we buy curtains and bedspreads and cushions and things.
>
> My bed is a YWCA one, very comfortable, but as it had a thick white iron frame I borrowed only the springs and had four wooden blocks made to stand it on. When I pull it out from the wall to make it the blocks all fall in different directions which of course adds zest to life. It is an awful rush in the mornings and we have to piece things in like a jigsaw puzzle. A microscopic amah helps us but she has had no training and three in our small apartment is about three too many. The effort entailed in having baths in the morning and cooking breakfast at the same time and then dressing while the table is being set is most wearing.
>
> Early next week we expect the first of our wandering staff and Board members to return from the interior. We have been such a small group at HQ and it will

be fun to have the others trickling in full of news from free China. They have had so many conferences up there that it will take days and days to get all the news from them. . . .

Ever so much love, Nessie

Letter home from Shanghai, 10 April 1939:

My dear Mother,

. . . Yesterday I went to breakfast with Lil and Talitha and then to morning service at the Cathedral. I have never seen the cathedral so packed. There were extra chairs up the aisles and in the side chapels and not a spare seat anywhere. It is wonderful how people turn out at Easter here. The Bishop [Bishop John Curtis], Stephanie Young's brother-in-law, preached. I was squashed in between two fur coats that had not been long enough out of moth balls and nearly had Hay Fever. It was awful. The singing was great. The Cathedral certainly has a marvellous choir.

On Thursday evening I went out to dinner with Maud French and Margaret Brown, two Canadian missionaries who work in the Christian Literature Society, and they took me to the sacred concert afterwards. Three choirs had combined for it, the Shanghai Choral Society, Shanghai Songsters and the Russian choir. The Shanghai Municipal Orchestra did the accompanying and Paci the conductor who ordinarily throws himself about even when one flute is playing a pp solo, worked overtime on his physical jerks. He is the most energetic conductor I have ever seen. The singing was great. A sprinkling of Russians certainly makes a difference. I have never heard chorus work to equal it in Shanghai. The soloists were good too. My only trouble was that I had the greatest difficulty keeping awake and the concert wasn't over till midnight. It must be the spring weather I think, but I seem even sleepier than usual. . . .

Much love to you all

Nessie

Letter to Eva Skinner, handwritten from Shanghai, 25 April 1939:

Dearie, you should see my new garments. But perhaps you will, only I fear the freshness will be off the feathers. I have gone gay in this very gay season – a defiant gesture in the face of middle age. Some of it is only alterations but the most vivid is new. Picture the enclosed with a black coat, the length of the sleeve and trimmed with colour. All I need is an elegant hand bag but I haven't got round to that yet. My hat is one I bought in Colombo re-blocked & my shoes were bought in New York so I am not altogether new. Now I shall have to starve till May when cotton dresses will have to be considered. Meantime there is a doctor's bill and a dentist and one more tailor. I remember when I had been in China three years in my first term I had to spend an awful amount all of a sudden on clothes & the same thing has happened again.

Of course when I think of the thousands of European refugees in Shanghai, literally thousands, I feel we should all go in sackcloth. I honestly don't know what Shanghai is going to do. There are 9,000 Jewish émigrés here now & another 11,000 are on their way. There is absolutely nothing ahead of them here but slow, hopeless starvation. Of course a few will find work. Already tailors, doctors, technicians have started in, but naturally this community cannot assimilate many and only about 2% of them have any money.

I talk two hours a week with two German doctors. One is a dental surgeon & the other a nose & throat man. The dentist is all temperamental and terribly depressed most of the time. At present he is ill 'lying in the wardrobe' his friend says & what he means I don't quite know. Dr Rosenberg, the nose & throat one, is one of the nicest men you could ever wish to know. His wife is not Jewish and need not have left Germany but of course chose to come. He had a big practice & they kept open house & now they are lucky to have a garret in Hongkew. What is going to happen to all these people? He is a man in the late forties I should say because he was all through the war. I like his mind so much. He is tolerant and humorous & objective and I just don't see how he can be when everything has fallen to pieces about him. If only there were something one could do, but short of a Nansen L. of N. Commission,[3] or <u>all</u> countries opening their doors wide, I don't see what can be done. It seems fantastic and incredible that here we shall soon be in the centre of a large group of fine intellectual professional people – all here in Shanghai.

[No ending]

Letter to Eva Skinner from Shanghai, 7 May 1939:

I hate to mention it dearie, but it is two weeks since I last wrote to you. The time flies away from me and nothing is accomplished. Of course I had plenty of time today to write letters and it has been sheer laziness that has held me back. We saw Margaret Brennecke off to Chungking this morning. I wonder how much she will be able to do up there after this last heavy air raid. I don't know whether you have had news of it in the NZ papers but reports here say it was the worst air raid of the war. Between 3000 and 4000 casualties. The British embassy was struck and the ambassador's private secretary is among the wounded. We have had no news from the YWCA, but we know that they were in the habit of taking refuge in the consulates, so we don't not know whether they were among the many killed and wounded in the British embassy grounds. What a world we live in. Chungking is a very crowded city and occupies a V formed by the two big rivers that join. There is no way of getting out of the city except by water or retreating inland and there is not time to do that. Thousands of people have moved out since the raid, but another like the last would kill thousands more. It seems absolutely unbelievable that indiscriminate raiding should have become as commonplace as it has here. The record of last week alone shows Ningpo, Foochow, Swatow and Chungking all badly raided; the residential areas in each case having suffered heavily and the Japanese spokesman here keeps busy saying that Japanese bombers have strict orders not to hurt civilians. Why they bother to go on lying about it I don't know. . . .

My letters from the north will be unsatisfactory I fear, because they are all subject to censorship and if the censors take exception to them they just don't send them on. I have a good mind to have all my mail pile up here for me till I get back because I would rather receive it late than never. Do you realise that I will be home in nine months!!! The latest travel plan for me is that I should make this visit the north seeing Chefoo, Tsinan, Tientsin, and Peiping and then come back to Shanghai for a few weeks work in the office. Then in August I should return to Chefoo and stay there for two months. . . .

I don't think I will be back in the interior before I return [to New Zealand on furlough] and I am sorry about that. The north will be a bit of a trial because our friends the enemy are infernally nosey and are always snooping around asking questions that have to be answered with a convincing plausibility that conceals the real answer. Also Japanese-run railways are subject to guerrilla attack and trains are frequently wrecked so it will be a merry business travelling even when I can manage to get a permit.

Ever so much love – Nessie

Letter home from Shanghai, 14 May, 1939:

My dear Mother,

. . . Next Saturday I am off to the north, I don't think I'll have my letters forwarded as the mails are very uncertain up there and go astray. I will be gone only about six weeks and in that time they can pile up here. The north is very much cut off because of the Japanese censorship of letters and papers and I shall go batty for lack of war news, but will take a day off to read periodicals when I get back.

Money is going to be an awful nuisance. I must ask the bank what to do about it. I think my bank has branches in all the places I am going to, but the Japanese have their own form of currency up there and you can't use Chinese national money. I will write to you, but don't be surprised if my letters don't get through.

They will not have much news in them anyway because I won't be able to say what I think. . . .

Last night I had supper with Talitha and Lil. Another guest was a Mr. Schippe [Shippe] whom I had met before. He is a writer just returned from ten weeks in Chekiang and Anwhei where he had been visiting the Fourth Route Army behind the Japanese lines. He talked and talked and told us the most interesting things about the way the Chinese army is making everything difficult for the Japanese. You can always tell when the Japanese are having a bad time because they carry out the most terrible air raids and recently there have been simply appalling ones in many places in the interior. There won't be air raids on the railway I will be travelling on but there may be Chinese guerillas tearing up the lines and sniping from behind boulders. I think that will probably be worse. . . .

Much love to you all,

Nessie

11

More Travels

May–August 1939

In Hankow, Nessie had been national city coordinator for the six associations of Central China. Now she was in Shanghai she was responsible for all ten city associations still operating: Canton, Chefoo, Chengtu, Chungking, Hongkong, Peiping , Shanghai, Sian, Tientsin and Tsinan.[1] From late May to August 1939 she travelled to Chefoo, Tientsin, Tsinan and Peiping. The first five letters in this chapter are handwritten on Nessie's Shanghai letterhead paper.

Letter to Eva Skinner, handwritten from Chefoo, 23 May 1939:

> Well dearie, here I am in Chefoo, and a nice spot it is. I'm staying at the Missionary Home and my room looks over the sea. After the ugliness of Shanghai it's wonderful to have hills and ocean and green trees and countryside not so far away.
>
> Last week was hideously busy. There were so many things to be done before I came away and I had to work overtime & even then didn't finish everything. Moreover, last week the Committee of Women's Organisations held their annual Institute – the subject being 'Shanghai City of Refuge'. They dealt with three waves of refugees, first Russians, second Chinese & third Europeans, & discussed the problems relating to each group. It was very interesting indeed, though I could wish that they had a few more practical ideas about what could be done about it.
>
> There are 8,000 German & Austrian Jews in Shanghai and very few of them have anything like a future ahead of them. Five percent have found work & another five percent have been set up in small businesses of one kind or another. By the end of the year there will be about 20,000. They are terribly crowded in the camps they are living in and last month there was a serious outbreak of scarlet fever. However more of the cases came from those living in rooms of their own which says a great deal for the sanitary conditions of the camp. The Committee has done marvels & all on next to no money at all & there is now a special

hospital and three ambulance dispensaries. . . .

Margaret [Brennecke] lived in the YWCA when she was here and I think I am going to follow suit. It's right away from the sea which I regret, but it is quite comfortable. All her good things have been lent to friends, but there are enough dishes & so on to make do and the bed is very comfortable. It will be a very lonely life and I'll go balmy talking Chinese all the time. If only I could find someone to live with me. There is a second bed room, a nice living room & a long wide porch so we would not be on top of each other. There's an amah who can cook simple meals so it would be comfortable. Perhaps I will be able to find a summer visitor. I must look up my old teacher & have some Chinese lessons. I've picked up some German books too and am going to have a shot at the language. I don't know whether I can find a teacher here or not. Probably not but I'll give it a go. It will be fun to start on something quite new. I've met so many Germans recently and have liked so many of them that I think it would be interesting to learn their language. . . .

I think I'm in for a new job in the fall. Our Business Secretary has to have three months' rest and such is my reputation for business acumen that I'm first choice to take her place. It will be very interesting; but it is a terribly complicated job at present with exchange as it is. I'll probably either go batty or wreck the finances, but I'll get some interesting experiences out of it first. We have a pretty sound advisory committee of business men & they will tell me when to sell and when not to sell gold. I'll have two weeks in which to work with the Business Secretary before her rest period begins and should learn the ropes in that time. . . .

Ever so much love. Every day adds to the things I'll have to tell you about when I get home. Life is full of surprises. You'd be surprised!

Nessie

Letter home, handwritten from Chefoo, 4 June 1939:

My dear Mother,

I'm still in Chefoo, though moving off to-morrow to Tientsin. The Missionary Home has a wonderful garden & from my seat on the top terrace I have a marvellous view of the sea.

Today has been glorious hot, hot sunshine and a perfectly glorious blue in the water. I can see a small Jardine Matheson coastal boat with its red funnel steaming across the bay to a point. I'll be doing the same thing myself to-morrow. I imagine that Tientsin will be lots hotter than this. I'll be into my summer uniform with a vengeance.

Did I tell you that the Vicar's wife called on me one day? I was out but I have met her since. She is a New Zealander & was at Canty College at one time. She came to China in 1913. I know some of her relatives in Christchurch. Marjorie Baker, the new head of Wanganui Girls' College, is a cousin of hers. I quite forgot to ask what her name was before she was married. I went up to the C.I.M. doctor to get an injection & found he is the brother of Peggy & Ramsay Howie of Dunedin. Ramsay was a Secretary in the SCM at one time & now teaches music in connection with Auckland Teachers' Training College. There are various other New Zealanders in the C.I.M. here. Mrs. Stocker (wife of Vicar), invited me to supper to meet one of them on the 12th but I'll be far away by then. I don't know yet whether I'm going to Tsinan or Peiping first. It depends on how soon I can get a pass. I'm due back here again in a few weeks. . . .

Love to you all,
Nessie

Letter to Eva Skinner from Tientsin, 10 June 1939:

Dearie it's absolutely ages since I wrote. I think you've only had one letter since I left Shanghai. This will be interrupted any minute by the graduating exercises of a primary school but I must make a start. I arrived in Tientsin from Chefoo last Wednesday. The boat left Monday evening about 7.p.m. and we reached Taku Bay about 11.a.m. after a lovely trip. There we had to wait for the tide & moved on again about 4.p.m. Just before we started a terrific gale blew up – a real old Hopei dust storm. The water is shallow of course so we didn't roll much, but all the junks and tugs and lighters we passed were having a riotous time. Some waves came crashing over our fore deck and drenched the third class passengers. Of course we ate dust all the way up the river. We berthed about 7.p.m. & and some of the passengers came on by train, but I waited for the small river boat next morning. It takes longer – much longer, but lands in the British Concession and there is no fuss with baggage. I always find coolies and ricshas a nuisance and avoid unnecessary changes.

13th June now and I am in Peking once more. One somehow, in spite of a rudimentary intelligence, expects to find things just the same, but that is absurd. There are still a good many of the old landmarks. It's grand to meet old friends again. I could spend weeks doing that and nothing else. Do you remember the ring I brought back with me to have mended? I'm so pleased with myself because I remembered to bring it to Peking with me. It's on my finger this minute and I am going to take it out to Bead St. later this afternoon when it's a little cooler.

It's certainly hot for June and everyone is hoping for rain. There was a slight shower yesterday but not nearly enough to do any good. This is the month for the rains but the season is evidently late. Peking seems lots hotter than Tsinan – I suppose because it's further from the sea.

Lots of love,

Nessie

Letter to Eva Skinner, handwritten on board the *SS Shuntein* en route from Tientsin to Chefoo, 29 June 1939:

I feel my dear as though I were getting back into civilisation once more after my wanderings in North China. I'm really getting off at Chefoo for another week tomorrow, but for 18 hours I can pretend I'm on the high seas going places. I'll try & write a long general letter on my way back to Shanghai & then type it when I get there. This trip has been full of interest & I'd like to get my impressions down before they're dulled off by other experiences.

Once more I'm separated from my belongings. I left two cases in Tientsin when I went up to Peiping and they are still there despite my efforts to get them on this ship. I don't know when I'll see them again or how I'll get on with only just enough to last a week in the way of garments. In all this heat it will be terrific, but I'll get another dress or so made in Shanghai and hope for the best. Shoes will be the biggest problem as my new white walking shoes, tennis shoes & black evening shoes are all in the British Concession. Of course I could have gone in to get them but there are a few things I just can't do – not kowtow – and being stripped and searched is one of them.[2] I just hate to give the Japanese that amount of satisfaction. People think the situation is going to ease up a bit as the Japanese are getting a little tired. It's interesting to see the British taking a leaf out of Gandhi's book & trying passive resistance for a change. They really are wearing the Japanese down. I sincerely hope the Japanese find themselves unable to take possession of the Concessions. They will try again because they cannot control exchange and currency unless they control the Concessions; but British policy seems to be against compromise with Japan in north China and may it remain their policy!

I've seen a little now of Tientsin, Chefoo, Peiping & Tsinan. The problem is basically the same in all four places but different aspects are uppermost in each place. I have an immense admiration for all the folk who are carrying on. The Association is really very worth while in all four cities even though its programme is somewhat restricted.

Time is an awful joke. All North China is supposed to run on Tokyo time which is an hour ahead of Shanghai. Chefoo is completely Tokyo time. Tientsin Concession keeps Shanghai time and outside the Concession is Tokyo. Peiping is mostly Shanghai except Government offices, railway, etc. When I went to Tsinan I arrived at 9.10 p.m. which is after the barriers are closed so I could not reach the home of my hostess. I went to Steins Hotel near the station & found a note from her asking me to come out in time for breakfast at 7.30 the next morning. I had no idea whether she meant Shanghai time or Tokyo time. If the latter I might arrive an hour late and if the former I might arrive an hour early. I compromised on 8 a.m. Tokyo time & got out there to find they kept Shanghai time & I was half an hour early. Imagine a guest on your doorstep at 7 a.m. We had a good laugh over it. You have to mind your step when you're catching trains though. I have two watches. I keep one at Shanghai time & one at Tokyo. This ship keeps Shanghai time. We do not compromise with the Japanese! But to-morrow morning I will be in Chefoo & must change watches between the ship and the shore. It's awful in the early morning if I'm wearing the wrong watch and too sleepy to calculate.

We've been having impossibly hot weather. Tsinan was awful and I felt prostrated. The temperature didn't go below 82° [27.7° Celcius] even at night and soared during the day. However Tangku was cool yesterday & today parts of the deck have been uncomfortably cool. Marvellous! Mail to-morrow in Chefoo if I'm lucky. I haven't had a letter in over six weeks. Ever so much love dearie.

Nessie

Letter to Eva Skinner from Chefoo, 5 July 1939:

Eva dear,

. . . Last night we had a regular downpour so today is hot and sticky – most unpleasant. I'm exceedingly uncomfortable especially as four mosquitoes have just bitten my stockingless shins, I'm sitting over a coil of mosquito incense too. I've just been down to the shipping office to find out what's what. I had a berth on the 'Hunan' on Friday but now it is going direct to Hgkg from Tientsin so the office is feverishly trying to get me other accommodation. Monday is the first possibility & if not then Tuesday. I really haven't enough work to do here at the moment and am wanting to get down to Shanghai. There's no way out except by sea, so if there's no accommodation, here I sit. . . .

I had a letter from Ethel [Law] the other day suggesting that I do my three months deputation work first & then have a three months clear vacation. Six months sounds awfully short time if I come back. She also wants to know if I want to come back for a third term. In the heat of July I would shout 'NO' in a large voice, but that isn't my real opinion. I'm not going to answer till I get to Shanghai. Maybe in a cool moment on the boat I will feel like writing a letter.

Ever so much love. In 7 months I'll be on the way.

Nessie

Letter to Agnes Moncrieff from the chairman of the national committee of the YWCA of China, Shanghai, 21 July 1939:

Dear Miss Moncrieff,

On behalf of the National Committee of the YWCA of China, it is my pleasure to forward you the action taken at our June meeting when it was voted unanimously to ask you to continue your service in the City Department as Coordinating secretary for that department until the time for your departure for furlough early next year. Although it was not part of the Committee actions, since the arrangement is but for a few months only, nevertheless I wish you to know that we as a Committee agree with the plan that you substitute for Mrs. Hsueh as Business Secretary with some clerical help during the period of her furlough absence this fall. We trust this double responsibility will not prove to be too taxing for your health and energy; we believe you can carry this dual responsibility to the satisfaction of all concerned.

In forwarding this invitation to you I wish to try to tell you how much we as a National Committee appreciate your presence and your work with us in China in this particular period of our history. It is not only for your work in strengthening our city Associations that we wish to express our appreciation, but also for your presence and the spirit in which you are helping the YWCA of China to carry on under most difficult conditions that we wish to express our gratitude. Your patience, your courage, your understanding of our need mean more to us in this time of struggle than ever before and we are grateful for your presence.

It is not within our province as a National Committee to send you a contract as is the practice with our Chinese staff, yet we wish you to know that we are counting upon your continued help in the City Department throughout the coming year.

With warm personal greetings and prayers for your continued safety.

I am,
Very sincerely yours,
Caroline Tsu
Mrs Y. Y. Tsu,
Chairman National Committee YWCA.

Letter home from Shanghai, 23 July 1939:

My dear Mother,

Alas your letter with scarf tucked in has gone astray. I think it must have been with a budget of mail that was sent up to Peking to me by hand. It was given to an American professor and his wife to take up. Said professor and wife have gone on to Japan. Someone had a letter from them from Korea but no one knows what they did with the packet of mail. No one has their address and so I fear everything is lost. I particularly did not have any letters forwarded to me by mail because the post is so unreliable in North China and I asked Talitha to open any letters from Wellington and take out my salary draft while I was away. She must have missed one because I think my May salary has gone astray with the letters. It has never turned up. There were other personal letters for me too, several from Chengtu and I suppose I will never see them again. Isn't it the limit. One of the minor trials of this crazy life. . . .

I can't remember when I wrote last, but not since I got back to Shanghai I think. I have been back ten days and in another ten I leave for Chefoo again. My berth is booked back to Shanghai on September 1st. Shanghai had an awful typhoon the day before I landed and we had a terrible trip that day as you can imagine. These coastal boats are not very large and pitch about in a typhoon sea. I had had such good trips that I had forgotten the sea is ever anything but smooth. I spent the day on my back with very little to eat. We had to stand out from the coast much further than usual because the typhoon had gone inland. The trip from Tsingtao down took twice as long as it should have.

We have had typhoon weather ever since in Shanghai. Very humid with strong winds that blow everything off your desk, cloudy skies and lower temperatures, but trying sort of weather. There has been a typhoon over Formosa and two or three days ago it got a move on and was expected slap in the middle of Shanghai, but turned off somewhere else. We got lots of wind and driving rain, but it was no worse than a good southerly only warm. You have to shut windows to keep out the rain and the heat is so awful you nearly pass out. The temperature in this room is only 82, but the humidity makes it feel about 92 [33.3° Celcius].

Did you wonder why you had such dumb letters from me in the north? Perhaps they never got through. I had to be careful to say absolutely nothing because everything is so heavily censored and when I was just raring to explode it was difficult to hold myself in. The Japanese are the most irritating and exasperating nation on earth and I sincerely hope they go bang crash before so very long. They have made a perfect mess of North China and Peking is a disgusting place to live with little brown monkeys crawling all over it.

There was an Anti-British campaign in full swing while I was up there and of course the blockading of the British Concession in Tientsin made things very disagreeable. I left Tientsin two days before it began which was lucky for me, but I left some of my things and a good deal of money behind and haven't got everything out yet. I didn't go back to the Concession to get my things because the Japanese were giving British subjects such a galling time at the barriers. One woman was stripped to her corselet in front of a Japanese sentry and in full view of the street. Most of them had had things stolen and had to wait two hours to get through. The Japanese certainly hate the British and now today's news says Britain has given in to the Japanese demands.[3] I feel perfectly fed up. We grouse about Germany not standing by her pacts, but if the news is true Britain is not standing by hers either. The only difference is that she is not quite so blatant about it.

Life up in the north is pretty bad. It was very interesting to go in for a few weeks, but I would hate to live up there. You get no news, unless you have a radio and you are not allowed to take a radio in these days. The only newspaper there is well censored by the Japanese and all mail in and out is liable to be censored. There are Japanese all over the place. They have 'bought' (it's called buying!) properties all over the city and every street has a brothel or something else unpleasant in it. Opium is as easy to get as rice. . . .

Ethel Law wrote and asked me the other day if I wanted to come back to China for a third term if China wanted and I have replied I will be very happy to come if I am wanted. Whether China will want a British Secretary now she has been so badly let down by the British Government remains to be seen. . . . [4]

Lots of love to everyone,

Nessie

Letter home from Shanghai, 30 July 1939:

My dear Mother,

I'm leaving for the north again on Wednesday and will not be able to write about anything so prepare to get short dissertations on the weather and perfectly innocuous things like that. Even this letter will not be sensible for it is the season the Chinese call 'Great Heat' and believe me today was it. For a few days we will have the most appalling hot weather, the very hottest of the summer. My room didn't go above 87° [30.5° Celcius], but the humidity and the lack of even the slightest breeze completely laid me out. I do hate this humid heat. However, I'll be out of it in a few days. It will be cool at sea and although the sun is fierce in Chefoo the nights are always cool with a breeze from the sea. August is always easier to bear anyway because you can look forward to a cooler month in September.

There isn't any news anyway for I've been busy at the office and have come home and lazed most afternoons. Last night Lil [Haass] came to supper and we all went on to Jessfield Park to hear an orchestral concert at 9.p.m. It is years since I have been to a concert out there. You recline in large deck chairs and get squirted with Flit after every item and believe me you need it. The mosquitoes are perfect cannibals and there are thousands of them. The path all the way from the main gate to the enclosure where the orchestra plays is lit with red and white lanterns. They are so pretty and then in the enclosure there are lanterns all the way round in three rows. They are hung up on wires. It was so cool out there I was actually glad of a light wrap about 10.30.

Our apartment has been haunted with a large rat. We came home late one evening and surprised it. We were told when we came that rats sometimes come in off the roof. The occupant who has really suffered is Stella's canary. He has been losing his tail feathers most mysteriously lately and then one night Stella woke and found that it was the rat that was pulling them out in his frantic efforts to get to the canary. The bird has not been singing for a long time and no wonder. We set a trap with cheese, but the rat prefers soap and eats a little of ours most nights when we forget to put it away in a cupboard. Today I set the trap with soap, but so far there have been no results. Our little maid is afraid of the trap and we are glad because we were afraid that she might get her hand caught in it. She thinks the rat is much too intelligent to come in when the trap is set. I hope someone along the terrace has caught him and that the canary will not be bothered any more.

Did I tell you that I have had some dresses made? I have had practically nothing new in the summer line for three years and looked it. It was alright up in Chefoo, but I looked awful against the smartness of Shanghai. Now I have three nice new dresses and a house coat and a length to be made up in Chefoo where tailors are cheaper. I shall have to give away some of my ancients. Everyone is collecting summer dresses for the European refugees who of course have nothing thin enough for this climate and no money to buy them. I think I can spare a couple of relics.

I am soaked through just with the effort of tapping the keys so am going to stop. It is most uncomfortable. Much love to you all,

Nessie

Letter to Eva from Shanghai, 3 August 1939. This letter and the remainder in the chapter are handwritten:

Well dearie, here I am all set for another northern trip. My boat leaves at noon and I'm going to taxi my baggage down in a few minutes & then toddle along to the office to sign some letters that I hope the stenographer will have ready. You never know what excitements a trip north will hold these days. There's a headline in the paper this morning about another British woman being stripped. They usually leave your corselet, but as I don't wear one there would be an element of uncertainty in the incident. They're taking money away from the British at

Tsingtao and I can't make up my mind whether to leave all mine or take it & pit my wits against theirs. Of course hiding places are limited when the person is gone over thoroughly, but I don't think they look inside your hat. Mine unfortunately doesn't have a lining.

How dull travel in NZ will be. Couldn't you arrange to have bayonets and revolvers issued to the police before I come back & a few blockhouses put up at street intersections just to make me feel at home. You needn't bother about air raids though. I can easily dispense with those. This is my last reasonable letter for a month. The next will be liable to censorship. Lots of love – Nessie

Letter to Eva Skinner from Chefoo, 10 August 1939:

Well dearie, I've just had your 21st July letter. Isn't that quick considering that it came up to Chefoo. Well, at that moment came one of the most alarming claps of thunder I have ever heard. It was right on the heels of the lightning so it must have been very close. July is ordinarily the wettest month up here, but there hasn't been even a shower since June though this last week it has been terribly sultry & we've expected rain any minute. About fifteen minutes ago the most welcome downpour began & I can still hardly see it is so dark. It has come very suddenly for it didn't look any more like rain than usual when I came to the office.

Gosh! That clap was even nearer. So here I am without even an umbrella. I'm afraid it's too late to save the crops. All but the sweet potatoes have been ruined & they seem to stand any amount of dry weather. But think how delightfully cool we shall be. I don't suppose we'll have any terribly unbearable heat after this for according to the Chinese calendar autumn began two days ago & the 24th is 'the passing of the heat'. I'll be wishing I had some warmer things with me before the end of the month.

There isn't a great deal to do in the Association this month so I've decided not to go to the office in the afternoons. This will give me a vacation of sorts and time for swimming which pleases me greatly. I had a gorgeous swim yesterday just before supper. I have known cleaner seas, but I didn't drink much. My swimming suit seems to be falling to pieces (Gosh! that was simultaneous!) and I don't suppose I can get one to fit here, so I shall continue to clutch the pieces round me & hope for the best. I have bought a voluminous towelling dressing gown for the walk down & back, so as long as I can keep under the water I'm all right. I've a good pattern for a knitted suit & will try my hand at it just as soon as the weather gets cooler. Folk say though that the knitted ones stretch so much that they're not much use.

Much, much love – Nessie

In the letters Nessie chose to keep from this time there is no mention of the reason for her returning to Chefoo, but an entry in the July 1939 minutes of the World Fellowship Committee of the YWCA of New Zealand records:

> Miss Moncrieff going to Chefoo for August as Secretary there has been taken into custody by the Japanese.[5]

Just over forty years later Nessie recalled, 'Next I was sent up to North China where the Chinese staff members were being annoyed by the Japanese and one of them had been arrested. I sat on the doorstep and said "shoo" to the Japanese when necessary, first in Chefoo and then in Peking.'[6]

Letter to Eva Skinner from Chefoo, 28 August 1939:

> Well dearie, here's another terribly hot day. Maybe there'll be a thunderstorm later on. I hope so, for this is the limit. Monday morning there's no newspapers – not that the paper is much use, but it's something. The radio news last night was pretty bad. I do wish there was some means of averting war. I'm sure no lasting good can come from it, but I can't see any other way out of the present situation. All these British coastal boats will be commandeered if war comes. They already have their orders. I'm wondering if I will be able to get away on Wednesday. Do hope so for I can't bear the thought of Chefoo any longer when it is so hard to get news. I'm counting the days. To be here indefinitely would be simply more than I could stand. The heat or something has got me down and I feel I just can't bear Chefoo. It will be wonderful to step on board the 'Shuntien' & feel I really am getting out. If British ships are commandeered the only ships running up and down the coast will be Japanese. I'll begin to pack tonight & that will make me feel I'm getting somewhere.
>
> The Admiral in charge of the Asiatic squadron of the U.S.A. fleet is in Chefoo this week-end & the American consul gave a party yesterday afternoon. Great discussion among the missionaries as to whether it was proper to go to a party on Sunday. Some went. Today there is a return party on board the flagship and everyone can go to that. I watched some of the 'navy wives' going along the beach road from the Cathay Hotel. They have such pretty dresses. How is it Americans always manage to look so chic? They seem to put more imagination into their clothes than we do.
>
> I started out to go to church at 6.30, but the beach was so attractive that I walked instead. A brisk wind is blowing my papers everywhere and heavy clouds are overhead. Perhaps it's rain. Chefoo is always so sudden. Mrs. Booth says there's always a breaking up storm about the third week in August & after that no more heat. It's late this year so maybe this is it. I don't want the heat to continue,

but I'd hate to have another trip down to Shanghai like the last one. It was awful. However I think the typhoon season is over or almost so. . .

Ever so much love – Nessie

12
Final Time in Shanghai
September 1939–July 1940

Nessie arrived back in Shanghai from Chefoo on 2 September 1939, and remained there until she departed for New Zealand on furlough in 1940. Her letters, both handwritten and typed, are on her headed paper.

Letter home, handwritten from Shanghai. 3 September 1939:

> My dear Mother,
>
> I'm listening to the most awful jazz & crooning coming over from the 'Shanghai Evening Post & Mercury'. It's really awful stuff, but it's interrupted from time to time by news flashes from Europe and we've just heard that war has been declared. It doesn't seem possible – simply not possible. I wonder what it will mean for us all. Well, it's no good talking about it at this stage.
>
> I'm terribly glad that I'm back in Shanghai. It was awful being in Chefoo & getting such little news. So often what we did hear turned out to be rumours. Of course, it remains to be seen how the situation out here will be affected. Meantime 'business as usual' I suppose.
>
> I arrived at 7.p.m. yesterday after over four days on that wretched boat. I went on board at 11.a.m. on Tuesday & we sailed about 2.p.m. in a wicked northerly gale. At Weihaiwei four hours later it was a terrific business getting passengers & baggage on board from the launches & sampans. We were packed as full as we could be, with two men in the Captain's cabin & one woman somewhere in the officers' quarters. All the time we knew there was a typhoon coming up the coast to meet us. I had dinner that evening – but only just. The night was rough but we reached Tsingtao next morning about 8.a.m. & rolled in the outer harbour while the doctor came on board & inspected us. He had to use a rope ladder to get on board & it was a perilous business. Then we moved into the typhoon anchorage & waited for the worst. There we stayed till Friday morning. It was a great old storm with howling wind & rain but the ship did not pitch as much as I thought she might.

'At Weihaiwei it was a terrific business getting passengers and baggage on board from the sampans.' August 1939.
ATL PA1-o-1191-30-4

The typhoon passed thirty miles east of us. Tsingtao suffered a good deal. Telephone & electric light were put out of commission & the bund broken in several places. A small American destroyer in the anchorage was driven up on the rocks where she is still sticking.

On Friday morning we moved a little nearer the shore & the pilot came on board & took us into the harbour. There we waited for hours for a launch which brought out nine passengers & took some of ours ashore. They had been very restive having to wait so long, but no launch could have got near us in the sea we'd been in.

About 4.p.m. we left and as soon as we were out in the bay we started to roll in grand style. I was all ready with two books out of the library & went flat on to my back before I had time to feel seasick. We knew it would get better as we went south which was a comfort. I was alright next day – Saturday, but there was a beast of a swell almost all day. It was a relief to get into the muddy Yang Tzu estuary. Stella [Purchas] was down to meet me & we taxied home. If everything goes as I expect it to, my next trip will be to HK en route for home in another five or six months.

I'm so relieved to be here because we all knew that the coastal boats are under orders & may all be taken off the run now war has been declared. It would have been hideous to have been stuck in Chefoo cut off from news. I would have been dippy in no time. . . .

Much love to you all,

Nessie

Letter to Eva Skinner, handwritten from Shanghai, 10 September 1939:

Well dearie . . . I got in on Saturday evening & then next evening we sat here with the radio turned on listening to the news flashes from Europe & nearly being driven mad by the awful jazz business going on in between. All the time I'm wondering how it is affecting people in N.Z . . .

I finished Norman Angell's 'You and the Refugee' the other day & am now reading 'Germany – What Next?' Both give such a realistic picture of where Europe is heading & I can't see any way out of the mess except by separating Germany from the Nazi leaders & that's a military business. I've seen enough out here in these last two years to realise how grim war is and also how grim is the life of those under military domination of a ruthless people. If the war is limited to the countries now participating I can't see how France & Britain can fail to succeed, but it's the unpredictable that makes one afraid to look ahead.

So far everything seems all right out here, but the massing of Japanese troops round the borders of Hongkong's New Territories made us all wonder what would happen. Fortunately Japan still seems to be dazed by the Russo-German Anti-Aggression Pact. It is exceedingly interesting living in an international community at a time like this and one sees the economic force of the regulations issued about trading with the enemy. I can't take German lessons from Mrs. Rosenberg, a German refugee, until the British Government decides whether refugees are to be included within the scope of the regulations. I can't buy ham at Lutherers – it's about the only really clean place to buy it cooked. (Have just listened to a news broadcast giving unpleasant facts about massing of Russian forces on Russo-Polish frontier. It looks jolly unpleasant.) Of course, out here we get news from everywhere & by the time Reuters has contradicted Berlin & Berlin denied Reuters we know exactly as much as we do when Domei[1] & the Central China News Agency has told us all about it.

Shipping has of course been affected out here. All the British coastal shipping was interrupted and is still very uncertain. No news is given till ships are almost up the river & their outgoings are veiled in mystery. I saw a Chinese Sec. off last night by a small launch at 9.p.m. & it certainly smacked of war conditions. Even the names of all the ships have been painted out & of course the Union Jacks on their side that have supposedly lent protection to British ships. We gurgled over the news that Japanese ships are now painting themselves with flags on their sides. That really is a turning of the tables. . . .

I haven't seen anything of my refugee doctors since I came back. There hasn't been time. Today we hear of 440 refugees on a ship & they can't land in Singapore, Manila, or HK & now Shanghai won't have any more. I don't know what will happen to them. Sometimes the realisation of all the suffering that is going on in the world is almost more than one can bear isn't it. . . .

Lots of love.

Nessie

In her letter of 23 May Nessie mentioned to Eva that, as she'd met many Germans recently whom she liked, she thought it would be interesting to learn their language and had obviously found a teacher.

Letter to Eva Skinner, handwritten from Shanghai, 24 September 1939:

Hello dearie, it's the loveliest day you can imagine and instead of puddling off to Church to be exasperated by the Dean I'm roasting in the sun in Jessfield Park. . . . I'm still listening in to about three broadcasts every evening & last night I found a new one at 7.20. An otherwise Chinese station rents itself to Germany and I heard 15 minute news and then another 15 minutes commentary. His English is very nearly perfect – only an occasional mispronunciation gives it away; but his method of commenting is so like the opposition in a rather poor V.U.C.[2] Debating Society effort that I hooted with mirth. I don't know enough about Hitler's style to recognise an imitation, but I should guess that Hitler is the model for this man, only the words don't come quickly enough for the emotional outburst and he attacks the incidental and the superficial rather than the fundamental differences between British and German news and propaganda. Shanghai is certainly a most interesting place to live. . . .

We're almost getting used to the war. After all it hasn't affected us yet as much as the Sino–Japanese war. This last week, or ten days, the papers have been full of anti-American ramblings. It's obvious that Japan is trying to sound out the American Government & it appears America will not interfere out here and Japan's next step will be to put into effect something violently anti-British in all probability. They are still anti-Britishing as hard as they can go up North & in the interior. What is going to be the end of all this business? There's been practically no news of N.Z. in the papers except that the Govt. followed Great Britain in declaring a state of war. I wonder what is happening, but it will be some weeks before I hear. . . .

I am busy taking over Mrs. Hsueh's job at present. She is going off on three months' holiday. I can see myself learning a lot. Even making a budget in three currencies nearly drives me crazy. I'm glad there's a competent accountant. When exchange rates all vary every day and you have to have a book rate to make book-keeping possible and your book rate is nowhere near the market rate things become quite impossible. Sterling has dropped considerably in relation to gold so sterling amounts and HK dollar amounts were transferred to gold and that complicated things more than ever. I hope I don't do the wrong thing all the time. . . .

Ever so much love.

Nessie

Letter to Eva Skinner from Shanghai, 23 October 1939:

My dear,

. . . Things have been rather tense here in Shanghai lately. The Japanese-sponsored puppet government egged on by the Japanese has been trying to oust the Municipal Council police off the outside roads that are controlled by the Shanghai Municipal Council. There was a perfectly wicked piece of shooting a few days ago, and since then the district is positively alive with police. The East Surreys are reinforcing the Municipal police and the puppets have placed five hundred of theirs on the same roads. You can imagine what it looks like. I am glad I don't live out there. Even the S.M.C. officials made pretty plain statements and the Chairman of the Council, who is American, notified Washington. Cordell Hull replied guaranteeing the protection of American life and property in the Settlement and Shanghai is delighted. America really is making herself felt and the Japanese are falling over themselves protesting their amiability towards Americans. January is coming much closer all the time and the Japs are wondering what results there are going to be to the abrogation of the Trade Agreement.[3]

Well, take back what I said. I have just been listening to another broadcast which says that the Hull guarantee is a myth and the puppet police have been smacking the Municipal police around again. Grenades and pistols were used and the account sounded like a real battle. Really Shanghai is an awful city; the puppets are determined to get the Council off the outside roads and the Council is just as determined to stay. The result is a miniature war. I wish the Japanese had some sense.

I haven't had any letters for a month. . . . I think it is not much use using the Hongkong address any longer. It was always quicker when the cheap air mail was in force, but now I think it better to write to me at the Shanghai address on this letterhead. Don't write anything too blatantly anti-Japanese for all letters into Shanghai are censored or rather subject to the censor. I post them out on ships so they don't go through the Shanghai post office so I can say what I like. There is censorship in Hongkong too now but I don't mind that. It's the Japanese I have to be careful about in case anything I write reflects on the organisation I work with.

Last week we were under water. It was no joke. I don't know quite what happened. The rainfall in a few short hours was abnormal and coincided with very high tides. Also the Japanese have refused to allow any dredging of the Whangpoo River during the last two years and more so with the gradual silting up there it is harder for the water to get away. It took me an hour to get to work the first morning. I took a ricsha to the bus stop and waited for about fifteen to twenty minutes for a bus. They were so crowded that they would not stop. You had to wade out to them and when I had to wade out to the first one that stopped the door was shut in my face so I had to wade back. I was wet half way to the knee by that time. Then a taxi took pity on me and gave me a lift. I don't know who the people were. We got in to a continuous line of traffic which was wallowing down to the city. Every now and then a car would get water in its carburettor or some other vital spot and everything else would be held up till the coolies arrived to push it to one side. Only the very centre of the road was navigable at all so there couldn't be the usual two lines of traffic. It was not so bad down town and as I had taken shoes and stockings to change I spent a dry morning. Then I changed back into the wet ones to come home. I had to step out of the bus into water half way up to my knee again and stood there till a ricsha happened along. The water was right up to our front door but I managed to step from the ricsha on to the step. After lunch I took a taxi in to town and we got into water in one place so deep that water came into the taxi. I thought that surely the engine would stop and was looking round for an empty ricsha but the car went on. Next day it was not so bad, but we still had to step into water at our front door or take a taxi. It was an expensive little week. . . .

My new job [business secretary] is proving very interesting. I really am quite thrilled with it though there is an awful lot I don't know yet. This business of dealing in several currencies makes bookkeeping a very intricate business. I would like to study business systems and filing when I come home. I wonder if Banks College in Wellington has courses like that.[4] It is difficult to combine my own job with the new one and I find I have to work very long hours. It was 7 o'clock every evening last week before I left the office and work is just piled high on my desk all the time. . . .

Lots and lots of love, dearie – Nessie

Letter home from Shanghai, 5 November 1939:

My dear Mother,

. . . On Friday evening I had to meet a Mrs. Manning who came in on an Empress boat from Canada. She was a YWCA secretary in India but married not so long and is on her way back to rejoin her husband in Calcutta after having a furlough at home. I found when I met her she was Irma Moyer whom I met when she was in Calcutta in 1936. We went shopping for undies in Yates Rd and I enjoyed helping her spend all her money. Then we went to a Chinese restaurant where some of the other secretaries had gathered and had a lengthy meal. After that Talitha and I took her to the Chocolate shop for ice cream. She had not used chopsticks before and we thought she needed a little more nourishment. Then we went to Talitha's apartment and waited for the 11.p.m. launch which she had to take back to the boat.

After all that when I got home near twelve I found myself locked out. The house door has a patent handle which can be opened from the inside, but not from the outside so my latch key was no use. The amah had not been told I was out so had not fixed the handle so that I could open it. I stood shivering on the doorstep and wishing I could get Stella out of bed. However at long last the amah arrived on the scene and I made a beeline for the kettle and my hottie. I was chilled to the marrow. . . .

I'm having a bad time at the tailor's. One has been ill for weeks and the new blouse he is making for me and the suit he is altering are still incomplete. I went in yesterday determined to bring them home with me finished or unfinished but he is engaging a substitute tailor and I was told they would be done this week. I hope he hasn't got typhoid or typhus or anything else catching. I think I'll sun the garments before I put them away in my wardrobe. Then another tailor promised to deliver a dress that I am having altered last Thursday so on Saturday I went along to ask why not and found the tailor out and the dress not yet begun. I told the Chinese in charge what I thought of the entire Chinese nation and I think he got the idea. Unfortunately the door was a swing door and wouldn't slam. You waste such a lot of time running round other people who say they will do things and then don't in this country. . . .

You should hear our canary sing. He has been completely silent ever since the rat got away with his tail feathers one by one. The tail feathers have come back but not the song. Stella got some bird tonic, one dose produced a warble. This morning 'Onward Christian Soldiers' coming over the radio was too much for him and he burst into ecstatic song – a real outburst. I shall have to make Stella keep her door shut in the mornings.

Lots of love to you all

Nessie

Letter to Eva Skinner, handwritten from Shanghai, 17 December 1939. This is the final letter to Eva that Nessie kept:

It's literally weeks since I wrote, but life has been simply hectic . . . The staff conference which begins to-morrow has to plan travel for the next year so we need to know whether I am going to be able to stay through till June or not. The YWCA sent a cable to N.Z. on Dec. 4th asking for a cabled reply so we are hourly expecting one. If it doesn't come to-morrow or the next day it will be too late & they will go ahead on the assumption I remain here. I am needed here to bridge over the next few months. They have hopes of securing a Chinese Executive Secretary to take over in the summer. I would feel my work both in the City Department & in the Business Office left very unfinished if I had to pull out in February. On the other hand my soul yearns for the open spaces and the peace and friendliness of N.Z. One isn't aware of the strain here – at least only sometimes; but I thought as I passed the Bubbling Well Police Station last night & and saw the half dozen armoured cars that patrol the streets at night how odd that would be in N.Z. if police had to take methods of that kind.

Rice is being held at a terrible price by the Japanese army. It is quite reasonable outside the barriers, but no one is allowed to bring it in and the people in the city just can't pay the prices. It's perfectly ghastly! There are rice riots most days & some days several shops are raided. People one knows quite well are held up & robbed on the streets. One woman had a pistol held to her ribs & couldn't call out even though she knew mounted Sikh police were less than a block away – within call. Another resisted & the pistol was fired into the ground which so scared her that she let them have her bag. The other day a revolver was held out in front of us as we drove past in a car, but it was a French police officer searching cars between the Settlement & the Concession. A proclamation has been issued against the hoarding of rice; but some are hoarding because they feel it is the only safe way of investing money. With exchange fluctuating and no one knowing what will happen to the Chinese dollar, rice looks a safe investment even though the Japanese may not be able to maintain the present exorbitant price. Everybody has to eat.

It's coal in Tientsin that the Japanese have been holding out on. Thousands of tons stored across the river and practically nothing allowed into the Concessions so that people are freezing to death. A journalist, or war correspondent, or someone, is said to have stated that there are a thousand missionaries in Central China & every one with murder in his heart. I'm afraid it's almost true. The Chinese are better than the foreigners are at the business of refraining from hating. We foreigners don't suffer; but you can't look on indefinitely at suffering & keep an emotional balance. . . .

I am going to break Sabbath & go out & do some Christmas shopping before so very long. It's hard to believe that Christmas is so close. Much love, Nessie

Letter home, handwritten from Shanghai, 25 February 1940:

My dear Mother,

I had a note from Cooks yesterday saying that Cabin 6 – a single berth cabin – had been allocated to me for my trip home. I don't know the name of the ship or when sailing but it's nice to know it's cabin 6! In five months I should be on my way home from Hongkong. I really must keep my mind off it as time goes more slowly if you look forward too hard.

I had a letter from Vee saying that she & Jesse & family are planning to come on to Shanghai to wait for their boat here. I'm so glad for I was very disappointed at the thought of having only a few hours with them. Vee says they had planned to wait in HK for their baggage to catch up with them but that now they are bringing only what they can carry on the plane so can come straight on . . .

The exchange value of the Chinese dollar is dropping again and prices are soaring. The cost of living is now more than three times as high as it was before the war began. Coal used to be about $32 a ton but it is now $270. Rice touched $70 a bag but I think is down a little again. It ought to be about $15. We don't eat much rice, but coal affects us because the Power Co. puts up its charges. Everyone has to give extra living allowances to employees & they have to raise prices to do it even on things that are not imported.

We've just had notice of another 15% increase in the price of milk. That makes 35% altogether. And our groceries soar & soar. We economise wherever we can but our prices go up & up. I'm lucky to be paid in pounds because I get more dollars to the £; but Stella is on a Chinese dollar basis and she finds it very difficult.

Very much love to you all from,
Nessie

Letter from the national committee of the YWCA of China, Shanghai, 14 May 1940:

Miss Agnes M Moncrieff
National YWCA
Shanghai.

My dear Miss Moncrieff:

Although you are already familiar with the action regarding your furlough which was taken at the last National Executive Committee, nevertheless on behalf of the National committee we wish to forward this recommendation to you in writing. Jointly we underscore the opening paragraph of the letter to the YWCA of New Zealand forwarding this action by air mail:–

'On behalf of the National Committee of the YWCA of China it is our happy privilege to forward to the YWCA of New Zealand the following action which was taken at the April 1940 meeting of our National Executive Committee:–

THAT the National Committee express its deep sense of appreciation of the co-operation of the YWCA of New Zealand in aiding our Association and of the contribution of Miss Moncrieff to the work of the YWCA of China and request that in continuation of that co-operation Miss Moncrieff return to China after furlough.'

At the same time we also wish to express to you our deep appreciation of your splendid help during this past eventful period of history in China and in the YWCA Movement – a period in which many totally new problems had to be faced and many adjustments made. Your part in living through this difficult period with us has not only saved us from many troubles, but has also strengthened our morale.

We know that you are returning to New Zealand for a well-earned furlough, for our national struggle entered the acute stage almost from the moment of your return from your last furlough. We are fully aware of the difficult problems you had to face in Hankow at the time when life was very tense and confused for us all. Your period of work as city department co-ordinator also came at a time of great disturbances, upheavals and transitions for our city associations. And lately your added contribution in the business office during Mrs. Hsueh's absence and after her return is another evidence of your splendid spirit of 'sharing the load' even at the expense of your own energy and strength. And at all times we have known that we could count upon your objective point of view and wise counsel for general consultation in other fields of association work than those included in your own responsibility.

To the YWCA of New Zealand we have expressed our appreciation of their contribution to China by including a secretary for China in their limited budget when they themselves need experienced staff members. We have expressed our gratitude and appreciation that you are the person through whom this contribution has been made to China.

Although it is hard for us to say farewell and to face the period of your absence from China, nevertheless we wish you well on your departure in July in order that you may return to us at an early date.

Very sincerely yours,

Caroline Tsu, Tsai Kwei

Mrs. Y.Y. Tsu, Chairman National Committee National General Secretary[5]

The letter under reference from the YWCA of China to the YWCA of New Zealand national executive, dated 10 May 1940, includes a personal comment:

I also wish to take this opportunity to supplement this formal action with a personal expression of gratitude and appreciation for Miss Moncrieff's splendid contribution during these difficult war-time years. Unforeseen problems, unanticipated complexities of work, have demanded flexibility, resourcefulness and patience to a degree undreamed of under peacetime conditions. Now that the time for Miss Moncrieff's departure for furlough draws near, we realize how much of this increased burden she has shared. We shall greatly miss her strengthening hand during her absence, but we shall count steadfastly and with confidence upon her return at the end of this period of rest and refreshment. We trust that the Y.W.C.A. of New Zealand will continue this co-operative relationship with the Y.W.C.A. of China by sending Miss Moncrieff back to us in 1941 for another term of service.

Sincerely (Signed)

Caroline Tsu

Chairman of the National Committee of the YWCA of China[6]

Letter home, handwritten from Shanghai, 27 May 1940:

> My dear Mother,
>
> I've had Committee meetings in my flat all morning & now its 11.30 & they're over – earlier than I expected. I'm lunching here, so have a little time before I need to move.
>
> I'm having such a busy time dashing round with Jesse & Vee that there's not much time for letters. Also I've had four late nights – after 12 – in the last week & am nearly dead for lack of sleep. I'm not a bit good at late nights in this climate or perhaps it is advancing age. Jesse isn't any good at them either. He likes to go to bed at 9.pm
>
> They all arrived in Shanghai last Thursday. I had the YWCA pass so got right down to the ship to meet them. I took the whole day off & went out to lunch with them at Elim House where they are staying. It's terribly full at present so they are all four in one big room which means very little rest for Jesse & Vee. The boys seem to have loads of energy though Vee keeps Robert on his back most mornings.[7] They have a private bathroom which helps a little.
>
> I got them started on their shopping on Thursday afternoon. They could only bring 33lbs a piece on the plane with them & had 8lbs excess. Their things are in split bamboo Chinese baskets with very thin oiled silk lining. Each basket with silk & the cord weighed 1½ lbs so they didn't lose much weight on the containers. They have to buy trunks here & Jesse needed suits & so did Robert. Jesse has lost 20 pounds in weight since I saw him last. He looks thin & tired & I'm glad they're out of West China for a while. The situation up there is not easy & bombings are a constant strain even though they're not aware of it.
>
> I've arranged to have my suppers with them, at Elim House so I see them at least once a day. I went there on Friday evening & we put the boys to bed & then went off to the second of the Tchaikovsky concerts. It was a Russian ballet, 'The Swan Lake' & was most interesting. Ballet seems to me like something from another world; it so vigorous compared to the modern 'walks' & 'swings' of the ball-room. It was full of colour & some of the dancers were very graceful. The prima ballerina was delightful. Some of the audience had seen Pavlova in the part so were more critical than I. The young Prince was on the elderly side; but he's the best of the male dancers in spite of his age
>
> On Saturday afternoon the family all came over here to tea after Jesse had taken the boys to see 'Gulliver's Travels'.[8] The boys love sardines which of course they have not been able to get in West China so I had an enormous plateful of sardine sandwiches prepared for them. There was not a crumb left to tell the tale.

I was glad my landladies were out for the boys made a great row dashing up & down stairs. I went back with them to supper & Vee & I window-shopped on the way.

On Sunday morning we went to the Community Church together & then out to West Gate to lunch with some friends of theirs at the Seventh Day Baptist Mission. They are people I have often heard Jesse talk about so I was glad to meet them. I had invited some of the staff to tea here to meet them and some of my guests had arrived by the time we got back. After that the third of the Tchaikovsky concerts. It was the orchestra this time. The first section was violin with orchestra, the second piano with orchestra & the third orchestra & oh boy oh boy was it good. They did the 'Pathetique' & someone had suggested it was a rather a pessimistic note to end on so they played Tchaikovsky's 'Slav March' which was grand. It brings in bits of the Russian National Anthem. I had never heard it played by an orchestra before and it was marvellous.

This morning I could hardly bear to get up, but I seem to be struggling through the day. Today is Jesse's birthday & they are all coming for dinner here. It is straining my household to the busting point, but I do have five of most things except places at table so I'm not sure how we shall manage. It's going to be a bit of a picnic, but I hope everyone gets enough to eat which is the main thing. We're going to have fried fish in breadcrumbs, new potatoes, beetroot, green peas & a salad of tomatoes and mayonnaise & then ice cream with bananas & pineapple & coffee & birthday cake. I feel like bulgy Algy at the thought of it.

I must make a dash for the office. Lunch has intervened & final instructions to the maid about tonight & and I must get to my desk and do a spot of work.

Much love to you all,

Nessie

Letter home, handwritten from Shanghai, 9 June 1940:

My dear Mother,

I've just got back from seeing Jesse & Vee & the boys off. They went down to the ship by the 5.15 tender & I had two hours on board with them before the tender came back. Dinner was early so I had an American dinner with them – huge ripe olives, lettuce crisp as can be & you didn't have to ask if it was safe to eat it, Californian oranges, ice cream, tomato juice, as well as fish & salad & a few etceterars. It was a delectable meal.

It was hard to say Good-bye; they are such dears & I don't know when we'll meet again, though if they & I both come back to China we should see each other again in Shanghai in a year from September. Robert's health will be the deciding factor as to whether they come back again or not. Jesse has been very busy here getting his book ready for the printer & they've been living a long way off; but we've seen a good deal of each other all the same. I would have liked to take more time off from the office; but we've been pretty busy. Today I have been almost the whole day with them helping pack. They have bought clothes & books & presents & of course trunks to put them all in. It was a grand rush getting everything pushed in in time.

And now I must think of my own packing. I leave just a month from to-morrow & there's an awful lot of work to be done. When I think of the sorting of letters & papers I just go tired. Wish I could be in NZ without getting there. . . .

I am told that I have to furnish the HK censors with a list of all the books & papers I take out of HK with me. Isn't that a horrible thought? I have lots of paper clippings & articles & so on for my deputation work. Think of the effort to list it. . . .

Much love to you all,
Nessie

13
The Burma Road
1940–1941

In mid-1940 Nessie returned to New Zealand on furlough. During her absence the headquarters of the YWCA of China was shifted inland to Chengtu. In July 1941 Nessie left New Zealand and made her way there via Rangoon and the Burma Road.

After the final letter written from Shanghai on 9th June 1940, in which Nessie wrote that she would be on her way home in a month, there is a gap of two months. This is explained by an item in the New Zealand YWCA monthly magazine, *The New Zealand Girl*, of September 1940:

> Miss Agnes Moncrieff has reached Australia on her homeward journey. Miss Moncrieff had the ill luck to contract pleurisy during her last month in Shanghai, but fortunately was able to make her steamer connection at Hong Kong and convalesce on the voyage.[1]

Letter to mother, on board *SS Taiping* en route to Sydney, 10 August 1940:

> My dear Mother,
>
> . . . Manila to Thursday Is. seemed a long stretch this time and we have been counting the days. But now it's well behind us and we feel nearer home.
>
> I am feeling heaps better, but get terribly tired still. I have done practically nothing but lie on a lounge chair and read all the way. Miss Read of the Canton Hospital staff is on board and she says it usually takes three months for a complete recovery from pleurisy and that I shouldn't do anything till the beginning of October. Scrabbling in the suitcases on the floor of the cabin tires me most and there is still a good deal of that ahead of me. Arrangements had been made for me to go through to Melbourne to do a spot of talking before leaving for N.Z., but I had to write to the NZ Association that the doctor had very firmly put her foot down on deputation work before I had had a good rest.
>
> Your last air mail letter arrived the last day before I left Shanghai; wasn't that luck. I was so glad to have it because I didn't think there would be any more

letters before I left Shanghai. All the time I was ill none came and I was pining for them. Just the day I left Shanghai Lydia [Johnson] arrived from Peiping bringing with her the mail that went astray a year ago. There were ever so many letters from NZ and yours with the scarf you sent me for my birthday. It hadn't spoiled at all in all its journeys and I am so glad to have it. Very many thanks.

I am still in summer garments, but not in Shanghai summer garments. In a day or two winter garments or at least silk dresses will be needed. But I am putting off the day as long as possible for everybody packed for me and I don't know where things are. There's a lot of repacking to be done and I hope that when I take out my fur coat there will be a bit more room in my boxes. I think I have 14 pieces so Customs will take a blue age when I get to Wellington. If I do come to Wellington and you come down to meet me remember the circular wave.[2] Try to get a permit to meet me otherwise with all these war restrictions I am afraid you will be held behind the barrier until I get through Customs.

No more news, but lots of love till I see you.

Nessie

Nessie arrived back in New Zealand on 10 September 1940. By October her health had improved sufficiently for the YWCA of New Zealand executive minutes to record:

> October 8: Miss Moncrieff has been given a satisfactory medical certificate.[3]

Beginning in October and carrying through to the following May, Wellington's *Evening Post* and other national newspapers carried numerous reports of 'Miss Agnes Moncrieff M.A.' speaking to differing groups about the current situation in China. Forty-five years later she recalled:

> . . . I just talked my head off round the country . . . six Rotaries in seven weeks . . . I'll never forget one meeting. . . All the secondary schools were invited to Wellington College so that I could just give one address . . . their huge hall was absolutely chockablock . . . their ears were flapping.[4]

The Wellington College talk was written about in her old school's 1941 magazine:

> A talk was given by Miss Nessie Moncrieff, an Old Girl of our school, who addressed the senior forms of most of the Wellington colleges at the Wellington Boys' College. She gave an illuminating account of the war conditions in China, stressing the courage and endurance of Chinese students who are recognized as the future leaders of the nation. She explained the importance of supply routes, the Burma Road in particular, and concluded with a tribute to the International Red Cross, whose work in providing medical help has enabled China to continue her struggle.[5]

Although the YWCA of New Zealand, due to the worsening world situation, was initially apprehensive about Nessie's returning to China for another term, the YWCA of China was 'counting steadfastly and with confidence upon her return at the end of this period of rest and refreshment.'[6] The May 1941 convention of the YWCA of New Zealand agreed Miss Moncrieff was to return to China for a further term at the end of her furlough in July 1941.[7]

Important to Nessie's future was a letter from Tsai Kwei, general secretary of the YWCA of China, to the YWCA of New Zealand. In it Tsai Kwei explained that as the situation in Shanghai was deteriorating with increasing limitations in freedom, and many people had migrated to the interior, the national committee of the YWCA of China had decided to shift their headquarters to Chengtu in Sichuan Province. Chengtu, not yet occupied by Japan, formed part of 'free China'.[8]

It was the World Fellowship Committee of the YWCA of New Zealand that was directly responsible for Nessie in China, and their minute book reflects concern for her welfare:

> March 8: Agreed Miss Moncrieff travel by sea to Hong Kong and then fly to Chengtu. Travel from Rangoon to Chengtu by the Burma Road ruled out.
>
> March 24: Members viewed with apprehension the suggestion Miss Moncrieff return via the Burma Road. A booking by sea to Hong Kong leaving on July 11 has been made with Cooks.[9]

In a letter to Nessie after that meeting, Ethel Law commented, 'the Committee felt a serious repugnance to that of you going via the Burma Road'.[10]

The 688-mile Burma Road, linking Lashio in Burma with Kunming in China, was built 1937–1938 by hundreds of Burmese and Chinese labourers. On 23 January 1938 Nessie had written to her mother that 'the first trucks had come into Chungking from Rangoon along the new highway'.[11]

On 26 March 1941, Ethel Law wrote to Nessie:

> Here is great news for you. A cable has just come from Tsai Kwei EXPECT MONCRIEFF CHENGTU. Somehow or another you will have to get from Hong Kong to Chengtu.[12]

Getting from Hong Kong to Chengtu 'somehow or another' was proving to be quite a challenge, and continued to be so, as minutes from the May World Fellowship Committee meeting show:

> May 6: Miss Moncrieff should take no undue travel risks. When making travel arrangements she should regard her safety as of <u>paramount importance</u>. World

> Fellowship Committee wish to lay this Safety First injunction upon Miss Moncrieff particularly if the question of air travel from Rangoon to Chengtu has to be weighed against surface travel on the Burma Road.[13]

In a letter to the YWCA of New Zealand written on 13 June 1941, Nessie commented:

> My last letter from Miss Johnson assures me that there is no way at present of getting baggage in from the China coast and advises me to travel via Rangoon. . . . I should make every effort to get some supplies in with me both for my own sake and because it is hardly fair to the others already in there to borrow extensively for bedding, medical supplies etc. I hope the Committee understands I will be as saving of the Association's funds as I possibly can be and I will make no decisions on the basis of personal inclination.[14]

The executive minutes of Tuesday 8 July recorded:

> Miss Moncrieff sails on Sunday by Monterey – route still uncertain but will be decided in Sydney.[15]

The final outcome is set down without comment in the YWCA executive's minutes of 3 September:

> September 3. News has been received that Miss Moncrieff has arrived in Singapore and now travelling to China via the Burma Road.[16]

Letter to mother from Rangoon, 27 August 1941. There is no greeting or ending, but at the top of the single piece of paper is typed 'Letter to Mother from Rangoon. 27.8.41.' The typeface is quite different from that in other letters sent from China, as is the paper. It obviously was retyped much later:

> The trip up from Singapore was absolutely awful. I have never travelled on such a tub. It was full of the most ghastly smells and a number of the Indian passengers ate their own food and kept it in their cabins. Imagine the odours. Miss Stanton and I shared an inside cabin so had no port even during the day. The first night while we were still tied up in Singapore Miss S. and I slept in the cabin. We vowed never again and the captain gave us permission to sleep in the smoking room. That had three ports which we were allowed to open as soon as our light was out so we didn't die of suffocation. The weather was pretty good. I felt a bit liverish one day and Miss S. went down to it properly and couldn't lift her head.
>
> We stayed a night at Penang. The afternoon we arrived five of us hired a taxi for an hour and went out to the Gardens and to a large Chinese temple. The gardens were full of monkeys and there was a large snake about six feet long

lying on the path. I managed to refrain from jumping out of the car and we got past without disturbing it at all. We had dinner on shore at the Swiss café and got back to the ship about 10.p.m. Next morning the others went up Penang Hill, but I had to make some Y.W.C.A. contacts. I went to call on the honorary general secretary. The name did not convey anything, but I discovered she had been studying at Selly Oak at the same time I had been there.[17] She is married to an Englishman in shipping in Penang. They have been there over a year but she doesn't like the climate and is very homesick for China. I know a number of her relatives in China and am to call on one here. He is in a position to give me good advice as to how to get into China for he is head of the Bank of China here.

Entering China via the Burma Road during the war years was an undertaking that posed no small difficulty. Nessie kept a diary of her road journey which she later transcribed as the basis of a report to her YWCA colleagues in New Zealand. At the top is 'National Committee YWCA, 87 San Sheng Chieh, Chengtu, Sze, China. January 1942'. It is in the same font as 'Letter to Mother from Rangoon'. At the end of each entry she records the miles travelled that day. The odd use of 'kilometres' five times shows it was typed sometime after 1976, when New Zealand changed to metric measurement. This reinforces the supposition that Nessie collated her correspondence when she was in her late seventies, possibly with an intention of turning it into a book.

Dear Friends,

As you know when I left New Zealand I had not decided whether to go Hong Kong or Rangoon. Information waiting for me in Sydney seemed to indicate that the only land route to the interior of China was the Burma Road. Other routes from the coast of China could not be used continuously and to attempt to enter by any of them might mean weeks and weeks' delay. I therefore booked a berth on a Dutch steamer to Singapore and after a very pleasant nineteen days at sea landed at Singapore and caught a small and very dirty tramp to Rangoon. That part of the journey was by no means pleasant for the weather was hot, the ship overcrowded and the accumulated smells of forty-one years overpowering. It was a great relief to land in Rangoon and leave smells and black-out behind.

The day after I arrived in Rangoon I began on the endless series of calls that are necessary before one can find a means of getting up the road. The men in charge of transport and allied services must be heartily sick of would-be passengers eating up their time in enquiries about possible trucks and convoys. One of my first calls was on Mr. Crane of the American Baptist mission. He gave me some very useful information which I followed up in the course of the next few days. One of his suggestions was to get in touch with a Mr. and Mrs. J.W. Rudd who were staying at the Baptist Guest House and were trying to get through to

Chengtu. I went out to see them to talk over possibilities. Mr. Rudd said they would be glad to add me to their party which included themselves and Dr. Joe Macrae of the Church of Scotland Mission who was going up to Chengtu for language study before moving on to the Mission Hospital at Ichang. Then began a series of conferences on our chances of getting up the Road. Several people at the Guest House were trying to get into China and one day we all met together to pool information and see if we could start a mutual society. We found that we had all been calling on the same people – Chinese Red Cross, China Industrial co-operatives, Bank of China, China Travel Service, Steel Bros, South-West Transport Co. The last named had instructions from the Chinese Government to transport missionaries free of charge as far as Kunming. The original instruction was intended for missionaries who could no longer work in occupied China and were trying to get into the interior. However it had been extended to include all missionaries. Baggage is limited to 200 pounds, but on more than one occasion baggage considerably in excess of this amount has been transported free. As far as I was concerned I knew that the difficulty would be to get any means of transport beyond Kunming and that was not very much more than half-way for me.

I had also been to see the secretary of the Australian Minister to China who was in Rangoon making arrangements for the baggage of the Legation to get through. I hoped there might be an opportunity for me to travel on the Legation truck, but the secretary was so overcome with the difficulties of cutting a way through the red tape of two oriental governments that he could offer me no assistance. I was however offered a seat on a Chinese Red Cross ambulance going as far as Chungking but I could not have taken all my baggage with me and I knew that if once I left it behind the chances were that I would not see it again. Also Chengtu is 300 miles beyond Chungking and I was not sure what means of transport there would be between the two cities. I would have had to travel approximately two thousand miles in a party of one with only a Chinese driver to work off my excitement on when the road became too thrilling for silence. I turned it down in favour of the Rudd party, but had I known how long I would have to wait in Rangoon I would have gone off with the Red Cross and hoped for the best.

John Rudd decided the best way to get himself, Joan and belongings into China was to buy a truck. That presented considerable difficulties. The few that came into Burma for private sale were booked in advance and some of the agencies had nothing to offer for six months. In the course of time John heard of an International two-ton truck and then began the long process of getting it on the road with all the necessary permits and papers. The truck had to be assembled and the body built. There was an export licence to be secured, and a police registration and several papers that took a long time. New regulations with regard to private trucks came into force and it looked as though the truck would have to carry a government load over the border before it would be allowed to carry a private load. Then the Buddhist long Lent[18] ended in a blaze of lights and the police had a partial holiday for ten days. I would be told that we were leaving in two days' time and would have all my boxes locked and labelled only to be told there was yet another formality and another three days must elapse. That went on for weeks.

At last the zero hour arrived and on October 13th, seven weeks all but a day after I had landed in Rangoon the truck arrived at the YWCA doorstep to collect my luggage. Later in the day I went out to the Guest House to spend my last night in Rangoon there for a new Burmese regulation had gone into effect permitting transit trucks to leave the city only between the hours of 10.p.m. and 6.a.m. The Guest House is several miles from the business section of the city so by leaving from that point we had a good start. John spent the last afternoon loading the truck. The load was not weighed but from the look of the springs it was as much as the truck could manage. We travelled the whole way with the tail-board down and odds and ends including two bicycles overflowing on to it.

<u>Oct. 14th</u>: We were up long before daylight, ate a hurried breakfast, piled on the over-night bags and at 5.40 a.m. started out on our long journey. As we left Rangoon behind us it began to rain and most of the day it poured in truly monsoon fashion. The road was tar-sealed and fairly level. It ran for miles and miles between paddy fields. It was low in parts and there were a few sections under water. One place proved rather deep for the splash got into the feed system and several stops had to made during the day to remove water from the filter cup and carburettor. Fortunately both John and Joe knew a great deal about the inside of an engine and what they did not know to begin with they knew long before the end of the journey.

We stopped for refreshments at the railway station at Pegu and at Toungyoo and reached Pinmana about 8.30 p.m. We had planned to spend the night at the PWD bungalow but were unable to find it in the dark. Instead we went to the railway station. As in India all large stations have rest rooms upstairs where passengers can sleep. We found three rooms each with a private bathroom and on the long balcony on to which the rooms opened we unpacked our food baskets and had a long overdue meal. 244 miles

<u>Oct. 15th</u>: We made an early start as we hoped to get through to Maymo some forty miles beyond Mandalay. After a good morning's run of almost a hundred miles we found that the road to Mandalay was flooded and there was a depth

of four feet of water in one place. No one could tell us whether it would be one or four days before the roads was open again. We had hoped to have lunch at a PWD or dak bungalow[19] but the road to both was under water and it was impossible to get through. We went to a municipal bungalow which was not so good and after lunch decided to continue our journey by a branch road that would cut out Mandalay and Maymyo and add another hundred miles to our trip, but we did not want to have a long wait at Meiktila.

We had gone only a few miles when we were once more stopped by floods. The road as far as we could see it was under water and we could not tell how deep the water was. Bullock wagons were coming through, but obviously the deepest part was a long way from where we were waiting and one could not tell whether the water or only the splash had reached the axle of the wagon.

As we were waiting a car drew up and a Burman stepped out who quite obviously wanted to get to the other side. He assured us that he had come through that morning in a Chevrolet. The water was rising but he was sure that we could get through in our truck. As we stood talking a British military truck came dashing through at a good speed. The driver, an Indian, told us we could get through if we removed the fan belt to prevent the water being thrown up into the engine. The surface of the road was good all the way and an avenue of trees stretched most of the way and would help to keep us to the middle of the road. The only difficulty was the trail of bullock wagons coming through. We should have to get off the middle of the road to pass them and we might get too far over. However John decided to risk it and with the Burman who turned out to be the deputy commissioner for railways in the district sitting on our front mudguard, we started off. About a quarter of a mile was under water and a curve in the road prevented our seeing what was ahead. It was alright till the trees petered out and one had to guess where the asphalt was. At that point we passed several wagons and had to get right off to the side of the road. For a few moments it seemed as though we would be brought to a dead stop at the deepest part and once stopped there would be no going on again till the waters subsided. After a tense moment we got back on to the road, the water gradually became shallower and just as the engine was getting dangerously hot we drove out of the water and up and over a small bridge. There we stuck and nothing could persuade the engine to start again. It looked like a long job so we stopped a military truck that had come through behind us and asked for a seat for our Burmese friend, Mr. Ah Bee (?) who had got very wet on the journey. John and Joe got busy on the feed system. Before very long our Burmese friend came back with the station master in his car and invited Joan and me to go to the station and wait there and have some tea. We were glad to accept and had an interesting time in Mr. Ah Bee's private carriage sipping tea and exchanging views on Burma and the world in general. He was a graduate of Judson College[20] and knew several of the people I had met in Rangoon. After a while we grew restive and the men did not turn up so our host suggested that he take us back to the truck to see how they were getting on and to take them a tray of tea. Just as we came in sight of the truck it began to move towards us. The men were glad of the tea. We piled into the truck again and they told us the tale of their efforts as we went along. Both assured us that they knew much more about the insides of the engine than they had before. We gather that there had been one moment when the petrol caught fire but happily it had been extinguished before any harm had done.

Once past Thazi where we had been entertained at the railway station the road was on a higher level and we had left the flooded districts well behind. It was late afternoon by that time and we still had sixty miles to go. The real climb to Kalaw which is a summer resort does not begin till within about fifteen miles of the town and it was well after dark when we began. The road was not as good as the main Rangoon-Mandalay road had been and all the bridges were marked for four tons only. Our gross weight must have been fully four tons, but we hoped the PWD engineers had left a good margin for safety. Only at one point was there any real difficulty. A new bridge was being constructed over a mountain stream and a short detour had been made over a temporary bridge. The approach on both sides of the bridge was bad and the bridge was labelled three and a half tons only. However we had to cross it. The main job was to keep going in that awful mud. Joe managed it though we held our breath till we got safely to the other side. Kalaw is 4340 feet above sea level. There are two hotels, both too expensive for us but our railway friend had given us a letter to the station master asking him to allow us to sleep in the waiting rooms. We had no difficulty in securing that privilege but the rooms were very dirty and smelly. By candle light we managed a meal then put up our cots and settled down for the night. It was necessary to keep the door open and we were afraid that thieves might visit us. I slept across the doorway with an elaborate erection of enamel ware that would fall at the slightest touch. Unfortunately I touched it myself during the night and proved the full value of the scheme. The only excitement was the arrival of the passenger train and the only noise that disturbed us was the prodigious yawns of the station watchman.

167 miles

<u>Oct.16th</u>: We were up and away fairly early. From Kalaw we travelled westwards through country that the guide book told us looked like the rolling Sussex downs. Paddy fields rather destroyed the resemblance, but it was beautiful country to drive through. During the morning we reached Taungyi, another hill station

about 4600 feet above sea level. We stopped at an Indian tea-shop for elevenses and bought some very good cakes for our lunch basket. On to Loilem another sixty miles westward we had the most winding road that we had met up to that time. We were right in the heart of the Shan states and the scenery was grand. We reached Loilem by the middle of the afternoon and called on the road engineer with whom the other members of our party had travelled from England. He sent us over to his home and we were regaled with the most delicious afternoon tea. There was a cordial invitation to spend the night but we knew that we would get an earlier start if we went on to a PWD bungalow so we set off again hoping to spend the night at Laihka about thirty-three miles further on. It was dark long before we reached Laihka and we failed to see the bungalow notice. The road was too narrow to turn the truck so we went on to Mongkung. There fortunately the PWD bungalow was well labelled and it was not long before we had we roused the servant and established ourselves for the night. I personally was delighted to come to the end of the day for I was running a temperature, felt extremely giddy and my back was aching as I did not know a back could ache. 165 miles

Oct. 17th: We left late with a run of about 120 miles before us. The road was narrow all through that part of Burma and for miles consisted of bitumen wheel tracks with grass growing between them. It was awkward passing other vehicles but we did not meet them for the engineer at Loilem had told us that the road that we had come by was closed to truck traffic because of the bridge we had had such difficulty in crossing east of Kalaw. We had a good run for ninety miles to a point about eight miles from Hsipaw. There we turned north-east to Lashio.

A few miles further on we had to pass a truck at a point where the road was narrow and very soft at either side. Our back wheel sank up to the hub and there we stuck. We had no tools with which to dig ourselves out and though people stopped to help, as night approached they had to go on. Finally it was decided that Joe should go on to Lashio and try to send help back to us. We hailed a passing truck and the driver agreed to take him in. The wheel for all our efforts was now completely buried. We had just decided to take the load off the truck when a break-down lorry came along. The situation was play to the brisk young Chinese in charge. He took the matter in hand, fixed a steel cable on to our front axle and the second effort succeeded in getting us on to the road again. When we reached the barrier at the entrance to Lashio Joe was waiting for us there. Some people who had been staying at the Guest House in Rangoon had seen us on the road and let him know we were moving. That night we stayed at a Government School. 123 miles

Oct. 18th: Classes began at 9.a.m. so we had to be packed up early. We had chota[21] and breakfast at the school and set off to the customs station about 11.30. There were several clearances to be secured. John was advised to get a certificate from the South-West Transport Co. and this certificate stood us in good stead at various points on our journey. Among other things it released us from the necessity of taking a government load over the border. After a couple of trips between new Lashio and Old Lashio and a little shopping we found ourselves free to go on. Prices were very high compared with Rangoon, but we knew they would be considerably higher farther on so we replaced several things that had been casualties on the trip. We knew that we were too late to reach the border that night so decided to stay at a PWD bungalow at Kutkai. It was only 48 miles further on but we had a very high climb ahead of us. It gave us a magnificent view of the sunset and the ranges beyond us. The bungalow proved to be the most luxurious we had stayed in. It was on a side road and commanded a good view of the main highway. It was cold at that height but the servant made a fire for us in the living room and we slept well in comfortable beds. 48 miles

Oct. 19th: We woke to pouring rain. The first day out from Rangoon we had discovered that the tarpaulin on the truck was not waterproof and there was no garage in which the truck could be put. We were tempted to stay there a day and hope for better weather on the morrow. Our anxiety to get to our journey's end was stronger however and off we set. At a town on the border which sounded like Chuckchuck we were formally passed out of Burma. Then only a few hundred yards and over a bridge and we were in China and the customs barrier was down before us. There followed several hours of waiting while the proper forms were filled out in the Customs Office. John had to take the truck round to the inspection yard, a terrible place where it was most difficult to find a spot where the truck would not sink into the bog. With transport the main problem of the country it passes understanding why they do not do something to level off that yard or provide some kind of surface that will prevent trucks sticking in the mud. Not so long before we arrived one completely overturned and it is not surprising

At last all our papers were properly filled and we were able to approach the barrier once more. But our troubles were only half over. The customs clearance was only one of several papers to be obtained. The truck had to be registered, a road maintenance tax had to be paid, a driver's licence secured and the registration was closed for the night. It was some time after dark but finally John persuaded the official at the barrier to see what could be done. Meantime Joe sauntered off to look for petrol. Both APC [Asiatic Petroleum Company] and Standard Oil offices were closed for the night and we needed petrol before we could move.

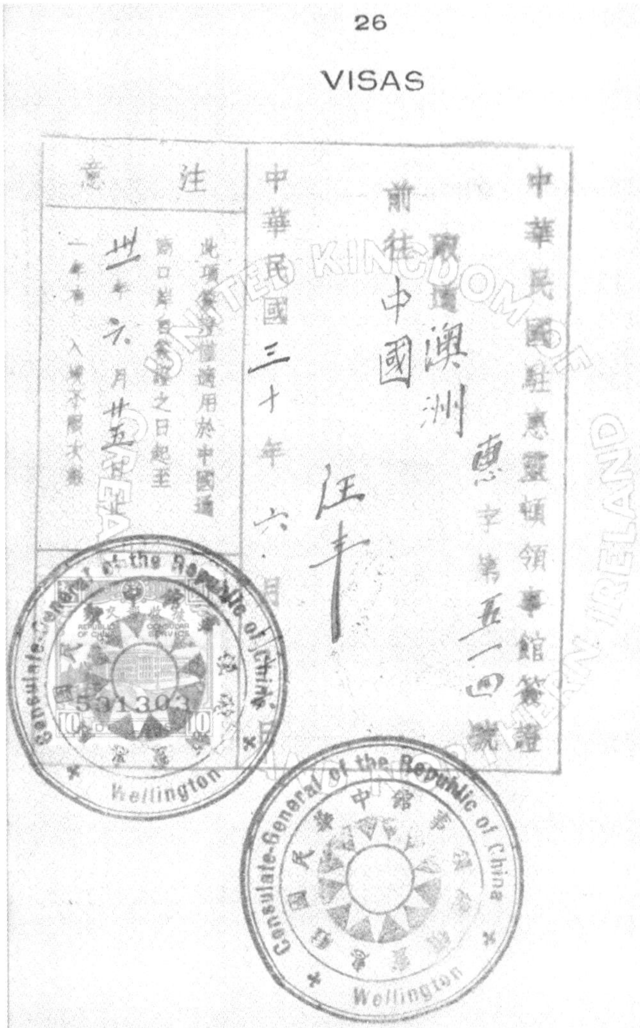

Visa issued in Wellington for return to China, 1941. Moncrieff family collection

Having got the registration on the grounds that we had to go on that night we had to go on. After looking round for a meal which proved to be unobtainable we decided to run two or three miles out of town and camp by the roadside returning in the morning to the Standard Oil yard for petrol. The road did not lend itself to camping but a few miles out we found a side road into which we drove the truck. The tent was pitched in front of it and we settled down to a meal. There was no water for washing but in spite of that we managed to sleep. 68 miles

Oct. 20th: Early next morning we were on our way back for petrol. The Standard Oil man in charge was late up that morning so it was some time before we could fill up the truck and go on our way. Along the next sixty miles or so we struck the worst surface of the whole trip. Our truck had a full load and we had to be careful of the springs. We didn't average more than ten miles an hour on any part of that day's journey and some of the time were well below that. At Chihfang we had lunch and there had the first of many shocks as far as food prices were concerned. The meal for four of us came to $68 which is about ten times the price of pre-war prices. It was quite a simple meal and at first I thought the waiter was talking in terms of the old Yunnan currency and meant $6.80 but no such luck. He meant $68 and we had to pay it.

We should have reached Lungling long before dark, but with such slow progress it was long after dark before we got there. When we reached the right kilometre post we still could not see the town and there were no other trucks about. Everywhere else we had stopped a double row of trucks had given away the location of inns. Joe and I got out to explore and found the main street running sharply down hill from the main road. This street was evidently part of the old trail that has been over those mountains for hundreds of years and we assumed, rightly as we found the next morning that the motor road took a wide curve and passed the lower end of the street further on. We enquired our way to the China Travel Service Guest House. On this part of the road the guest houses have been taken over by the Transport Board but the CTS staff remain and for the most part they were very comfortable to stay in. The Guest House was not difficult to find. Every few yards down that uneven stone path I would enquire the way and be pointed down hill. At last we came to it and found to our relief that there were empty rooms. It was not possible to bring the truck off the main road so we had some little distance to carry the food baskets and overnight bags. Guest Houses and inns for the most part do not provide any food so travellers must go to a restaurant or provide their own. Arriving after dark as we mostly did we found restaurants closed so were glad of the provisions that Joan and I had bought in Rangoon. Joe had to go back to sleep on the truck but the rest of us were moderately comfortable. 76 miles

Oct. 21st: Our first job was to change our rupees into Chinese currency. From Lashio on the rate of exchange was very high, but we knew that it dropped sharply after Lungling. John had been told that Lungling was the best place to change, but as it turned out we could have got a better rate at Wangting on the border. John and I tried a shop or so but they did not want to change as much as we had. We were directed to the Finance Office at the end of the street. John had expected to have to pay duty on the truck so was well supplied with money. He had over 1500 rupees and I had about 200. I had been advised to bring nothing larger than five or ten rupee notes. John had hundred rupee notes and did not get such a good exchange rate as I did. My rate was $8.50 for each rupee and his was $8. We came away with large parcels of money that had to be wrapped up in brown paper for none of the notes given us were more than over $10. I have never had money in such bulk to look after before. The paper was not strong enough so finally the money had to be wrapped up in my green pao fu.[22] Just imagine a pao fu of money. John and I felt very self-conscious carrying so much money and expected to be robbed at every step. But we got the loot safely on to the truck and drove off. The money transaction had taken a long time and it was 10.15 before we left. The road led over the mountains that day as indeed it did most days. There were few villages and little sign of cultivation. Wild flowers grew in abundance through a great deal of that country and many of the plants that we regard as garden flowers were growing wild – marigolds and michaelmas daisy and a little yellow daisy rather like a single chrysanthemum. There were so few houses that we thought we would never find a place for lunch. In many places small restaurants had been opened to serve drivers and passengers and often the food had to be brought a considerable distance. At last we saw a banner floating out across the road and above it on the side of the hill was a new restaurant. We climbed up to it and ordered a meal. The girl in charge was a member of the CIM [China Inland Mission] at Longling and asked if we knew Mr. Moore. The rest of the party had met him in Rangoon so cordial relations were quickly established. They landed us in an embarrassing position for the girl refused to take money from friends of Mr. Moore. We had to press it upon her and of course she really meant to take it, but we did not know how much to give her and don't know to this day whether what we left on the table was adequate or not.

This day gave us one of the great thrills of the trip for we suddenly came out over the Salween Valley. We must have been about four thousand feet above the river which we could not see because the sides of the valley were so steep and the valley so narrow. But we could see bits and pieces of the road winding below us at many different levels. Some were on our side of the river and some on the other and we had a grand view of parts of the road winding round steep precipices on the other side. It was twenty-four miles from the top of that range down to the suspension bridge that spanned the river. The road was mostly wide and well graded but there were several corners where it would have been awkward to meet a truck. The bridge had been bombed but had been repaired though trucks moved over it very slowly and only one at a time. It is too narrow for more than one-way traffic. It was a great thrill to get on to the bridge and pass slowly over that deep and swiftly moving stream.

For several days John and Joe had been talking of the necessity of stopping somewhere to grease and oil the truck. We were then over a thousand miles from Rangoon and they decided to stop that afternoon. By the time we had crossed the river it was late afternoon so about two miles up the other side at a place where the road widened sufficiently to allow camping we stopped for the night. As it turned out it would have been much better if we had gone on farther and left the greasing till the morning for we were all bitten by mosquitos that evening and probably John got the bite that gave him malaria in Kunming. However the greasing and oiling was done and then our tent was pitched on the side of the road. The tent was Joe's. It was very small and there was just room for two camp stretchers side by side with not an inch between them. It was raining by the time it was up and we were glad to get to bed. Joan and I slept in the tent, John in the cab and Joe under the tail-board of the truck. Getting in and out of bed was something of a circus with so little room and I never once slept in that tent without getting a wet slap on the shoulders when I sat up in the morning. 50 miles

Oct. 22nd: It rained most of that night. The water ran under the tent and my shoes were in a pool when I got up. Joe fared worst for the draping of waterproof over the tail-board had not kept the water off and one end of his bed was very wet. It was still raining when we got up and dressing was a problem. However the weather cleared and we had breakfast and started off.

Most of the morning was spent climbing out of the Salween Valley. It was steeper on this side though not so high. We had not gone very far before one of the back tyres went flat. The tyre and tube were both perished and good for nothing. Someone in the International Agency in Rangoon had put very old stock on the truck instead of the new ones that should have gone on. John put the spare on and we wondered how long the other back tyre would last us. That day we reached Paoshan just before dark. We pulled up at the APC depot but discovered that they hadn't any petrol left. We drove on to the gate of the city and I got out to find a hotel and to see if I could get news of any other commercial supply of petrol. At the Nanyang hotel, which we had been told was the best in Paoshan, I met the manager of the APC. He had a copy of the letter of introduction Joe had received from the APC in Rangoon and promised to see what he could do for us in the morning. We had rather a long way to carry things from the truck to the hotel, but the truck was left in the APC yard so we all slept in the hotel that night 55 miles

Oct. 23rd: We had to go back to the APC installation with Mr. Li who had got in touch with a friend at the aerodrome who promised him a drum of petrol. The morning was spent waiting for it and finally Mr. Li's man came back to say that the petrol would not be available. Thereupon Mr. Li took us back to a private company that sold petrol at higher prices than the APC and we secured a drum there. This was the men's first experience of filling the tanks from a drum. It proved fairly simple with the right equipment, but filling the reserve tank without the necessary 'elbow'[23] was always a slow and tedious business.

It was about 3 p.m. when we left Paoshan and we all agreed that we wanted to go on before having any lunch. We lunched along the way and travelled for some time after dark to try and make up a little for our late start. We went for miles along a narrow gorge with a river below on our right. We thought it might be the Mekong. The gorge seemed never-ending and finally when we came to a widening in the road we decided to stop and have our supper. Our tent was right on the road that night in front of the truck and when other trucks began to pass about 4.30 a.m. it seemed as though they were almost running over the ropes. 51 miles

Oct. 24th: We found that we had indeed camped in the Mekong Valley, the worst for malarial mosquitos on the whole trip. However we had not seen or heard one all night. A few miles further on we crossed the Mekong over the suspension bridge that has given the Japanese so much trouble. They have had raid after raid trying to destroy that bridge, but have only once been successful. It has been out of action for some time, but has been repaired. We were asked by the police on guard to go over it very slowly. Like the Salween bridge it is very narrow and will take the weight of only one truck at a time. A new bridge has been built a little further down the river and the new road approaches were nearly completed.

It was a stiff climb out of the Mekong Valley. We had hoped for a longer run that day, but late in the afternoon the second of our back tyres gave out. We hadn't a second spare and it was beyond repair. The only thing seemed to be for one of us to go on into Hsaikwan about 50 miles further on and come back the next day with a spare. However a convoy of sedan cars that we had seen for the first time at Wangting caught up with us at this point. They had passed us several times and we were on waving terms with some of the drivers. The leader stopped to see what was the matter and saved the situation by lending us two new tubes. The canvas lining in the cover was very rough but the cover itself had not split as the first one had done so the men put the new tube into the cover and we were able to move on. That night we camped again by the roadside. This time it was near a waterfall so the water supply was no problem and there was a pool under the bridge where it was possible to have a good wash. The moon which was a few days old gave us a little light by which to prepare our evening meal and pitch the tent and put up the stretchers. 57 miles

Oct. 25th: The road was not quite so mountainous as before. We lunched at Yang Pi which is about halfway from the border to Kunming. In the afternoon the road ran into a narrow gorge and though we were going upstream there did not seem to be a range of any height in front of us. We had been watching a trail of pack animals on the old trail above the road when suddenly we rounded a corner and saw the valley we were in almost closed by a small hill in the middle. On the hill was an ancient fort that must have guarded the pass for hundreds of years. The pack trail came down to meet the road and we realised that we were passing a point that must have made a good deal of China's history. The valley opened beyond into a broad plain and we were soon on the outskirts of Hsiakwan. We did not want to stop there as we had been told that it was a bad place for malaria and also for dysentery. We had however to find some petrol and pulled up at the Standard Oil installation. There we bought another drum and filled our tanks with what remained of the Paoshan drum. As we had expected petrol was much more expensive here and it was well over $1000 for fifty-three gallons.

At Hsiakwan a road goes off to Talifu and Hsichow where the Central China College is situated in refugee quarters. It would have been an interesting side trip and I knew a member of the faculty because the College was in Wuchang before the war. We were all, however, anxious to get on. There is a beautiful lake on the plain near Hsiakwan and the road winds round it for a considerable distance and then follows up a valley and runs into the mountains again. Along the plain is an avenue of Australian blue gums. I got out and picked some leaves and sniffed eucalyptus and felt homesick for the rest of the day. Soon after leaving the plain we found a good camping spot. It was dark before we arrived but our technique for getting a meal and making our beds in the dark was improving and we were soon asleep. 75 miles

Oct. 26th: In Rangoon we had heard many stories of wild driving. We had been agreeably surprised for they had not seemed to be as reckless as they were reputed to be. Certainly on those tremendous mountain ranges we had come over they were moderately careful. From this point on we had to revise our opinion. At a point where the road was wide enough for two trucks to pass easily we were bumped by a passing truck. It was nothing but careless and incompetent driving.

It could have been a good deal worse, but our tarpaulin was badly ripped and the cooking utensils that were poked in along the side of the truck were bashed out of shape. My wash basin was a total loss. Joan's pot and kettle will never be quite the same again. We spoke a piece to the driver of the truck but it did not have much effect. As John was standing at the side of the truck considering repairs another truck passed and with all the width of the road at its disposal caught John in the back and gave him a bad bump. The driver was so scared that he dashed on without stopping more than a moment. Joe and I dashed off uphill after him but it was no use. He picked up speed and was soon far beyond us. I had thought for a moment that John was done in entirely. He was alright though his back was badly bruised and his shirt torn to pieces. The shock was considerable. Joe's professional services were called in and John was soon resting comfortably. We drove on a little way where the road was even wider and there remained for some time till the worst effects were over. Joe hammered the pot and kettle into a better shape and I mended the tarpaulin so our bits and pieces would not fall off the truck.

We stopped at Siangyun for lunch and there noticed that the tyre with the new tube in it was slack. It was duly removed and revealed that the rough canvas inside was wearing the tube badly. John had not brought a repair outfit with him so the bicycle repair outfit was requisitioned and the tyre was mended with it. Then the men changed the tyres putting the weak one on a front wheel.

We found out afterwards that the new road through to Chengtu leaves the highway at Siangyun and has only just been completed. Whether it is at all possible for motor traffic I do not know, though we heard good reports of it later on at Kunming. That night we found a most delightful camping spot, easily the best of the whole trip. It was after dark when we arrived and had to carry our things down a steep path from the road, but there was an open grassy space and a stream and we were glad that the day had come to an end. 40 miles

Oct. 27th: In the morning the men decided that if the worn tube was to stand up to the road ahead they had better reinforce it as best they could. They therefore took the rolls of rubber they had brought for their bicycles, cut them into three long strips and patched the tube the whole way round on both sides. This took considerable time and the clearing up of the pots and pans and the filling of thermos flasks were done long before John and Joe were ready. I wandered off and found a pool in the stream out of sight of the road and I had my first real bath since leaving Rangoon. I had not had my clothes off for several nights and that bath did much to restore my self-respect.

It was late before we were on the road and we had not gone far before we began to climb the highest range on the whole road. We were some thousands of feet above sea level when we left our camping place but the top of the pass was some 8,800 feet. We climbed 2600 feet in 26 kilometres. The guide book led us to believe magnificent scenery but we soon found ourselves in thick mist and had difficulty in seeing the road more than a few feet in front of us. We travelled with our lights on and it was eerie to see lights coming towards us long before we could see even the outline of the approaching truck. Some did not have their lights on and we narrowly avoided hitting one or two of them. We had a fine view when we got down below the level of the mist on the other side. Down on the level again we had the worst bump of the trip. We were rounding a blind corner and meeting another truck when a third truck hooted behind us. Joe signalled it to wait, but it came straight on cutting across in front of us and bashing our right mudguard so that the headlight was left hanging and the mudguard bent in so that the edge was immediately over the wheel. The truck hit the bank ahead of us and turned into the road again taking some of the earth from the bank with it. There was a lengthy and somewhat heated conversation. The driver admitted that his foot brake was completely useless and he was coming at such a pace that he could not stop. He was thoroughly scared and willing to admit that the fault was his. He gave his name and address and said that he would leave a written statement at the next city Chuhsiung. His mudguard was damaged and his radiator was leaking. His was a military truck and John put the case into the hands of the British consulate when he reached Kunming. Our mudguard had to be removed before we could go on and that took a long time. Joe went back and made notes of the distance between our position and the spot where the other truck hit the bank and took a photograph which was afterwards handed in to the consulate. Once more it was after dark when we arrived. We had decided to stay at an inn in Chuhsiung so we did not have to get a meal and put up the tent. Joe and I went prospecting for the China Travel Guest House. Unfortunately it was full and the inn to which they directed us was so unprepossessing that we decided to ask if there was a chapel in the town. A small boy earned a dollar taking us to the C.I.M. chapel where we roused the pastor to see if we might sleep there. He however took us round to the home of an American missionary, Miss Morgan. It was a considerable distance from the road where we had left the truck and we were doubtful about carrying our bedding rolls so far. Miss Morgan had beds and bedding to spare and promised us a meal. Back we went to the truck with the gateman in tow to look after the truck while we all had a meal. We were soon all four tucking away fried eggs and beef and sundry other Chinese dishes as well as cups and cups of tea. Joe had to go back to the truck which he brought inside the city gate but we others passed a quiet and comfortable night in the mission compound. 75 miles.

Oct. 28th: We were called early and after a good breakfast we set out for the truck. We needed petrol which was hard to find. After several enquiries I went to the Post Office and found the address of the Standard Oil agents. We went back on our tracks to the side road leading to the West Gate and after poking round for a while I found the office. There I had to order and pay for the petrol and then set out with two men and an assortment of utensils to their petrol dump some distance along the road we had come. We met the truck and I walked while the men were taken on the step. It was about 11 a.m. before our tanks were full and we could set out for Kunming. We had heard a good deal about the climb before Chuhsiung but no one had mentioned the climb on the Kunming side, which was almost as high. The day was clear and we had a wonderful view from the summit. The grade was good and at the top we ran along a long ridge before we began the descent.

The day before we had seen the embankment of the new railway here and there. In the Ipin Gorge, which is very narrow, the road and the line run on opposite of the river. In the gorge the road was narrow and the surface bad. Some of the tunnels on the line are completed but stand isolated as it were with the approaches not formed. We saw only about half a dozen men at work on this section of the line. Every effort is being made to complete the westerly section near the Burma border so that it will be easier to bring in material for the eastern section.[24] We saw piles and piles of sleepers at various points along the road but no other supplies.

Again we had to travel after dark. About 8.30 we arrived at the top of the last hill and looked down on the lake on the shores of which Kunming is built. We did not intend to go into the city that night because since the heavy bombing raids many people have been living on the other side of the lake. The C.M.S. [Church Missionary Society] Hospital is there and two of the women missionaries are living in a small house at Kao Chiao across the lake from the city. Into their yard we drove the truck and there it remained for almost two weeks. In spite of the fact that we had not been able to let them know the date of our arrival baths, for all four of us were prepared and a large and satisfying meal. 110 miles

Oct. 29th: We spent the morning washing hair and writing letters and in the afternoon went across the lake to the city in a sampan which takes anything up to two and a half hours according to the wind. John and Joan went to the C.M.S. Compound, Joe went to Mr. Arnold's and I went to the YWCA.

Nov. 3rd: I returned to Kao Chiao expecting to leave next morning for Kweiyang, but John developed malaria and we had to wait.

Nov. 4th to 11th: This time was spent at Kao Chiao. It was a bit of a picnic especially for our hostesses. They had only one guest room which John and Joan occupied. Joe put up his tent on the lawn and I slept on the verandah and kept my things in a suitcase under the bed.

Nov. 11th: We left Kao Chiao at 10 a.m. and proceeded ten miles to the West Station on the outskirts of Kunming. There we were held up by a demand for a $1000 road maintenance tax. Joe went in to the British Consulate to secure a letter that might get us off. As offices do not open till about 3 p.m. on account of air raids we had a long time to wait. It was raining and rather cold. After about five hours Joe returned with the letter and we got away at 3.45 p.m. Our troubles were not over because we had been given wrong directions about the road to Kweiyang and almost encircled the city before we found out our mistake. Finally we discovered the right turning and passed through the East Station without difficulty. We had expected to get as far as Chuching that night, but the long delay had made that quite impossible. Before Ta Pan Chiao we found a South-West Transport compound and were allowed to spend the night there. The man in charge of that section was very friendly and gave us a good deal of information about the road, also a small map which proved most useful all the way. 30 miles

Nov 12th: We left at 7.40 a.m. and had not gone far before we were bumped by another truck which cut across in front of us too quickly. Again our mudguard was dented, but not seriously. The road was fairly level to Chuching, about 100 miles from Kunming and the terminus of the railway that is being put through to Suifu. We had been invited to stay at the C.M.S. Hospital there but went straight through. Chuching is the starting point for trucks that travel the two roads that lead to Szechuan. Goods are brought to Chuching from Kunming by train and convoys of trucks are loaded there. We went on to Ping Yi where there is a China Travel Service Guest House. Unfortunately it was full and so was the hotel they directed us to. The only place we could find for the night was a very rickety and dirty little inn. It had only one room with four beds in it, but I took that as it seemed the only available spot in the town. At one end the wall did not go up to the ceiling. There was a kind of mezzanine floor or loft reached by a ladder just outside our door. Several soldiers were sleeping up there. Not only did we have no privacy but we did not dare leave the room in case our things should be stolen. We had a meal served in our room and hoped that we would not be disturbed by thieves in the night. All along the road from Kunming to Kweiyang and even beyond we passed columns and columns of soldiers on the march down to the French Indo-China border. Many of them were well equipped but we saw very few guns of any size on the move. The soldiers walked in single file, a long line of them on each side of the road. Most of them had twigs and leaves in their hats to serve as camouflage should any Japanese scouting planes come over. The only disturbance from the soldiers during the night was caused by one of them falling down the ladder to our floor level. He did not seem to be hurt. We none of us slept very well that night because it was so cold. 123 miles

Nov. 13th: We woke to a white world. Ping Yi is fairly high and there was a hard frost. We were away at 7.a.m. and had breakfast by the roadside some little distance out and well up in the hills. This day we had a very mountainous run up and over one range after another. We had to stop at one point and transfer petrol from the drum on the back of the truck into our tanks. We were seen by the driver of a truck who had lost a drum of petrol on the way and were accused of having picked up his drum. At lunch in Pan Hsien this accusation was repeated but we firmly refused to let them look at our drum and referred them to the consul at Kunming if they were not satisfied.

Again we had to travel after dark because we wanted to reach Annan. We were in a valley when suddenly the road rushed a hillside and in a series of 24 hairpin bends climbed right out of the valley and ran on into Annan. We had been told of this giant zigzag and were very sorry not to see them by daylight. It was easier to drive over this section at night because lights showed up the approaching trucks. On the other hand the bends were so sharp that it was very difficult to judge the grade and we had to reverse on one or two of the corners. We arrived at 9.15 and were very fortunate to find room in the CTS Guest House. It was very comfortable and we enjoyed it after our experience of the night before. 115 miles

Nov. 14th: We had to transfer petrol from the drum so did not get away till 9.30 a.m. The road wound uphill for some distance and suddenly came out over a steep river valley something like the Salween but not so deep. At the bottom of the valley was a sizeable river and a pontoon bridge. The descent to the bridge was very steep and we had to wait while a truck ahead of us went down and over the bridge. The bridge was well secured though the stream was very swift. We had to move very slowly. The ascent was steep to begin with, rising in a long straight slope and then winding round curves and hairpin bends to a tremendous height above the river. The road here was not so well graded as the stretch from the border to Kunming. We had a marvellous view of range after range. The road seemed to make for the highest points on the highest ranges and still keep climbing. As the day wore on we began to drop to somewhat lower levels. At Ling Chuan we thought of spending the night. It is a fairly large town with both Roman Catholic and C.I.M. missions. However we still had a little daylight left so decided to go on to An Shun. Again Joe and I went hunting an inn after dark. The first one we approached was occupied by soldiers and I was stopped by a rifle as I got near the door. We found good accommodation at the Ta Hua Hotel and parked the truck nearby. 90 miles

Nov. 15th: We left at 8.30 after transferring petrol from the drum and covered the 60 miles to Kweiyang before lunch. The truck was not allowed in the city. So we had lunch at a restaurant outside and went to the Standard Oil installation for another drum of petrol. This necessitated a trip into the city to their office. Joan and I bought bread and I paid a flying visit to the YWCA. Unfortunately the General Secretary was out.

At 3.30 we were again back to the checking station where we had registered that morning. We had another bump as we waited there. The chain was torn off the right end of the tail-board and the hinges bent so that the tail-board could not be lifted up. The road was fairly level but the surface poor so we did not make much progress. Shortly after dark we reached a checking station on the outskirts of a village. The officer in charge told us that there were inns and restaurants and we found both without much difficulty. 105 miles

Nov. 16th: We had a fairly level road all day with humpy hills to right and left. We reached Tung Tzu after dark and found both CTS Guest Houses full. We secured inside rooms at the Hua Sung Hotel. There were no windows and the coal gas both night and morning was very unpleasant. 85 miles

Nov. 17th: We left at 7.a.m. This day there was more trouble than usual with the petrol. Every few miles we had to stop while the men cleaned out the filter cup, sump and filament. As soon as the petrol was low enough they decided to stop and empty the tank and wash it through with petrol. This and the refilling of the tanks took nearly two hours, but the truck ran much better for the cleaning. It was just as well for we had a tremendous range to climb. We reached the top of one range and had the most remarkable view of the whole trip. The road ran down in a series of loops and hairpin bends into a valley that was much lower than the one we had climbed out of. The mountain ranges beyond us were magnificent and we stopped to have a look about us.

We had hoped to have lunch in Szechuan Province but at Sung K'an we were held up for a road tax. At Kunming we had been assured that no further tax would be necessary, but this one was a special Kweichow province road maintenance tax and collected we were told on behalf of the department of Foreign affairs. No amount of argument or discussion would move the officials. They would not accept any of John's varied collection of documents; neither

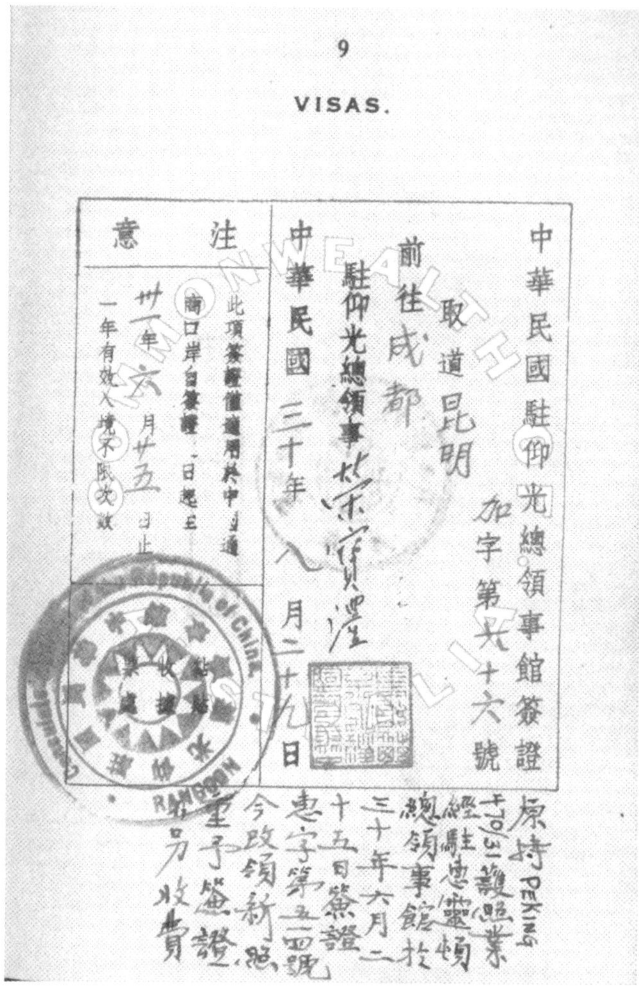

Visa issued in Rangoon for entry into China, 1941.

Moncrieff family collection

would they accept a guarantee. We were getting very short of money, but managed to find the $460 and went into the village for lunch.

Just before we set off again we discovered that Joan's overnight bag was missing. It must have fallen off the truck. Altogether we were rather depressed as we set off. We had another high range to cross that afternoon with a grand view in all directions. It was so high that it gave much the same effect of being on top of the world as flying does. We wondered if we would ever see plains again. We reached Chichiang at 7.30 and went optimistically to the Guest House. Our late arrivals always meant that the best inns were full. Chichiang was no exception. A small boy escorted me round the town calling out at the entrance of every inn to see if they had rooms to spare. After calling at nine or ten I went back to the Guest House. There they let us put up our cots in a central room, off which most of the bedrooms opened. Everyone else had gone to bed so we prepared a meal as quietly as we could, set up our cots, took off our shoes and got under the blankets. 115 miles

Nov. 18th: We did not get away till 8.30 as petrol had to be transferred. The road was much more level. We reached Hsi Tang Chi on the south bank of the Yang Tzu before noon. We passed the checking station about eight kilometres out and fortunately had lunch there. Having reached the ferry we discovered that no trucks could cross at that point but that we must go back eight miles to the junction to find the right ferry. Back we went only to find that we needed a permit to cross the river and that that must be obtained at the South-West office at Hsi Tang Chi. One of the juniors was sent in with us to help to secure the permit because the only man who could attend to such business would not be back in the office till 4 p.m. Eventually the permit was forthcoming and we started back to the checking station feeling that we knew that eight kilometres of road only too well. The bright spot in the day was the news when we reached the checking station that Joan's bag had been picked up and was at the Sung K'an checking station.

At the station they were anxious to get us on our way because the ferry does not cross after dark and there were already several trucks waiting. The man in charge did his best to get us over first but he was told that personal baggage could not take precedence over Government supplies and we would have to wait our turn. Another eight kilometres or so brought us to the ferry and there we found about seven trucks ahead of us. The ferry could take only one loaded truck or two empty ones at a time. The river is fairly broad at that point and the current swift so it took half an hour for the ferry to go and return. It was so late that we knew there was no chance of getting over that night. We knew if we went off to look for an inn we should lose our place in the line. We therefore decided to camp on the road alongside the truck. A grand audience collected around us. Drivers, ferrymen, and a number who seemed to spring out of the landscape, participated as onlookers in our evening meal and preparations for the night. The only water was the muddy Yang Tzu. We boiled it well, but there was so much sediment that it was not attractive. The tea was not bad but by the time it had stood in our flasks all night it was a frightful colour. Fortunately the night was very mild and we did not have the heavy river fog that we had been warned against. We had no shelter but spread yu pu[25] over our beds to protect them from the dew and mist. 51 miles

Nov. 19th: We were packed up and ready long before the ferry was ready to take us. By 8.45 our turn came and John drove the truck onto the ferry. The trip across, which was upstream, took twenty minutes. Two men were busy all the time baling water out of the lighter keeping the level of the water almost at the same height. The ferry went upstream out of the main current to a point well above the pontoon on the other side. Then still going full steam ahead it moved into the current and was carried down stream doing a crab-like side step across the river.

On the other side we had a long run of ten miles or more before we reached the main road and drove into Chungking. We had been told that we would require a special permit to enter the city but there was no checking station of any kind and we drove right to the top of the steps above the Canadian Mission Agency. I shall never forget the Chungking skyline as one sees it at several points near and in the city. Just an irregular broken line of ruins. Away out in the western suburbs the bombers had been busy as ruined buildings testified. Chungking is well supplied with dugouts. For miles along the road they have been cut every few yards in the rock. The Agency afforded us all the comforts of civilisation again except a bath. Something was wrong with the hot water system. One can however do a great deal with a basin of water though I have to admit that I used three without making much impression.

Nov. 20th: We all had business to attend to in the morning so did not get away till 3.30 p.m. It was pouring with rain but we wanted to arrive in Chengtu on Saturday so decided it would be well to get a start on the road. At Kunming John had been given sealed papers for the Chungking customs station. All along the first ten miles or so of the road we kept a look out for it expecting to be stopped round every corner. However there was no checking station of any kind till we were about thirty-five miles from Chungking.

We had no idea where to stay that night so kept going till we found a village with inns. I don't even know the name of the place we stayed at. We had to stop for registration and the officials told us there was an inn nearby so we stopped there. It was one of the poorest we stayed in. Joan and I had a room on the first floor, Joe was above us and John slept on the truck. The beams that supported the first and second floors seemed quite strong but the flooring boards creaked and swayed alarmingly. I was not sure that Joe would not descend upon us in the middle of the night. 35 miles

Nov. 21st: We were on the road at 7.a.m. It was extremely slippery after the heavy rain of the day before and the mud was deep in. The surface was poor and every time we passed another truck and got over to the side of the road our back wheels had a tendency to skid. The road winds up and down and round and round but does not climb high at any point. The countryside seemed to consist of a series of hummocks that get very monotonous. The soil is a picturesque red which makes the landscape very colourful. There were acres and acres of sugar cane, and field after field of sweet potatoes was being harvested. Our objective was Tzuchow but we did not reach it. We reached the ferry about the middle of the afternoon but were held up by a tank truck that had run off the boards on the pontoon and could not be put back on them. After many fruitless efforts they decided to take the pontoon over to the other side of the river. We watched this ill-balanced and drunken looking ferry being rowed to the other side. Soon it was our turn and John had the greatest difficulty in getting the truck on to the ferry. From the river bank to the ferry there were only two very slippery planks and each time his back wheels got on them they skidded dangerously. The fourth attempt was successful. Getting off the ferry is never so difficult and he managed it well though the planks were equally slippery.

The crossing took so long that we decided to spend the night at Neichang which was just as well for the hotels are much better there. Fortunately there were rooms to spare in the CTS Guest House and we had about the most luxurious night of the whole trip. The Guest House is scrupulously clean and for the first time on the trip we used the bedding provided and left our own on the truck. There was even a bath room at this Guest House but we did not bother because we were so near the end of the trip. I had just booked the rooms and was hurrying back to the truck when I met Mr. Edwards of the YMCA and with him Tsai Kwei who was on her way to Chungking. TK and I sat down and had a long talk while the others coped with baggage and preparations for supper. We both had to get up at 4.a.m. the next morning. Otherwise we might have talked through the night. 120 miles

Nov. 22nd: We were away at 8.a.m. and had a good run through though the surface was poor. Our minds were not so much on the country we were passing

> through as on our destination and in the early afternoon it was good to see the last range of hills that we would have to cross rising up ahead of us. It is I think the highest point between Chungking and Chengtu but is a mere rise compared with the ranges we had come over in Yunnan and Kweichow. We were soon at the top but there was so much mist that we did not have a very good glimpse of the Chengtu plain. The summit is only seventeen miles from the city and since the road across the plain is good we made better time.
>
> Before long we could see the radio station and then we were in the east suburb and making for the city gate. The actual gates had been removed so that people could get out of the city more easily during air raids. We went straight to Pi Fang Kai, the compound of the CMS, arriving there about 3.30 p.m.in good time for tea which we all needed. The trip from Chungking had been cold and this last day the coldest of all. I came out to the WCUU [West China Union University] campus by ricsha and so ended a 2400 mile road journey that had brought us right into the heart of free China.

The YWCA of New Zealand national executive minutes of 1 December 1941 recorded:

> Miss Moncrieff has cabled 'Safe arrival in Chengtu'.[26]

On 7 December 1941, just fifteen days after Nessie arrived in Chengtu, Japanese planes bombed Pearl Harbor. In her 1985 interview, she commented: 'I was very fortunate. I was always just out of the way.'[27]

14

Third Term: Chengtu

December 1941–October 1945

For almost four years from the end of November 1941 to the end of September, Nessie held three key positions in the YWCA of China's temporary national headquarters in Chengtu. From this third – and what would prove to be her final – term she kept only two letters.

She did however write to the YWCA of New Zealand, who included extracts from them in their monthly publications. Often the letters weren't received in New Zealand for several weeks, as is shown in the World Fellowship committee minutes of 15 April 1942:

> Letter from Miss Moncrieff, written 7th February, came from Chengtu via Calcutta, Lagos, USA to NZ.[1]

The following extracts give a glimpse of what life was like for those in blockaded central China at that time:

> FROM MISS MONCRIEFF, CHENGTU 7th February 1942.
>
> We have come to the end of a series of Conferences up here. First we had a regional conference of Y.W.C.A. leaders, both secretarial and volunteer; then there was a training conference for general secretaries and thirdly our national staff setting-up conference. That is not over yet. We have two more days of it next week. After that is over the Training Department is holding an acquaintance conference for a selected group of women students from this campus. I am glad to say that I have no responsibility in that. I am longing to get on with my own job. My job is composite. I am English secretary to the General Administration. I have no responsibility for that department, but I keep the English minutes and all of Tsai Kwei's English correspondence. This means a good deal of work for Tsai Kwei writes many of her letters to Chinese people in English. It is a very convenient half way between the formal Chinese and the Chinese they use in personal letters. Then I have all the work of the business office and the book keeping. Now we are cut off from Shanghai it means setting up our books on a

more elaborate system than we had and it is taking me a long time to work out a system that is suitable and adequate.

While Zia Tsoo Yi is away from Chungking I am Coordinator of the City Department and that means more work than it used to, because I have to keep Tsoo Yi in touch with all the developments in what is really her department.[2]

The same issue also published:

FROM MISS MONCRIEFF:

It is marvellous the way the work goes on. We are even planning some expansion this year. Our Secretary to General Administration is at present in Kweilin discussing the opening of Y.W.C.A. work there. She is also visiting Hengyang, on the Hankow railway. We hope for a Service Centre for Transients even if it is not ready for a regularly organized Y.W.C.A. This would be something more than a hostel for refugees passing through the other parts of China and would be a very useful first step for the Y.W.C.A. Tsai Kwei keeps marvellously steady in the midst of all these problems. She is much better in health and is working full time though the doctor still insists on a rest each day. I am working very closely with her on National staff problems and it is most interesting. My admiration and respect for her grow apace.

Winifred Galbraith is at present is on her way down from Sian. She was held up by snow for two or three days. Imagine travelling over bad roads and high mountain ranges on the top of a loaded truck with weather like that. I take my hat off to the travelling staff and hope I may continue to stay put.[3]

Five months later the October issue published:

FROM MISS MONCRIEFF: July 3, 1943

I leave for my vacation about July 8th. I am going up to Behluding again this year to keep house for my cousin [Jesse Moncrieff]. It really is a lovely spot and I am thoroughly looking forward to another thoroughly domesticated summer on top of a mountain. This year we are going to save expense by cycling across the plain. My cousin is lending me the bicycle that belongs to his youngest son. It is not full size and is much too small for me so I look over grown on it but it runs easily so I think I will get there.[4] . . .

A letter from New York has stimulated us to do a little more profound thinking about post-war plans ourselves and we hope to have a meeting of the National Executive Committee next month and give most of the time to a discussion on what we see as the place and function of our movement in post-war reconstruction. One of our problems, of course, is the future of the Associations on the interior. A city like Chungking, for instance, will probably have a difficult

> period of adjustment when the Government moves away (if it does move away) and the population shrinks to a more or less pre-war figure. How can we help the association over such a period of transition when members leave and contributors leave and the city is dependent on its own normal resources? This is only one of the questions that must be faced. Our questions are not yet in a complete or comprehensive form, but I hope to send you more about the discussions later in the year.[5]

The YWCA of New Zealand's executive minutes of 10 February 1944 record:

> It was felt any further increase of expenditure on behalf of the China secretary was impossible; at the end of 1944 only sufficient money would be left for Miss Moncrieff's return to NZ. Miss Moncrieff's statement in her letter of October 11 1943 re the functions and limitations of western secretaries in China was carefully considered and in the light of this statement it appeared probable Miss Moncrieff would not be returning to China for a further term after her furlough in 1945.[6]

The YWCA Review of June 1944 featured a two-page article headed 'A LETTER FROM MISS MONCRIEFF'. In it, the comments she makes about seven years being a long time obviously applied to her own exhaustion too.

> A LETTER FROM MISS MONCRIEFF Chengtu, March 14, 1944
> SLOW MAILS
>
> Yesterday a sheaf of mail came from the World's Y.W.C.A. It was all dated January and February 1942 and obviously came by an overland route. Folk say that slow mail is coming in by way of a pass in Northern Burma where the Ledo road may eventually come, but it is impossible to know the route. Recently magazines, all at least a year, many two years old, have arrived. We are very glad to see them even at this late date but they do emphasise our isolation. So much is happening in the world and we hear so little. Our reading material consists of a daily news bulletin published by the British Ministry of Information and very limited in the news it gives. Then there is an 'American Digest' which comes from Chungking and contains news of the week on all war fronts and articles taken from American magazines. The American 'Time' comes in by air mail which takes anything up to two and a half months from America and is passed around the community. The 'Readers' Digest' is photographed by a Chinese publishing firm in Chungking and is available several months later. The price is fabulous so groups of people go in together and buy one copy. But we lack up to date articles of opinion and interpretation and feel very isolated.
>
> When I feel particularly restless I think of Leila Bridgman and the hundreds

of other internees and feel like a thrupenny bit for complaining and a bent one at that. I don't know how all those people, cut off as they are, keep human at all. . . .

SEVEN YEARS IS A LONG TIME

I do think that there is a war weariness prevalent. Not that anyone's morale is low but there is a general exhaustion that is not to be wondered at. It is partly physical. Standards of living are all lower with the rising costs and folk are not getting nourishing food as they should. Some people are of course making pots of money out of the situation but as in any time of inflation it is the salaried people who are hardest hit. I think lots of the young things find it hard to look forward. Life doesn't seem to hold for them what they thought it would and they are discouraged. Seven years is a long time for a war to last.

DAILY FEEDING OF THOUSANDS

We had a report from far away Macau the other day. There is a staunch group there who were part of the Canton Y.W.C.A. Their chief work is relief. They feed 1000 to 2000 destitute people every day with some assistance from the Governor. . . . We passed a grant of 28,000 dollars to them last September, but the Japanese were making a bee line for Macau at that time and we thought they would surely be occupied. However they were not. The question was how to get the money down there. One can't do it through a bank. However they discovered a mother who wanted to get money to her daughter in Chungking. The mother paid the money into the Y.W.C.A. and we paid the daughter in Chungking. That is quite an acceptable way of getting money round the country. When we want to get one of our trained secretaries up here from occupied areas we are frequently stuck because the office in Shanghai has no money to spare for travel expenses. Sometimes we can find a student here who needs money and his relatives pay it into the Y.W.C.A. in Shanghai. I have just made the final payment on a transaction of that kind. Letters so often go astray between here and Shanghai that we do not hear for months and months whether the money has been paid. I don't know whether I will ever be able to work at a respectable pace again. One has to be content with such slow motion in China. . . .

My greetings to the Committee.

Love from NESSIE MONCRIEFF[7]

In the 1980s Nessie wrote to some newly discovered relatives in Scotland about her life in China. In just over two pages she summed up her fifteen years there. She described her third term of YWCA work as:

> I had to make myself useful in any way I was asked to in the YWCA National HQ. Our accountant was still in Shanghai so I had to look after the money, trying to hold its value in a period of runaway inflation and trying to keep an account

of it in six currencies with a book rate and a black market rate of exchange. It has left me allergic to inflation. Few people in NZ know what a runaway inflation is like and Mr Muldoon is not one of them.[8]

Five months later things were looking a little brighter, as is shown in November's issue:

MISS MONCRIEFF ON HOLIDAY 15th August 1944

Behluding is really a wonderful place for a vacation. It is on the top of a somewhat isolated 'know' which means that there is an extensive view all round. There is a wonderful sweep of mountains, valley and plain with snow-capped peaks in the distance. We had a wedding during the holidays the bridegroom is a New Zealander, Harry Haines, who came over to the C.I.M. on the same boat as me in 1941. He has married an American girl, a most charming person with a beautiful singing voice. . . . We were all so proud of the fact that the Changsha Y.W.C.A. was the first of our Associations to move back from its refugee location though we knew it might prove a little premature. It is very discouraging at this stage to have lost two more local Associations and to have two others very seriously disturbed. Kweilin Y.W.C.A. bought a houseboat, hired boatmen and ran a travelling hostel of refugees down south to a spot where they are continuing to cover expenses with the houseboat. We are a little uneasy about the place they have chosen as it will be in the line of Japanese advance from north and south if there is an advance. Miss Shin Tak Hing who was General Secretary in Hongkong is now the Kweilin General Secretary and she had had just about enough of Japanese occupation, I think. The General Secretary from Changsha has just arrived in Chengtu. She and her staff evacuated to Kweilin but had to leave when the Government issued general evacuation orders. She came north but had to spend seven days and seven nights sitting on her luggage on a train which should have taken about twelve hours to make the journey to Tusan. She could not put her head down or stretch out in all that time. I don't know how she managed. . . .

Warm greetings, NESSIE MONCRIEFF[9]

The YWCA Review of April 1945 published:

A LETTER FROM AGNES MONCRIEFF December 3, 1944
HOLDING ON

Kweiyang is our only Association in Kweichow province now and that may break up when the Chinese order a general evacuation of the city. This year has certainly been a year of shrinkage. Kweilin is gone, Kukong Y.W.C.A. has moved back to Kukong but at present communications are cut and we have not been successful in finding a way to get money to them though we have not given up yet. Sian secretaries went back to Sian after the spring evacuation but they have

> had to build from the beginning again and if the situation does not improve in that area the whole thing will close again. That leaves Kunming, Chungking, Chengtu and some work still going on in far away Macau. Four associations are still operating after a fashion in occupied China but we practically never hear of them. Secretaries recently returned from America straight from the tremendous activity of American Associations are apt to be critical but I think it is a tremendous achievement to be still functioning at all over seven years of war and in the face of all the problems such years bring. . . .
>
> A LARGE HOUSEHOLD
>
> My household becomes more and more interesting. When I started keeping house for my cousin we knew our combined salaries would not be sufficient to run this house on our own so we prepared to share it with others. But I did not count on such a large family. We have three American Army Officers who have their meals at a hospital Mess, a technical representative of Allison Airplanes Engines, a Chinese member of the West China University English faculty and our latest arrivals are two doctors; one is Chinese and a student at PUMC [Peking University Medical College] when I was in Peking and I knew her there. Her husband is a Viennese doctor of Jewish extraction who has been working with the Chinese Army and Chinese Red Cross for the last three years. They are refugees from Chengchow which the Japanese took last spring. Then two LMS [London Missionary Society] members of Ginling Women's College faculty come on alternate days for dinner with us. It is a most interesting household but a bit on the large side. My early mornings and late afternoons and week-ends are very domesticated but I am fortunate in having a very good cook. I could not swing it otherwise.
>
> Last week Winfred Galbraith arrived back from touring round the Sian area and stayed with us. She is always fun to have about and I enjoyed her visit immensely. I saw her off last Thursday at 6 am with a frightfully chilly north wind into which she would spend all day driving and not in the cab but on top of all the cargo to a place called Mienyang a hundred miles north of Chengtu. The next day she would spend on a river boat and on another bus going east to Santai where there is an isolated University. She has seen more travel of that kind in China than anyone else I know.[10]

Nessie's comment about keeping house for her cousin referred to her living situation in the Mission house with Jesse, who, just before Nessie's arrival in Chengtu, had returned from furlough, but without his wife and family, as the US Government forbade missionaries' children to return. When the YWCA of China moved to Chengtu, the accommodation situation was very difficult, as rapidly soaring inflation in China, especially in the Chengtu area, saw prices double and treble from month to month. It was logical for Nessie and Jessie to combine resources, slim as they were, and improve the situation with boarders. What Nessie didn't mention was that the house at the West China University campus was an hour's walk to the YWCA, over rocks and often through mud.[11]

In May 1945 *The YWCA Review* published the full text of a letter from the YWCA of China regarding New Zealand's decision to discontinue supporting a representative in China. It was through the publication of this letter that YWCA of New Zealand members were informed of what was happening to their China secretary.[12]

CHINA SAYS THANK YOU

Dear Miss Law.

Thank you for your letter of September 1944. It is indeed sad news for us that the New Zealand YWCA does not feel that they can continue to send a direct representative to China. The contribution made by the two secretaries whom New Zealand has supported has been a very real one. We appreciate the reasons that have made this change of policy necessary, but we would like to assure you that if at any future date circumstances permit you to send a member of staff from New Zealand she will be sure of a very hearty welcome.

I would like to take this opportunity of expressing on behalf of the YWCA of China our deep appreciation for all Miss Moncrieff has done for the YWCA during her fifteen years of service with us. She has been a real strength and stand by in many ways and during these last difficult years of financial inflation and mounting budget has rendered a very great service and carried a heavy burden. We are going to miss her greatly both for herself and the work she has done and we shall find it difficult to find anyone who can fill her place adequately. Though she is leaving China we are glad she is continuing in the service of the YWCA and we are sure that she will be a very real link for many years to come between the YWCA in New Zealand and the YWCA of China. She will carry with her our best wishes for her work in Wellington.

With many thanks for all your help in the past thirty years and all good wishes for the future of your Association.

I am

Yours sincerely

Ren Ying Gao

Secretary to the General Administration (acting during Miss Tsai Kwei's absence)

July's issue reported:

LIFE IN CHENGTU 1945

Dr Decker is in Chengtu at present and is staying in our home. I well remember him and his statesman-like view from the time I met him in Shanghai in 1939. It is grand to have this opportunity of getting to know him so well. We are to have a conference with him on Thursday afternoon and will be discussing post war problems. I hope Tsai Kwei will be back. She has been in Chungking but transportation between Chungking and Chengtu is horrible. Buses and postal trucks are booked up weeks in advance and a plane only one every two weeks. We do need her back so badly and are counting on all the fresh enthusiasm her visit to America will have given her. Lil Haass, writing from India, made me laugh by writing she still thought bread and butter one of God's precious gifts. We have just had a pound of butter given us for a present. Yesterday I spread some really thin NZ style bread and butter for our tea and we ate it lingeringly. It was the greatest luxury.

I read the other day a review of a novel that had been written about an internment camp and what happens to personality under the strain. It seems to me the same thing happens, though perhaps not so extreme, under the difficulties of being on the wrong side of a blockade. One certainly sees a lot of lowering of moral standards and a kind of disintegration of personality that is one of the tragedies of war. On the other hand there are folk who are pure gold even though they are utterly weary.

The rapid advance of the Japanese towards Kweiyang and along the Canton–Hankow railway has closed down two more of our precious city associations – Kukong is now occupied territory and Kweiyang so nearly was that the Association ceased functioning. However a grand opportunity to open in Lanchow has developed and we lack only the right person to send up there. The National Committee took action some time ago to start work up there just as soon as personnel could be found so we sent up some money as an earnest indication of our intentions; and are hoping against hope that we can find someone to go up. Personnel is easily our greatest problem, even worse than finance, thanks to the American War Fund. However we have people combing Lanchow to find someone.

My greetings to the Committee,
Love from Agnes Moncrieff.[13]

September's issue featured an undated report:

FROM CHENGTU TO CHUNGKING 1945

The National Executive Committee decided last month to move our headquarters from Chengtu. When we came up here several other national organisations had their offices here, e.g. National Christian Council, Church of Christ in India, National Student Relief Committee and so on. They have all moved one by one to Chungking [the wartime capital].

When we came, communications were easy between Chungking and Chengtu. Now the plane service is only one a week and public buses and postal trucks slower and slower. There are more delays and road accidents as the buses get older. In Chungking we are much closer with the national women's organizations, and groups both within and outside the government that are most concerned with plans for post-war reconstruction. Also it is much easier, or should I say somewhat less difficult, to build up financial support from Chinese sources. . . .

Someone will go down to Chungking mid-June to see about an office building and the move will take place about September. Personally I hope I do not have to go as I have told Tsai Kwei that I will be leaving at the beginning of October. In some ways it would be good to see them established in their new quarters before I go. If they do not find a business secretary in time I may have to go down and hand over the books to a firm of accountants in Chungking. I wouldn't be surprised if I had to give the YWCA up to get a month's grace, but I do not want to get away later than the middle of October. I will keep you informed of plans as they develop.

Agnes Moncrieff[14]

Nessie's final correspondence from China to the YWCA of New Zealand was published in November 1945's *The YWCA Review*:

HOMEWARD BOUND 1945

I thought you would be interested to know that I have just had a reply from Cook's in Calcutta to say that they have registered me for accommodation to Sydney by the earliest available departure after the 15th October. Ships, they say, run at irregular intervals to Australia, averaging about one every six weeks. That sounds quite promising and I think it is sufficiently definite for me to secure an endorsement of my passport for India with two months stay in India.

This is the very hottest time of the year in Chengtu. I have never been on the plain in late July and I certainly don't enjoy the heat. I am going to get away for a break next month before I begin to hand on my job to my successor. I plan to go up to Ya-An, which is 110 miles south-west from here, and over the border of

16

VISAS.

No. 3.

29 SEP 1945

Produced to me. Valid for departure within 60 days to New Zealand via India. Good for two months stay in India.

CONSUL GENERAL

Top: 'My household becomes more and more interesting . . . We have three American Army officers, and a technical representative of Allison Airplane Engines.' Nessie (second left) and Jesse (third left) with their boarders. 1943.
Moncrieff family collection

Left: 'In Chungking I had a great time securing all the necessary permits and endorsements.' Note at top of page: 'Produced to me. Valid for departure within 60 days to New Zealand via India. Good for two months' stay in India'. Issued by the British Consul General in Chungking, 29 September 1945. Visa for departure from China. 1945.
Moncrieff family collection

Sikong province, which in some maps is part of Tibet. It takes about nine hours by Chinese bus if you are lucky, but there is just a chance that I may get army transport part of the way at least. I will stay with friends at a temple up in the hills and it sounds cool and restful. The great joy will be bathing. Note that I do not say swimming. I gather that there is a pool deep enough to sit in and that is about all. I will be back in Chengtu again before the very end of August and have a very busy few weeks tidying up the loose ends of my job and helping break up this household and selling everything that is saleable. Getting my things down within 33 pounds for the air trip out will take some careful planning, though I don't seem to own anything but rags. I insist on bringing my coffee percolator,[15] because I could not find one in the length and breadth of New Zealand last time I was home. One grand thing about housing bits and pieces of the American Army, as we are doing, is that there is sometimes coffee available.

The National Y.W.C.A. is in the throes of preparation for a training conference next month. We are going to hold it at our Headquarters which is an American Baptist Mission House in the city with a big compound. There will be about 30 secretaries I think, some of them entirely new and some with a few months' experience. My part in it so far has been to send travel money out to the local associations, and travel is a huge item these days. In fact every kind of expenditure is in hundreds of thousands and some in millions. The cost of living continues to go up. Fortunately, however, the exchange rate on the open market is going up too, so our days of extreme poverty are over. U.S. $1.00 brought N.C. $1505 this month so we are trying hard to build up work while money is a little freer. Personnel has been at a very low ebb in the Y.W.C.A. for a long time, but I think that is on the up and up too at the moment. Tsai Kwei has been able to add some interesting experienced members to the staff and that will be a big help. Two more secretaries have just returned from study in America. Huang Siu Chi, the Executive Secretary of our Student Department is back, and Helen Nyi who has accepted the General Secretaryship in Kunming. We have not seen her yet because it was too expensive to bring her over to Chengtu and then send her back to Kunming. Expensive in both time and money, the former being more serious, I think.

Secretaries newly arrived from America find it very difficult to adjust to conditions of life and work here. These are the latest arrivals from Shanghai before Pearl Harbour and they find all sorts of problems in West China. We are fortunate to have such a nice place for them to live but, of course, there are no luxuries, and some of the necessities are pretty scant.

The piece of work that is booming at present is the work with soldiers' families. Cora Deng is in charge of promoting it and there are centres here and in

Kunming and Chungking as well as the experimental project at Headquarters and a rural experiment project a few miles out that we run in co-operation with the sociology department of West China Union University. Money is not in the least difficult to raise for such work, and it seems to appeal to the public imagination. Everyone realises that the families of the soldiers suffer horribly under the present conscript system, and there is not much difficulty in getting support and workers.

Did I tell you in my last letter that the National Headquarters is on the move again? This time we are going to Chungking, where the national women's organisations and most of the national Christian organisations have their offices. It will be a good move in many ways, but housing will not be so good, both for living quarters and for office accommodation and the cost of living will be higher and transportation in the city is impossible. No one likes living in Chungking, but as long as the Government is there it will continue to be a crowded city. The climate is awful and I am very glad I will not have to live there.

There is a movie to-night and as it is our night for no electricity I think I will go over and see what it is like. It will be cool out of doors even if the movie is not interesting.

Hoping to see you soon.
Yours with love,
AGNES M. MONCRIEFF[16]

The two phrases, 'I don't seem to own anything but rags' and 'our days of extreme poverty are over' are the only references Nessie made of the privations she endured. However in 1984, when she was 85, Nessie wrote to a friend:

> It gave me so much pleasure to have something so practical and thoughtful. Ever since the years spent in west China, where a cake of soap or a tin of nugget was more welcome than a diamond necklace would have been, I've never liked a gift that was not practical.[17]

Nessie did take the break that she'd mentioned in the *Review* article. The letter below is one of the two letters Nessie kept from this time. The font of both is similar to her Burma Road diary. This letter, which has no ending, is to her sister Jean from Ya-an, 15 August 1945.

My dear Jean

I dropped you a note the day I left Chengtu just two weeks ago today. Hope you got it. I meant to write such lots of letters up here but today for the first time I wrote to Jesse and maybe I will have the energy to write one more.

We all left Chengtu with Captain Taylor at 3 p.m. which was the time we were supposed to be at Shin Chin airport. We got there at 4 p.m. and found the jeep supposed to take us on the next lap had already left. Captain Taylor got one of his men to take us on the next 30 miles to Chung Lai. We had three rivers to cross, the first and largest was the Min. We were lucky in finding ferries on our side of the river. The airfield is five miles beyond the town and the last two miles it ran along the bitumen runway – wonderful after Chinese roads. It used to be a base for B29s when B29s were in this part of the world and now being abandoned.

The Captain in charge was a delightful host. He had been to the Vickerts in Ya-An several times and they were paying a return visit. Connie and her youngest, aged three, came into Chengtu to meet us but the other two boys had waited at Chung Lai. Eva Spicer and I had a tent and the Vickerts another tent and we had the run of the officers' ablution block. You never saw such a spread of good things; things that do not appear in civilian life in West China. I had 3 cups of coffee and 2 cups of grape juice and sandwiches of Vienna sausage and 'spam' and goodness knows what else.

About 9.30 next morning we set out in a jeep for Ya-An. It is 50 miles from Chung Lai and over the first of the passes into Tibet. Ya-An is in Siking Province and used to be part of Szechuan. It is an attractive little city on the banks of the Ya River, on the opposite side from the highway. You cross over by a very long steel cable suspension bridge. I felt quite sea sick by the time I got across it.

We had dinner then everyone but Connie and me left for the mountain. I was very glad to put off the climb for one day because what with the rush to get away and the shaking in the jeep I was so tired and couldn't bear the thought of anything energetic.

Next morning it was raining, but we decided to leave and had a seven mile walk in and climb in the rain. The biggest climb is 500 steps that brought us almost to the door of the temple. We were a bit bedraggled and my luggage hadn't arrived so I had to spend the next few hours in a housecoat and mules belonging to Eva. It was worth it. The next few days were very wet indeed and we mightn't have been able to get up at all. The path for a mile is very slippery; it runs along a steep hillside and is not so good in wet weather. I got a lot of sleeping in the next few days. Since then I have worked hard on my quilt, read several books, learned a new game of patience and played bridge. The party consists of Connie and Clarence Vickerts, the three boys, Eva and myself. Sgt Weist who brought us had to go back.

There is a pool in the rocks close to the temple and we all go and sit in that with a cake of soap every day. Water comes dashing down over a rock face from a pool and a succession of falls higher up and is very clean and cold.

Yesterday was so lovely I decided to try to get to the top of the ridge behind the temple. It was very steep and the path not well defined so I had to go carefully.

> I got within thirty feet of where some men were cutting bamboo for fuel. Then I lost the path. But I got a thrill. I heard noises of an animal just above me and the men called 'leopard, leopard' and started calling to each other. This is their way of scaring off animals. It seemed to be successful for we didn't see the leopard. I wondered if I would meet one on the way down but was so taken up with trying to keep on my feet I soon forgot everything else. I had Chinese straw sandals tied on over my shoes but even they were useless once they got wet. I sat down hard on my beam end at least a dozen times and today am a mass of aches and pains. One knee is very stiff and swollen, so don't think I'll be doing much climbing this month, but otherwise seem intact.
>
> Corn is growing all round the temple and a lot of animals come down for that. We always know when leopards come because the dogs bark. I am woken up in the night quite often by dogs barking or servants shouting to scare away porcupines. One of the farmers who was having corn eaten by a bear wanted Sgt. Weist to go over and kill it with his pistol but there was no moon and it only came at night.
>
> Exchange prices have dropped considerably with the Japanese offer of surrender but I can't tell at this distance what is happening in Chengtu. With such exciting things happening in the world this temple seems very remote. A carrier brings a Chinese paper for Clarence every day but Chinese papers are apt to get ahead of the news. However we hope for word today of the Japanese reception of the Allied reply to their proposal to surrender. I can't help think of all the internees and prisoners of war. What a release.

Nessie departed from Chengtu on 28 September 1945, almost four weeks after Japan's surrender, and after delays in Calcutta and Sydney, arrived back in New Zealand some seven months later on 21 April 1936.

With her she brought the quilt she worked so hard on. The small triangular patches are of worn material, stitched somewhat haphazardly, and there is a very simple backing.[18]

Letter home from Calcutta, 10 October 1945. This was the second of her retyped letters and has no greeting or ending, only the heading 'Letter to Mother 10.10.45'.

> Jesse and I reached Calcutta on Sat. 6th and I'm still dazed by the luxury of life this side of the hump. Electricity that works, electric fans, porcelain baths, flush toilets, comfortable chairs and a general sense of spaciousness and comfort. I find myself homesick for the more primitive life in China.
>
> We left Chengtu on September 28 by air for Chungking. We had to be at the Airways office at 7 a.m. but did not leave the field until 1 p.m. owing to bad landing weather at Chungking. It is only an hour's flight. We came down on the

airstrip on an island in the river. In the rainy season the strip is about twenty feet under water for the Yang Tzu rises from 80 to 100 feet in summer. It is a very short strip and pilots call it the worst in the world. They say it would be absolutely condemned in America but so far there has only been one accident on it. We stayed at the C.I.M. in Chungking and had a great time securing all the necessary permits and endorsements. Chungking is all up and down hill and I wore out shoe leather at a deplorable rate. Our papers came through and we had a booking for Oct. 4th.

Something happened to the schedule and it was postponed until the 5th. We had to be at the airfield at 5.30 a.m. but did not take off until 8 a.m. as it takes a long time to get everyone and everything weighed and the papers made and checked out. It was raining at Chungking so we didn't see much but it cleared as we went south with sunshine, but no view of the ground until we began to lose height about fifty miles from Kunming. We landed at 10.45 and there a blow awaited us for our plane was commandeered by the Generalissimo and after hanging about till 3.30 for official confirmation we were told to take our stuff off the plane. There was fighting in the city so we weren't anxious to go there in case we couldn't get out next morning. Jesse telephoned the American Air Transport Commission to see if we could be billeted there; it was only half a mile away. A Red Cross driver ran us across in his jeep and there we stayed. Supper at 5 p.m. was good because we had had only a sandwich since breakfast. We took in a movie on the field and then to bed.

Next morning brekkie was at 7 a.m. and it was the last food we saw for fourteen hours. We were at the field by 9 a.m. but the plane had to come in from Chungking. Finally it was 1.15 when we took off. The route to Calcutta is much more direct now that the war is over. We came down on an airstrip in upper Burma for fuel, then flew direct to Calcutta 3.30 to 7.45. There were a good many clouds about, but we saw the Mekong, the Salween, the Chindwin and the Ganges Rivers. For about half an hour or so we had mean weather and the plane felt like a first class buck jumper.

The final issue of *The YWCA Review* for 1945 recorded:

> Miss Moncrieff is held up in Calcutta awaiting a ship to Australia. She expects to sail by the end of December.[19]

In the letter she wrote her relatives in the 1980s, Nessie ended with, 'I hope all this hasn't bored you. It is "bare bones" of course. Those years in China were tremendously satisfying, maddeningly frustrating and just about everything else in between.'[20]

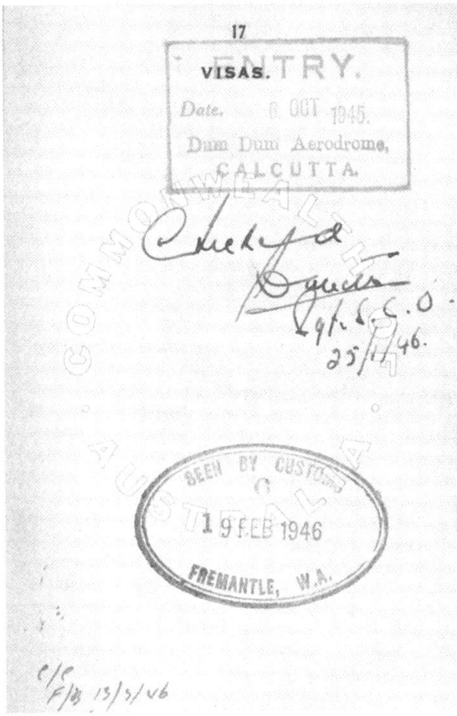

Top: Stamps in Nessie's passport showing her arrival at Calcutta airport on 6 October 1945, departure by ship from Calcutta on 25 January 1946 and arrival in Australia on 9 February 1946. Moncrieff family collection

Right: Agnes Moncrieff arrived back in New Zealand on 21 April 1946. Moncrieff family collection

15
After China
November 1946–June 1988

Nessie had written to the YWCA of New Zealand that Cook's had registered her for accommodation from Calcutta to Sydney by the earliest available departure after 15 October.[1] She arrived in Calcutta on 6 October, but had to wait over three months for a berth to Australia:

> Troops were on their way home and ships crowded. I found plenty to do in the YWCA War Service while I waited.[2]

Nessie left Calcutta on 25 January 1946, arriving in Fremantle 19 February, and staying in Sydney until mid-April. The only explanation for the two-month stay in Australia is an entry in the executive minutes of the YWCA of New Zealand, 10 April 1946:

> Correspondence from the Prime Minister's Dept assuring the YWCA of transport facilities for Miss Moncrieff as soon as Miss Moncrieff has recovered from her hospital treatment in Sydney.[3]

Agnes Moncrieff arrived back in New Zealand on 21 April 1946, just three weeks before her forty-eighth birthday and sixteen years since she had left to be the YWCA of New Zealand's foreign secretary to the YWCA of China. Four days later she met with the national executive of the YWCA of New Zealand and then had three weeks' rest before setting out to visit all the New Zealand local associations, until the end of July when she was to take up the position of general secretary of the Wellington YWCA.[4]

> GREETINGS FROM MISS MONCRIEFF
>
> It is good to come back to sunshine and gorse-covered hills and colourful gardens and all the beauties of mountain and valley and sea that make New Zealand one of the loveliest countries in the world. It is even better to be welcomed by friends everywhere, to feel the gap of long absence closing and to look forward to working among you all again.
>
> I'm glad that it has been possible to arrange a visit to all the Associations this

winter. There is so much I want to know about what had been happening in New Zealand and so much to share with you about China. As I've travelled in China and India and Australia and met with Association groups, two convictions have deepened. One is a sense of the solidarity of our Movement. Differences there are of course, but no differences of outlook, pigmentation, language or stature can destroy the bond we have in our common purpose. The more vital the purpose, the greater the reality of fellowship that makes us feel at home in Association groups wherever we may find them.

And the second conviction is how much the Y.W.C.A. is needed in the post war world. 'To encourage friendship and understanding among the peoples of the world,' reads the final clause of the purpose of the Y.W.C.A. of Great Britain. What a task – what an inspiring task is ours! Beyond the immediate objectives of local activities, Y.W.C.A. members all over the world are striving towards this great aim. Nothing but the most devoted and enlightened effort of people of goodwill everywhere will be able to heal the terrible sickness of the world, and bring the nations together as one family. . . .[5]

AGNES MONCRIEFF IN SOUTH ISLAND

Miss Moncrieff was at the National Office on her return from the South Island and reported the highlights of her visit to the three South Island Associations. . . . She had visited Dunedin where as well as speaking to YWCA groups and other women's and youth groups she had been invited to speak to the University Men's Club who told her she was their first ever woman speaker. In Timaru new YWCA rooms were opened and in Christchurch as well as meeting with the various YWCA groups she spoke to geography classes and the 250 strong Travel Club.[6]

Unfortunately, the years of privation in wartime China had taken their toll of Nessie's health, as is reflected in successive executive minutes:

25 July: Owing to her indisposition Miss Moncrieff had been compelled to cancel her visit to Napier and New Plymouth.

29 August: Miss Moncrieff's doctor's certificate received advising Miss Moncrieff be given three months' leave of absence. The National executive expressed their sympathy with Miss Moncrieff during this period of ill health and unanimously agreed a sick leave allowance should be made to Miss Moncrieff.

12 September: Miss Moncrieff still having hospital treatment; wrote thanking National Executive for the sickness allowance arrangements.

It was twelve months before the minutes of 4 October 1947 recorded:

> Miss Moncrieff – Letter to be written congratulating her on her improved health.[7]

Nessie herself summed up this time in her review letter:

> It was some time before I was fit for a job. Class teaching and YWCA work were beyond me physically so I joined the staff of the Correspondence School[8] and was there for the next fifteen years.[9]

Interviewed in December 1985, when she was 87, Nessie recalled the difficulties of her last term in China:

> Up in west China we had to live off the land, there was nothing. There were no dairy products at all and there was such rapid growth up there that the foods that were grown up there don't have the same nourishment in them that they do when they grow more slowly in a climate like ours. So we were all at the mercy of certain nutritional diseases, which over a period of time became serious. And it was the bigger people who suffered most![10] . . .
>
> I was very ill when I got back from China. We'd been living under rather impoverished circumstances up in West China, and I always remember the doctor saying to me when he finally discharged me, 'fit for anything but return to China'. And I never went back.[11]

Agnes Meikle Moncrieff died on 26 June 1988 at the Woburn Presbyterian Home in Lower Hutt, six weeks after her ninetieth birthday.

Many tributes were paid to her, among them the YWCA of New Zealand's:

> Many in the YWCA regarded Nessie as a living legend. Although she is no longer with us physically her spirit will endure and her life will serve as an example for many generations to come.[12]

Notes and References

Abbreviations:

ATL: Alexander Turnbull Library

1. A Different Course

1 *The Reporter,* Wellington Girls' College magazine 1913–1922, Wellington Girls' College archives.
2 Nessie to her mother, 17 October 1936, MS-Papers-7492-02, ATL.
3 *New Zealand Listener,* Wellington, New Zealand. Published for the National Broadcasting Service by S. R. Evison, 9 May 1941.
4 Transcription of interview with Nessie by Chris Elder and Michael Green, 8 October 1985.
5 'A Brief History'. YWCA Ireland. http://ywca.ie/about-us/brief-history/
6 Nancy Boyd. (1986). *Emissaries: The Overseas Work of the American YWCA 1895–1970.* New York: The Women's Press, 59.
7 Ethel Law to Sarah Lyon, 23 February 1927, MS-Papers-7492-09, ATL.
8 National Executive Minute Book, YWCA of Aotearoa New Zealand, 27 October 1927, MSY-0857, ATL.
9 Ibid, 18 November, 1927.
10 Chris Elder (ed). (2012). *New Zealand's China Experience: Its Genesis, Triumphs, and Occasional Moments of Less Than Complete Success.* Victoria University Press: Wellington, 120.

2. First Term: Peiping, 28 February 1930–July 1934

1 Transcription of interview with Nessie by Chris Elder and Michael Green, 8 October 1985.
2 In the 1920s and 1930s, the YWCA of New Zealand's Girl Citizen Movement involved thousands of fourteen- to twenty-year-olds. The Girl Citizens learned how to run conferences and meetings, speak in public and fundraise, and enjoyed holiday camps, dances, plays and outings. 'Herstory', YWCA of Aotearoa New Zealand. http://ywca.org.nz/who-we-are/herstory/
3 The Great Flood of the Yangtze River in 1931 caused much devastation. Much of Wuhan was under water for more than four months. www.disasterhistory.org/central-china-flood-1931

4 Sir Frederic Truby King founded the New Zealand Plunket Society in 1907 to provide advice and support to mothers and babies. See www.teara.govt.nz/en/biographies/2k8/king-frederic-truby
5 The Red Swastika was a voluntary organisation founded in China in 1922 as an eastern answer to the Red Cross. It is now the Red Swastika Charitable Foundation. www.eytanuliel.co/20/12/08/redswastika
6 Ginling College was founded in 1913 in Nanking by American missionaries; in 1919 it became the first Chinese university to grant bachelor degrees to female students.
7 When Japan invaded Manchuria.
8 In the colder regions of China, a 'kang' (oven) was normally built into the main living room. Made of clay or brick, the kang would be heated from underneath and used as a bed and general living space.

3. Home, Travels and Return to China, 1934–1937

1 (30 August 1934). 'News from China'. *Evening Post*, vol. CXVIII, no. 52, p. 19. www.paperspast.natlib.govt/nz
2 The offices of the Shanghai YWCA. Now Nanjing Road West.
3 Jean Stevenson to Nessie, MS-Papers-7492-01, ATL.
4 All offices and businesses, and many homes, employed a delivery boy to deliver notes or 'chits'.
5 As Nessie was well-built and 1.77 metres in height, she no doubt exceeded the weight limit.
6 On 14 August 1937 the Chinese air force, in the course of an attack on Japanese shipping, accidentally dropped bombs on the International Settlement, killing more than 1700 people.
7 As Nessie held a British passport she would have been admitted to Hongkong; but Pearl, with an American passport, would not have been.
8 (October 1937). *The New Zealand Girl.* YWCA of New Zealand, p. 11.

4. Hankow, September–December 1937

1 Hannah Pakula. (2009). *The Last Empress: Madame Chiang Kai-shek and the Birth of Modern China.* New York: Simon and Schuster, 284.
2 A 'bund' is an embankment.
3 Transcription of interview with Nessie by Chris Elder and Michael Green, 8 October 1985.
4 On 26 August 1937, as Sir Hughe Knatchbull-Hugessen, the British ambassador, was being driven from Nanking to Shanghai, a Japanese aeroplane machine-gunned his car. The ambassador was severely wounded.
5 Suiyuan was part of the puppet state of Mengjiang (1937–1945), under Japanese rule. In 1954 under the People's Republic of China, Suiyuan became a part of Inner Mongolia.
6 Spelled backwards, 'Milk'. An American product of dehydrated milk powder.
7 (11 November 1937). 'Chinese Scene'. *Evening Post.* Vol. CXXIV, No. 115. p. 9. https://paperspast.natlib.govt.nz/newspapers/EP19371111.2.49
8 (10 March 1938). *The New Zealand Girl.* YWCA of New Zealand. p. 8.
9 On the Yangtze River about 135 kilometres east of Nanking to control the lower Yangtze.

5. Hankow and the Godown, January–March 1938

1 The Eighth Route Army was one of the main military forces of the Communist Party of China, active during the Chinese Civil War and Sino-Japanese War. See http://www.fact-index.com/e/ei/eighth_route_army.html.
2 A sacred mountain in Sichuan where Nessie's cousins, who were missionaries in Sichuan, often holidayed.
3 The Panay was a United States Navy gunboat which was attacked and sunk by Japanese bombers on 12 December 1937 while anchored in the Yangtze River near Nanking. Three men were killed, and forty-three sailors and five civilians wounded. The Japanese claimed that they did not see the United States flags painted on the deck of the gunboat. They then apologised and paid an indemnity. Two newsreel cameramen who were aboard (Norman Alley of Universal News and Eric Mayell of Movietone News) filmed the attack, and after reaching the shore filmed the sinking of the ship.
4 Rustat was, and still is, the name on the gate of 26 Tweed Street Dunedin, which at this time was the home of Dr H. D. Skinner, his wife Eva and their son Richard, then age fifteen. Incidentally Charles Brasch, the well-known New Zealand poet, literary editor, publisher and arts patron, wrote in his memoir, 'I was born higher up the hill, in a house in Tweed Street, Littlebourne, which belonged years afterwards to our friends the Skinners and was called Rustat.' Charles Brasch. (1980). *Indirections: A Memoir 1909–1947.* Wellington: Oxford University Press, 118.
5 'Our First Delegates', New Zealand Red Cross. See https://www.redcross.org.nz/about-us/centenary/aid-workers/our-first-delegates/
6 The Canossian Daughters of Charity is a religious order around the world. See www.canossiansisters.org.

6. After the Godown, April–July 1938

1 I Fang Girls' Collegiate School at Changsha was unusual in that it was established in 1917 by Zeng Baosun (Tseng Pao Swen), who was the University of London's first Chinese graduate, to give Chinese Christian women a higher education. www.bbcconline.net/en/stories/z/zeng-baosun.php
2 Steamed buns.
3 In the early stages of the war, this was China's greatest victory over the Japanese.
4 Madame Chiang Kai-shek's speech was printed under the title 'A Broadcast over Two Hemispheres' in *The New Zealand Girl.* (July 1938). p. 8.
5 On 29 April 1938, the Japanese air force launched major air strikes on Wuhan to celebrate their Emperor's birthday. The Chinese, knowing this beforehand, were well prepared. This battle was known as the Battle of Wuhan, one of the most intense air battles of the Second Sino-Japanese War. The Chinese air force shot down twenty-one Japanese planes at a loss of twelve. See en.wikipedia.org/wiki/Battle_of_Wuhan.
6 Butterfield and Swire was one of two British companies (the other was Jardine Matheson) that controlled a considerable portion of travel and mercantile interest, not only on the Yangtze but also up and down the China coast. www.willysthomas.net
7 On 12 May 1938, Nessie was 40.
8 Two biographies were written. See Munroe Scott. (1979). *McClure, The China Years.*

Toronto: Penguin; and Munroe Scott. (1985). *McClure: Years of Challenge*. Toronto: Penguin.

9 On 9 June 1938 Japanese forces began moving up the Yangtze River in order to capture Wuchang and Hankow. See www.ibibilo.org/pha/monos/144/144chap3.html

10 The 1938 flood of the Huang He (Yellow River) was caused by National Revolutionary Army (Chinese) troops under Chiang Kai-shek breaking the levees in an attempt to turn back advancing Japanese troops. The strategy was partly successful, but there were over 500,000 civilian deaths. http://epicdisasters.com/the-worlds-worst-floods-by-death-toll/

11 The New Life Movement was set up by Generalissimo Chiang Kai-shek and his wife Soong Mei-ling in February 1934. It attempted to counter Communist ideology with a mix of traditional Confucianism, nationalism and authoritarianism.

7. Travels, July–October 1938

1 This is a reference to Nessie's plans for leaving Hankow, which she intended to do on her return from Chengtu. Going via Kowloon rather than to Canton meant she would travel all the way by rail to Kowloon and then take a brief ferry trip across Hong Kong harbour. (Nessie to Eva, 22 May 1938, MS Papers-7492-04.)

2 In 1902 the Presbyterian Church of New Zealand established the Canton Villages Mission at Kong Chuen, twelve miles north of Canton. Many New Zealand missionaries served there. See http://www.archives.presbyterian.org.nz/missions/cvmhistory.htm.

3 In 1929 André Michelin invented an automotive train that used tyres instead of steel wheels. It was popular in France and its colonies, including in French Indochina (now Vietnam). See http://www.openbeelden.nl/media/149143

4 Manuals for the YWCA Foreign Secretary had: 'in China in the summer white shoes are worn exclusively'. Nancy Boyd. (1986). *Emissaries: The Overseas Work of the American YWCA 1895–1970*. New York: The Women's Press, p. 55.

5 Official stamp or seal.

6 They would have met in 1922 when Nessie was at the World Student Christian Federation conference. When Nessie was a schoolgirl in Carterton, Jesse and his parents had spent some time with her family.

7 Jesse and Vee's sons. Robert was then eleven and Douglas eight.

8 Nessie to the YWCA of New Zealand, 3 September, 1938. MS-Papers-7492-04, ATL.

9 As the main airfield at Chungking was some distance away from the city, passengers were then rowed out to a hydroplane which took them back to a smaller landing place nearer Chungking.

10 At river ports with seasonally changing water levels, steamers actually tied up to large floating pontoons – called hulks – that were reached by floating bridges. The slant of the bridge was a ready gauge of how high (or low) the river was. John S. Service (ed). (1989). *Golden Inches. The China Memoir of Grace Service.* California: University of California Press, 155.

11 'Detailed description of travel through the Yangtze Gorges in the 1920s by the leading expert of the time, S Cornell Plant.' in S Cornell Plant. (1921). *Glimpses of the Yang Tzu*. Shanghai: Kelly & Walsh. See www.classicbooksandephemera.com/shop/classic/001525.html.

12 When a ship is flying Blue Peter, its voyage is about to begin. See http://oceanservice.noaa.gov/education/for_fun/WhoBluePeter.pdf

13 Scottish word for disturbance/confusion.
14 Yale-in-China was the informal name for the Yale Foreign Missionary Society, founded in 1901 by a group of Yale graduates and faculty members committed to establishing a Christian missionary presence overseas. See www.yalechina.org
15 'All is well.'
16 'Bias Bay, now known as Daya Bay, is about 80 kilometres east of Hong Kong. The landing of Japanese troops there led to them occupying Canton on 21 October 1938.' en.wikipedia.org/wiki/Daya_Bay
17 Bocca Tigris is a narrow strait in the Pearl River Delta down which the steamers travelled to Hong Kong.
18 *The New Zealand Girl*, November 1938, p. 2.

8. Back in Shanghai, October–December 1938

1 On this day in 1937, Walt Disney's *Snow White and the Seven Dwarfs* – the first full-length animated film – had its premiere in Hollywood. (21 December 2013). 'Your Weekend'. *The Dominion Post*, p. 29.
2 National Executive Minute Book 1925–1927. (3 October 1928). YWCA of Aotearoa New Zealand Records. MSY-0857, ATL.
3 Pelmanism is the system of scientifically training the mind, devised by William Jospeh Ennever.
4 As Nessie's father had been born in Scotland and then immigrated to New Zealand with his parents, Scottish idioms were sometimes used in her letters. Perjinct means 'exact; precise; minutely accurate'. Etymological dictionary of the Scottish Language. www.electricscotland.com/history/jamieson

9. Sojourn in Hong Kong, January–February 1939

1 The Church Guest House was part of the Hong Kong Anglican Church complex. Originally built in 1919 as a hostel for students, it was then used as a guest house for missionaries and other church people passing through Hong Kong. What remains today is now called Martin House. See www.gwulo.com/martin-house-former-church-guest-house
2 *Red Star Over China*, a book by Edgar Snow, is an account of the Communist Party of China written when they were a guerrilla army still obscure to Westerners. It was first published in London, 1937.
3 *Sixty Glorious Years* is a 1938 British film starring Anna Neagle as Queen Victoria.
4 Nessie to Eva, 30 April 1938. MS-Papers-7492-04, ATL.
5 Danny is with Nessie and Mary Ochiltree in the photo taken at the Peiping YWCA residence during Nessie's first term, and also in the 'YWCA Spring meeting'. There are other references to her but only as Danny.

10. Return to Shanghai, March–May 1939

1 'Fairy Flats, 25 miles outside Woosung in the estuary where the river meets the sea, is the main hindrance to ships entering the port of Shanghai. The bar is 17–18 ft at lowest water and 28–30 ft at neap high water.' H von Heidenstam. (1922). 'The Growth of the Yangtze

Delta'. *Journal of the North-China Branch of the Royal Asiatic Society*. Vol. LIII. See libweb.uoregon.edu/ec/e-asia/read/yangtze-grow.pdf

2 The New Zealand Centennial Exhibition, 8 November 1939–4 May 1940, celebrated 100 years since the signing of the Treaty of Waitangi at Rongotai, Wellington. See https://nzhistory.govt.nz/culture/centennial/centennial-exhibition

3 Fridtjof Nansen (1861–1930) was a well-known Norwegian explorer and scientist. In the final decade of his life, Nansen devoted himself primarily to the League of Nations following his appointment in 1921 as the League's high commissioner for refugees. See https://www.nobelprize.org/nobel_prizes/peace/laureates/1922/nansen-facts.html

11. More Travels, May–August 1939

1 Nessie to the National Committee of the YWCA of China, October 1939, MS-Papers-7492-05, ATL.

2 'On June 14, 1939, Imperial Japanese Army forces surrounded and blockaded the foreign concessions over the refusal of the British authorities to hand over four Chinese who had assassinated a Japanese collaborator and taken refuge within the British concession.' See research.omnicsgroup.org/index.php/Tientsin_incident

3 Eventually the British chose to turn over the four Chinese fugitives to end the standoff; the Chinese were later executed by the Japanese. See research.omicsgroup.org/index.php/Tientsin_incident

4 At this time Nessie held a British passport, so was considered a British subject.

5 YWCA of Aotearoa New Zealand World Fellowship Minute Book 1939–1952, MSY-0877, ATL.

6 Nessie to Jessany and Arthur, MS-Papers-7492-08, ATL.

12. Final Time in Shanghai, September 1939–July 1940

1 Dōmei News Agency was the official news agency of the Empire of Japan.

2 Victoria University College, where Nessie was a student from 1917–1920.

3 In July 1939 the United States gave notice of its intention to abrogate the 1911 Japan–US Treaty of Commerce and Navigation, with effect from January 1940.

4 Banks' College Wellington offered secretarial courses.

5 YWCA of China to Nessie, MS-Papers-7492-06, ATL.

6 National Executive Minute Book, YWCA of Aotearoa New Zealand, 1938–1941, MSY-0859, ATL.

7 Although Robert was then only twelve, for several years he had suffered from tuberculosis, a common disease in those days. Many of Nessie's letters mention concern at the state of his health. Robert remained in the America, where he became a doctor of pathology in California. He passed away there in his eighties. Moncrieff family history.

8 *Gulliver's Travels*, released by Paramount Pictures in 1939, was the second ever cel-animated feature film and Paramount's answer to Walt Disney's *Snow White and the Seven Dwarfs*, released in 1937 (which Nessie saw in Hankow, December 1938).

13. The Burma Road, 1940–1941

1 (September 1940). *The New Zealand Girl.* YWCA of Aotearoa New Zealand, p. 8.

2 This was very much part of the YWCA culture. 'We exchanged the international Y.W.C.A. wave. And she [Florence Pierce, American YWCA foreign secretary] was so excited she dropped her hat.' (5 September 1930). 'Latest News of Miss Moncrieff'. *Every Girl.* YWCA of Auckland, p. 18.

3 National Executive Minute Book, YWCA of Aotearoa New Zealand, 1938–1941, MSY-0859, ATL.

4 Elder (2012), 120.

5 *The Reporter.* (1941). Wellington Girls' College archives, p. 22.

6 YWCA of China to Nessie, MS-Papers-7492-06, ATL.

7 National Executive Minute Book, YWCA of Aotearoa New Zealand, 1938–1941, MSY-0859, ATL.

8 Tsai Kwei to YWCA of New Zealand, YWCA of Aotearoa New Zealand National Executive Minute Book, 27 February 1941, MSY-0859 ATL.

9 YWCA of Aotearoa New Zealand World Fellowship Committee Minute Book 1939–1952, MSY-0877, ATL.

10 Ethel Law to Nessie, 24 March 1941, MS-Papers-7492-07, ATL.

11 Nessie to her mother, 23 January 1938, MS-Papers 7492-04, ATL.

12 Ethel Law to Nessie, 26 March 1941, MS-Papers-7492-07, ATL.

13 YWCA of Aotearoa New Zealand World Fellowship Committee Minute Book 1939–1952, MSY-0877, ATL.

14 Nessie to YWCA of New Zealand, 13 June 1941, MS-Papers-7492-07, ATL.

15 YWCA of Aotearoa New Zealand National Executive Minute Book 1938–1941, MSY-0859, ATL.

16 Ibid.

17 In 1936, after a short tour in Denmark, Germany, Holland and Belgium, Nessie returned to England for a term of study at Woodbrooke, the international college of the Society of Friends in Birmingham, in the suburb of Selly Oak. In her letters she refers to the college as Selly Oak. See MS-Papers-7492-02, ATL.

18 October marks the end of the three-month Buddhist lent. en.wikipedia.org/wiki/Buddhism_in_Burma/

19 The Public Works Department of the government maintained bungalows for the use of their staff and other travellers in most of the towns along the roads of the Shan States. Dak bungalows fulfilled a similar purpose: 'They were maintained by the government for use by their travelling workers on dak-(postal routes). When not needed by the workers others travellers could use them for a fee.' www.kipling.org.uk/rg_bungalows

20 'Known since 1989 as Yangon University, Rangoon University was founded in 1920 when University College and Judson College (Baptist affiliated) merged. By the 1930s, the university was the hotbed of Burmese nationalism producing a number of future senior Burmese politicians, including Aung San, U Nu, Ba Maw, U Thant . . .' en.wikipedia.org/wiki/University_of_Yangon

21 A light meal eaten very early in the morning.

22 A traditional wrapping cloth or bundle handkerchief.

23 The elbow coupler valve is a manual control which is used to start and stop the flow of fuel.

24 '. . . construction of the line was abandoned due to Japanese advances, and was never resumed. Today the Yunnan side of the line lies in ruin.' See en.wikipedia.org/wiki/Yunnan–Burma_Railway.
25 Woven grass mat.
26 National Executive Minute Book 1941–1946, YWCA of Aotearoa New Zealand, MSY-0860, ATL.
27 Elder (2012), 116.

14. Third Term: Chengtu, December 1941–October 1945

1 YWCA of Aotearoa New Zealand World Fellowship Minute Book 1939-1952, MSY–0873, ATL. Also from December 1951, 'Miss Moncrieff joined the Committee.' Later this committee became the Public Affairs Committee, with Miss Moncrieff its chairman from 1955–1969.
2 *The YWCA Review,* May 1942, p. 3.
3 Ibid., p. 9.
4 The bicycle belonged to Douglas, who was nine when the family left for their 1940 furlough.
5 *The YWCA Review,* 1943 October, p. 5
6 National Executive Minute Book 1941–1946, YWCA of Aotearoa New Zealand, MSY–0860, ATL.
7 *The YWCA Review,* June 1944, pp. 4–5.
8 Nessie to Jessany and Arthur, MS-Papers-7492-08, ATL.
9 *The YWCA Review,* November 1944, p. 25.
10 *The YWCA Review,* April 1945, p. 23.
11 World YWCA archives, Geneva, Switzerland.
12 *The YWCA Review,* May 1945, p.13.
13 *The YWCA Review*, July 1945, p. 21.
14 *The YWCA Review*, September 1945, p. 8.
15 The editor remembers Nessie's battered aluminium coffee percolator which she'd 'brought home from China' and used on the gas stove in her home at 32 Tanera Crescent, Brooklyn, Wellington, introducing the editor to 'proper coffee'. Nessie also possessed a long battered aluminium torch which she had carried on the Burma Road.
16 *The YWCA Review*, November 1945, pp. 8–9
17 Nessie to the editor, 16 January 1984.
18 The quilt is currently with the editor.
19 *The YWCA Review,* December 1945, p. 3.
20 Nessie to Jessany and Arthur, MS-Papers-7492-08, ATL.

15. After China, November 1946–June 1988

1 *The YWCA Review,* November 1945, pp. 8–9.
2 Nessie to Jessany and Arthur, MS-Papers-7492-08, ATL.
3 National Executive Minute Book 1941–1946, YWCA of Aotearoa New Zealand, MSY-0860, ATL.
4 Ibid.

5 *YWCA Review* [renamed], June 1946.
6 *YWCA Review,* July 1946, p. 12.
7 National Executive Minute Book 1946–1952, YWCA of Aotearoa New Zealand, MSY-0861, ATL.
8 In Wellington in 1951.
9 Nessie to Jessany and Arthur, MS-Papers-7492-08, ATL.
10 Transcription of interview with Miss Moncrieff by Chris Elder and Mike Green, 8/12/85. Nessie would have definitely been one of the 'bigger people'.
11 Elder (2012), 121.
12 Pauline McKay (then national co-director of the YWCA of New Zealand) to Peg Hutchison. In possession of the editor. Also see Barbara Francis. (2010). *Our Secretary in China*. YWCA of Greater Wellington, 189–191.

Bibliography

Archives

Alexander Turnbull Library, Wellington, New Zealand:

Moncrieff, Agnes Meikle, 1898–1988
MS-Papers-7492 from 1920–1988
'Comprises correspondence from Agnes Moncrieff to her mother and friends regarding her life in China and her work with the YWCA and NZSCM. Also includes testimonials, certificates and genealogical information for the Braithwaite and Moncrieff families.'

Young Women's Christian Association of Aotearoa – New Zealand Records,1899–2004
MS-Group-0233
National Executive Minute Book 1929–1937, MSY-0858
National Executive Minute Book 1938–1941, MSY-0859
National Executive Minute Book 1941–1946, MSY-0860
National Executive Minute Book 1946–1952, MSY-0861
World Fellowship Committee Minute Book 1939–1952, MSY-0877

Wellington Girls' College Archives:

Pupil Enrolment Register.
The Reporter, 1913–1922; 1941

World's YWCA, Geneva, Switzerland:

Correspondence and reports from YWCA of China 1941–1945.

Periodicals and Serials

The Chinese Recorder and Missionary Journal. October 1933; March 1935; October 1936; March, November 1940; February 1941; China: various protestant missionary publishers.

Every Girl, YWCA of Auckland: 8:1, 5 September 1930; 8:6, 5 February 1931; 8:9 5 May 1931; 9:1, 5 September 1931, ATL.

New Zealand Listener. Journal of the National Broadcasting Service, Wellington, New Zealand, May 1941, ATL.
The New Zealand Girl, YWCA of New Zealand: 1:1, December 1935 to 6:12, December 1941, ATL.
The YWCA Review, YWCA of New Zealand, February–December 1942, ATL.
The YWCA Review, YWCA of New Zealand, 8:1, March 1943, ATL.
YWCA Review, YWCA of New Zealand, 10:1, February–March 1945, ATL.
Evening Post, Wellington, 1922–1946, as in Papers Past online, https://paperspast.natlib.govt.nz/

Books

Berry Christine. (1996). *The New Zealand Student Christian Movement 1890–1996: A Centennial History*. Christchurch: Outreach Press.
Bertram, James. (1993). *Capes of China Slide Away*. Auckland: Auckland University Press.
Bianco, Lucien. (1971). *Origins of the Chinese revolution 1915–1949*. California: Stanford University Press.
Boyd, Nancy. (1986). *Emissaries: The Overseas work of the American YWCA, 1895–1970*. New York: The Woman's Press.
Brasch, Charles. (1980). *Indirections: A Memoir 1909–1947*. Wellington: Oxford University Press.
Challis, Derek and Rawlinson, Gloria. (2002). *The Book of Iris: A Biography of Robin Hyde*. Auckland: Auckland University Press.
Coney, Sandra. (1986). *Every Girl: A Social History of Women and the YWCA in Auckland 1885–1985*. YWCA of Auckland.
Dunn, Margaret. (1991). *The Dauntless Bunch: The Story of the YWCA in Australia*. YWCA of Australia.
Elder, Chris (ed). (2012). *New Zealand's China Experience: Its Genesis, Triumphs, and Occasional Moments of Less Than Complete Success*. Wellington: Victoria University Press.
Francis, Barbara. (2010). *Our Secretary in China*. YWCA of Greater Wellington.
Garner, Karen. (2003). *Precious Fire. Maud Russell and the Chinese Revolution*. Boston: University of Massachusetts Press.
Howe, Renate. (2001). 'The Australian Student Christian Movement and Women's Activism in the Asia-Pacific Region, 1890–1920s'. *Australian Feminist Studies*. 16:36. London: Carfax Publishing Company.
Hyde, Robin. (1984). *Dragon Rampant*. Auckland: New Women's Press Ltd.
Ip, Manying (ed). (1990). *Home Away from Home: Life Stories of Chinese Women in New Zealand*. Auckland: New Women's Press.
Law, Ethel. (1964). *Down the Years: A Record of the Past, for the Women of the Present and the Future*. YWCA of New Zealand, Taranaki Newspapers, New Plymouth.
Lovell-Smith, Hilda Kate. (1961). 'The Story of the Christchurch Young Women's Christian Association: A Venture with Youth from 1883–1894; 1901–1960'. YWCA of Christchurch.
Newnham, Tom. (1995). *New Zealand Women in China*. Auckland: Graphic Publications.
Newnham, Tom. (2002). *Dr Bethune's Angel: The Life of Kathleen Hall*. Auckland: Graphic Publications.
Hannah Pakula. (2009). *The Last Empress: Madame Chiang Kai-shek and the Birth of*

Modern China. New York: Simon and Schuster.
Petersen, G. C. (ed). (1971). *Who's Who in New Zealand.* Wellington: A.H. & A.W. Reed Ltd.
Porter, Robin. (1994). *Industrial Reformers in Republican China.* Studies on Modern China series. London: M. E. Sharpe.
Rees, Ronald (ed). (1939) *Christians in Action: A Record of Work in War-time China by Seven Missionaries.* London; New York: Longmans, Green and Co.
Sargent, Inge. (1994). *Twilight Over Burma. My Life as a Shan Princess.* Hawaii: University of Hawaii Press.
Service, John S (ed). (1989). *Golden Inches. The China Memoir of Grace Service.* California: University of California Press.
von Randow, Tyl. (2016). *Red Dust over Shanghai.* Auckland: Eunoia Publishing.
World YWCA. (1955). *The YWCA Today and Yesterday: A Handbook of National Associations 1855-1940.* Geneva: World YWCA.

Other

Transcription of interview with Miss Moncrieff by Chris Elder and Michael Green 8/12/85.

Unpublished

Moncrieff family history.
Tremewan family history.

Photographs

Alexander Turnbull Library: Agnes Moncrieff Collection, PA1-o-1191.
Moncrieff family.
Gillian Pope.
Skinner family.
J C Beaglehole Room, Victoria University of Wellington.
Barbara Francis

Index of Names

*The following is a list of names Nessie mentions in her letters. Corresponding page references follow. References in **bold** refer to illustrations.*

Adlam, Suzanne, was an American schoolteacher in Shanghai with whom Nessie was friends. 171

Amaron, Estelle, was a foreign secretary of the YWCA of Canada from 1926–1957 and later in Burma, Ceylon, Sierre Leone and Ghana. 170

Anderson, Eleanor (née MacNeil), was Nessie's predecessor in China 1915–1926, who then married Harold Anderson, a Church Missionary Society doctor in Chengtu, but still remained with the YWCA there. **75**, 88, 148

Bates, Dr Miner Searle, was a teacher at the United Christian Missionary Society at University of Nanking. From mid-December 1937 onwards, he worked for the international committee to create a Nanking Safety Zone for the Chinese. 101, 104, 106

Bentham, Alice May, was general secretary of the YWCAs of Dunedin, Christchurch and Auckland, and in 1941 Perth, Western Australia. 184

Bertram, James, was a 1932 New Zealand Rhodes Scholar Oxford and 1936 Rhodes Travelling Fellow in China. Bertram was the first foreign correspondent to reach Sian following the 'Sian Incident', which he wrote about in *Crisis in China*.[1] He was in Hankow at the same time as Nessie[2] and from 1945–1975 was a lecturer and professor of English at Victoria University of Wellington.[3] 141

Brennecke, Margaret, was an American YWCA foreign secretary in China from 1923–1950. 190, 194

Bridgman, Leila, worked with the YWCA of Auckland from 1920, and in 1924 was YWCA of New Zealand's Girl Citizen national chief counsellor.[4] She was general secretary of the YWCA of Wellington from 1932–1941 and national general secretary of the YWCA of Singapore in 1941. She was interned by the Japanese in Indonesia from 1941–1945; national general secretary of the YWCA of Australia from 1947–1955; and with the YWCA Canada from 1956–1959.[5] 249

Carlson, Brigadier General Evans F, worked for the American military in China from 1937 as an observer with Chinese forces, and was so affected by the danger of Japanese aggression in the Far

East that he resigned his commission as a captain in 1939 in order to be free and to eventually write and lecture on the subject.[6] 171

Chang, Dr Francis. See Pih, Kathleen.

Chang, Hsueh-liang (Zhang Xue-liang), also known as 'the Young Marshall ', was a one-time warlord who attained a position of command in the Nationalist forces of Chiang Kai-shek. In 1936 he held Chiang captive in order to secure an agreement towards a united front against Japan. 32, 141

Chen Miss, Ya-Chun, was a secretary of the YWCA of China. 136, 140–41

Chiang Kai-shek (Jiang Jie-shi), was a military and political leader who headed China's Nationalist Government from 1928–1949. The communist victory in 1949 saw him exiled to Taiwan. 36, 82, 87, 89, 114, 122, 125, 140, 179–80, 261

Chiang Kai-shek, Madame (Soong Mei-ling), was first Lady of the Republic of China and wife of Chiang Kai-shek. In 1918 Soong Mei-ling had been a secretary in the YWCA of Shanghai industrial department. 87, 116, 120, 122–24, 140

Curtis, Bishop John, was an Anglican missionary to China in 1904, and from 1929–1950, Bishop of Chekiang. In 1914 he married an English missionary doctor in China, Eda Bryan-Brown.[7] (Eda was the older sister of Nessie's great friend in New Zealand, Stephanie Young.) 189

Danuser, Maybel, was an American YWCA foreign secretary in China from 1918–1933. 37

Decker, Rev Dr J W, was in 1943 the Far East secretary of the International Missionary Council in New York.[8] 254

Deng, Cora [Deng Yuzhi], began YWCA work in Shanghai in 1923, from 1929–1931 studied at the London School of Economics, which included an internship at the International Labour Organiation in Geneva. From 1933 onwards she was the YWCA of China National Industrial Secretary.[9] Deng was also a member of a Marxist study group which included her colleagues Talitha Gerlach, Lillian Haass and Maud Russell, as well as Rewi Alley and several other Chinese and Western progressives.[10] In 1950 Deng became general secretary of the YWCA of China. 126, 129–30, 134, 138, 187, 257

Dexter, Elise G, was a missionary of American Church Mission in Wuchang from 1917–1925 and in Hankow from 1936–1939 with Bishop Logan Roots, where she coordinated public health services with the International Red Cross.[11] 96, 127, 140

Donald, W H, or Bill Donald, was a young Australian newspaperman in China at a crucial time in that country's emergence as a modern nation.[12] 125

Elliott, Nell, was the YWCA of Canada's foreign secretary in Hong Kong from 1920.[13] Nessie had met up with Nell when they both attended the YWCA of China's 1933 convention. 68, 73, **75**, 119

Farmer, Rhodes, was a journalist from Perth who spent 1937–1939 in China. As well as reporting on the conflict with Japan he was requested by Madame Chiang Kai-shek to edit her speeches, newspaper articles, broadcasts and letters into a book.[14] Later his own book, *Shanghai Harvest: A Diary of Three Years in the China War*, was published.[15] 110, 133

Feng Yu-Hsiang, was also known as 'the Christian General', a warlord who threw his support behind Chiang Kai-shek's Nationalist forces. From 1928–1930 he was vice premier of the Republic of China. In 1922 he married Li Techua, who was a student work secretary in the YWCA of Peking.[16] 36

Galbraith, Winifred, was a YWCA of Britain foreign secretary in China and later a World YWCA secretary. In September 1951 she came to New Zealand for a brief visit. 119–21, 161, 248, 252

Gerlach, Talitha, was an American foreign secretary in China from 1926–1940 and 1946–1948, and a member of the Marxist study group. In 1951 she was invited by Soong Ching-ling (Madame Sun Yat-Sen) back to China to manage the China Welfare Institute and remained in China for the rest of her life.[17] 54, 65, 170, 185–87, 189, 192, 199, 211

Grey, Dr Robert, was one of the two doctors sent to China by New Zealand Red Cross from 1937–1938.[18] 110, 115, **118**

Haass, Lil (Lily; Lillian), was an American YWCA foreign secretary in China from 1914–1945. She was initially the national industrial secretary, then national personnel and training secretary, and was also a member of the Marxist study group. 95, 97–99, 185–86, 189, 192, 200, 254

Haines, Rev Dr Harry, was born in New Zealand and studied in Australia, England and America. He and his wife Loma Housley, a daughter of missionaries, were married in 1944. They served in China until 1951.[19] 251

Hancock, Annie, of Dunedin, was a teacher with Canton Villages Mission 1912–1924, and later taught in Hong Kong. 146

Hansen, Mr, was manager of the Lutheran Mission Home. 'The Lutheran mission had an enormous six-floor boarding house-cum-offices-cum everything else and everybody who went through Hankou in the way of foreigners – and some Chinese too – stayed in the Lutheran mission place.'[20] 134, 148, 169

Hawkings, W J, 'Two persons very much at the heart of the British community in Shanghai are Billy Hawkings and his wife Mavis Hawkings. They lived at "the Limit" their house and garden at the furthest western outpost of Shanghai. There they witnessed the Japanese armed offensive. . . .'[21] 174

Helde, Mrs Erma (née Forbes), was an American YWCA foreign secretary in China from 1919–1924, who later married George Helde, a YMCA secretary in China from 1916–1943. 181

Hsueh, Mrs Wei Taeg-bae, was a YWCA of China national business secretary. 198, 209, 215

Hull, Cordell, was the American Secretary of State from 1933–1944. 210

Johnson, Lydia, was an American YWCA foreign secretary in China from 1926–1943. 65, 220, 222

Kepler, Dr A R, was an American missionary in China from 1901–1942 and became the director of the National Christian Service Council for Wounded Soldiers.[22] 101, 104, 106

Knatchbull-Huggessen, Sir Hughe, was a British diplomat, civil servant and author. In 1936 he was Britain's ambassador to China.[23] 74n4

Koo, Mrs Gee-tsun (Helen), wife of Dr T Z Koo (a renowned Chinese Christian leader and at one time secretary of the World Student Christian Federation who was at the 1922 WSCF conference which Nessie attended. In 1931, 1937 and 1941 he visited NZ.)[24] Nessie frequently visited Mrs Koo in Peking and later in Shanghai. 28, **35**

Law, Ethel, MA Victoria University College, was a teacher from 1910–1919; general secretary of the YWCA of Christchurch from 1920–1926; national general secretary of the YWCA of NZ from 1927–1930 and 1937–1947; and secretary of the YWCA of Canada from 1931–1937. 22, 84–90, 96, 102, 135–36, 143, 197, 200, 221, 253

Li Keng, was a rural secretary for the YWCA of China. 95

Little, E S, was in 1886 with American Episcopal Mission in China, then became founder and general manager of Brunner Mond (later ICI).[25] In 1927 Little travelled to New Zealand to become an early member of the Alderton's Group Settlement which purchased substantial land holding in Kerikeri for horticultural production. 'It was through the enthusiastic advocacy of Mr. Little that many expatriates from China settled here.'[26] 174

Liu, Rev Newton and Mrs (Nessie gives name as Rev Nelson Liu), of the American Church Mission, Ichang.[27] Newton Liu (Liu Yaochang) was consecrated Bishop of Shensi in the Church of the Holy Nativity Wuchang on 28 October 1947.[28] 128–29, 131, 157

Liu, Vera, was a secretary in the student department of the YWCA of China. 36–37, **44**–45, 134

MacRae, Dr Joe, was a Church of Scotland missionary doctor at Ichang and a member of the party Nessie travelled with from Rangoon to Chengtu in 1941. 224–29, 231, 233–34, 236–39, 241, 245

Maxwell, Dr James Laidlaw Jnr, was a son of well-known medical missionary Dr J L Maxwell Snr. He was English Presbyterian medical missionary to Formosa from 1901–1924 and 1940–1948; and to China from 1924–1940 and 1949–1951. He was director general of the China Red Cross from 1937–1940.[29] 76, 82, 87, 97, 110–11, 116, 158

McClure, Dr Robert, was a Canadian physician, medical missionary and great mechanic, frequently mentioned in publications about missionary work in China. He was an International Red Cross field agent when Nessie was responsible for despatching their supplies to mission hospitals that treated the wounded Chinese and also for some time after. 93, 111, 115, 132–33

McNeur, Rev George Hunter, of Otago, was one of the first missionaries with the Canton Villages Mission.[30] 150

Miller, Dr Harry W, was an American Seventh-day Adventist missionary doctor, also famous for pioneering work with soy milk, which was linked to the Sanitarium Company. From 1937–1939 he worked in Hankow establishing the Wuhan Sanitarium Hospital. 134

Moncrieff family, then included Catherine Agnes, Mrs (1865–1953), Nessie's mother and recipient of letters; brother Doyle (1901–1970); Janet (1904–1994); Catherine (1897–1982); and the twins Dora (1909–1994) and Jean (1909–1948). 18, **20**, 53, 77, 119, 136, 258

Moncrieff, Jesse (cousin), and his wife travelled from the USA to China in 1915 as missionaries with the American Baptist Foreign Mission Society and were based in Chengtu, Szechuan, West China. Jesse became a professor of languages at West China University. His wife, Virginia (Vee), was affiliated with the Seventh-day Adventist Church, taught music. 99, 107, 126, 143, 150–55, 213, 216–18, 248, 252, **256**, 258, 260–61

Moore, Mary, of Dunedin, was a teacher in the Ichang area of China with Church of Scotland Mission from 1897–1948. 129

Muldoon, Robert, was Minister of Finance for the National Government of 1967–1972, and again between 1975–1984 when he was also Prime Minister of New Zealand. In 1984 Mr Muldoon was knighted. 251

North, Margaret, of Nelson, was a New Zealand nurse with New Zealand Church Mission Society on staff at Hangchow Hospital from 1932–1941, which was then the largest hospital in China. In 1941 she was sent to work in Hong Kong, and from 1942–1945 interned in the Stanley Internment Camp, where she was awarded Royal Red Cross First Class. In 1947 she returned to China, where in 1949 she married Rev Anthony Spurr of the UK. 173, **175**

Packard, Ruth, was an American foreign secretary in China from 1937–1943. 171

Perkins, Jeanne, (later Mrs. Hilbert van Hengel) was an American foreign secretary in China from 1927–1940. 54, 171

Phelps, Dryden and Peggy, were American Baptist missionaries in China from 1930–1951. Dryden taught English literature at West China Union University, specialising in Shakespeare. 154

Pih, Dr Kathleen, was born in China but brought to New Zealand at age five by Margaret Reid of Dunedin. She studied medicine at Otago University Medical School and travelled to China in 1930 as a missionary with Presbyterian Church of New Zealand. After then studying opthamaology at London University (1935–1937), Pih returned to China in 1937 and married Dr Francis Chang of Shanghai. Nessie attended their wedding in Hong Kong in 1938. Both were on the staff of Shanghai University, and they retired in Tauranga in 1969.[31] 148, 150

Pollock, Pearl, was an American YWCA foreign secretary in China from 1923–1943, and a good friend of Nessie's. 61–**62**, 64, 68, 71, 73–74, 95–96, 98, 122–23, 137, 158–59, 181

Purchas, Stella, of Christchurch, was a member of Canterbury University College's SCM at the time that Nessie was an SCM travelling secretary. She was a New Zealand Church Missionary Society (CMS) teacher at Hangchow from 1932–1940; a CMS financial secretary based in Shanghai from 1941-1943; interned at Lunghua Civil Assembly Centre from 1943–1945; CMS financial secretary in China from 1946–1951; and was with CMS in Uganda from 1953–1963.[32] Stella and Nessie remained good friends until Nessie's death. 173, **175**, 186, 188, 201, 207, 211–12, 214

Read, Professor Bernard Read, was an American scientist in China from 1909–1949. He was director of the Henry Lester Institute of Medical Research in Shanghai between 1941–1945.[33] 173–74

Reibe, Deaconess, was with the American Church Mission in Ichang. 127–28, 131, 157

Roots, Bishop Logan H, was a China Episcopalian (Anglican) from 1896–1938 and Bishop of Hankow from 1904–1938. 124, 141

Rudd, John and Joan, were Nessie's companions on her journey from Rangoon to Chengtu in 1941. 223–26, 229, 231–33, 236–39, 241, 243–45

Russell, Maud, was an American YWCA foreign secretary in China from 1917–1943, later an advocate for China in America, and a close friend of Rewi Alley and Talitha Gerlach. See *Precious Fire, Maud Russell and the Chinese Revolution*.[34] 171

Shepherd, George W, was a New Zealand missionary in China from 1919. In 1925 he transferred to the American Board of Commissioners for Foreign Missions and became involved in programmes for rural reform, then subsequently took a leading role in the New Life Movement, spearheaded by Soong Mei-ling (Madame Chiang Kai-shek).[34] 140, 180

Shippe, Hans, was a journalist who travelled to Shanghai in 1925. 'As a journalist, he was active and sharp, and stopped at nothing to gather information that told the true story of China.' In November 1941, Shippe died on the battlefield in the Yimeng Mountains while fighting with the Chinese against the Japanese army.[35] 192

Skinner, Eva, wife of Dr H D (Harry) Skinner,[36] was on the board of the YWCA of Dunedin when Nessie began training there in 1928. They became good friends, with Nessie frequently staying there while on furlough and for many years after she returned from China. They corresponded regularly all the time Nessie was away. Eva passed away in 1963. 11, 17–18, 91, 146, 182

Smedley, Agnes, was a left-wing American journalist and writer in China as correspondent of the Frankfurter Zeitung from 1929. She became fluent in Chinese and during China's civil war wrote a number of books supportive of the Communist forces. She met James Bertram in Sian at the time of the 'Sian incident' in December 1936.[37] 101, 141

Snow, Edgar, was an American journalist and author who reported on the Communist movement in China in *Red Star Over China* (1937), followed later by *The Other Side of the River: Red China Today* (1962).[38] 179

Soong, Mei-ling, see Chiang Kai-shek, Madam.

Soong, T V, was brother of Soong Mei-ling, a prominent businessman and official in Republican China. 112

Spicer, Eva, was a graduate of Somerville College, Oxford. She spent 1923–1950 in China with the London Missionary Society on the staff of Ginling College for Women, initially in Nanking.[39] Like Nessie, with whom she became good friends, she too had been on holiday in Kuling, and then was in Wuchang when the college briefly moved there before moving permanently to Chengtu. 259

Stevenson, Jean, of Dunedin, was a secretary of the YWCA of Australasia in Adelaide and Melbourne and general secretary the YWCA of Auckland from 1911–1932, then general secretary of the YWCA of New Zealand from 1932–1937. Between 1938–1947 she was a YWCA worker in Burma, Calcutta, Delhi and Madras. 31, 34

Stocker, Rev Ives, spent 1910 in North China with Church of England Mission. In 1917 he married Shantung Dorothy Bartrum of Creek Station, Geraldine, New Zealand.[40] 194–95

Sun, Yat-Sen, was a revolutionary and political leader who became the founding father and first president of the Republic of China. 42, 61

Tang, Yu Lin, was a Chinese warlord and chairman of the government of Rehe (Jehol) from 1926–1932. 31–32, 34

Tremewan, Dr H C, graduated from Otago Medical School in 1937. He spent 1938 in China under the auspices of the New Zealand Red Cross working in the Sino-Japanese conflict,[41] for which he was later decorated by the Chinese authorities.[42] 115

Tsai Kuei, (Tsai Kwei; Cai, Kui), was in 1937 appointed national general secretary of the YWCA of China. 'In the difficult years of national crisis and then war, evacuation, destruction and reconstruction the YWCA of China has looked to Miss Tsai for advice, consolation, and leadership. Those who have had the privilege of knowing this unusual little woman will never forget her; those who have yet to have this privilege have much to anticipate.[43] 54, 70, 95, 97–98, 181, 215, 221, 245, 247–48, 253–55, 257

Tsu, Caroline (née Huie), was a foreign secretary of the YWCA from 1919–1920 who married Rev Yu Yue (Andrew) Tsu, PhD. In 1935 she was Dean of Women at St John's University in Shanghai, and the national chairman of the YWCA of China from 1938–1940. Nessie attended her husband's consecration as Bishop of Kunming in Shanghai Cathedral on 1 May 1940.[44] 198, 215

van Hengel, Jeanne (See Perkins, Jeanne).

Wang Ching-Wei (Wang Jing-wa), was a Chinese revolutionary and political leader. He was premier leader of the Kuomintang from 1932–1935. He later broke with Chiang Kai-shek and formed a Japanese-supported collaborationist government in Nanjing.[45] 179

Wang Hsiu King, was a secretary of the YWCA of China. 138–39

Warren, Rex, was a New Zealand *Melbourne Sun* journalist in China from 1937–1938. 124

Weiss, Ruth (also known as Wèi Lùshī), was a Jewish Austrian-Chinese educator, journalist and lecturer whom in 1933 went to China and received Chinese citizenship in 1955.[46] 153

Wenger, Mr, of the Missouri Synod Lutheran Mission. 162–65, 167

Wilkinson, Iris, was a New Zealand poet, writer and journalist who wrote under the pen-name of Robin Hyde. Between February and July 1938 she visited China to gather material for a book, published in 1939 as *Dragon Rampant.* At her own insistence she was permitted to visit areas close to the front lines in Kiangsi Province, where she was trapped in Hsuchow and suffered ill-treatment by the Japanese before being escorted out to Tsingtao.[47] Although both she and Nessie wrote about the same Hankow incidents, there is no mention in any of Nessie's letters of them having met. However in her 1985 interview Nessie recalled, 'I was one of the people who tried to dissuade her from going up to the front lines, but she was very stubborn and she was just determined to do it, and of course she got caught.'[48] 133

Young, Stephanie, MA (Oxford), was a long-time friend of Nessie's who came to New Zealand in early 1919 with her husband, who died two years later. She was a teacher and later principal of St Margaret's College, Christchurch.[49] 189

Zia Tsoo Yi, was a secretary of the YWCA of China. 248

Index of Names source list

1 James M. Bertram. (1937). *Crisis in China: The Story of the Sian Mutiny*. London: Macmillan.
2 James M. Bertram. (1993). *Capes of China Slide Away.* Auckland: Auckland University Press.
3 'James Munro Bertram'. Te Ara Encyclopaedia of New Zealand. See www.teara.govt.nz/en/biographies/4b27/bertram-james-munro
4 (1931). *The Girl Citizen.* National Board of the YWCA of New Zealand. Dawson Printing Co Ltd.
5 Sandra Coney. (1986). *Every Girl: A Social History of Women and the YWCA in Auckland 1885–1985.* YWCA of Auckland, 136–138.
6 *The Chinese Army* Institute of Pacific relations, 1940; Evans Carlson. (2014). *Twin Stars of China: a behind-the-scenes story of China's valiant struggle for existence.* New York: Dodd, Mead and company. Original work published 1940.
7 'Obituary Notice: Eda S. Curtis', *British Medical Journal*, 22 February 1964, 506.
8 'Reestablishment of Missions in Pacific Islands', *The Argus,* Melbourne, Victoria, 9 December 1944. See www.trove.nla.gov.au/ndp/del/article/11374152
9 Daniel H Bays (ed). (1996). *Christianity in China: From the Eighteenth Century to the Present.* California: Stanford University Press, 243–262.
10 Him Mark Lai. (1985). *Chinese American Transnational Politics.* Chicago: University of Illinois, 93.
11 Archie Crouch. (1989). *Christianity in China: A Scholar's Guide to Resources in the Libraries and Archives of the United States.* New York: M. E. Sharp Armon.
12 'The Reporter and the Chinese Warlords', 9 November 2013, Saturday Extra, ABC Radio. http://www.abc.net.au/radionational/programs/saturdayextra/bill-donald-story/5078594
13 Yeung Kwok-keung. (2006). *Protestant Voluntary Associations and the Development of Civil Society in Early twentieth Century Hong Kong.* Taiwan: Taiwan Baptist Theological Seminary, 64.
14 Hannah Pakula. (2009). *The Last Empress: Madame Chiang Kai-shek and the Birth of Modern China.* New York: Simon & Schuster, 294; 299; 302.
15 Rhodes Farmer. (1945). *Shanghai Harvest: A Diary of Three Years in the China War.* London: Museum Press.
16 (1922). *Women Leaders of Present Day China: Chinese Christians Worth Knowing.* Boston: Woman's Board of Missions. See https://archive.org/details/ldpd_11013585_000

17 Karen Garner. (2003). *Precious Fire: Maud Russell and the Chinese Revolution.* Boston: University of Massachusetts Press, 210.
18 'Our First Delegates'. New Zealand Red Cross. See https://www.redcross.org.nz/about-us/centenary/aid-workers/our-first-delegates/
19 See The Methodist Church in Malaysia. http://www.methodistchurch.org.my/index.cfm
20 Transcription of interview with Nessie by Chris Elder and Michael Green, 8 October 1985.
21 Tyl von Randow. (2016). *Red Dust Over Shanghai.* Auckland: Eunoia Publishing Ltd, 346–347
22 'American Presbyterian Mission'. Biographical Dictionary of Chinese Christianity. http://www.bdcconline.net/en/stories/by-affiliation/american-presbyterian-mission/
23 'Sir Hughe Montgomery Knatchbull-Hugessen'. Revolvy. See www.revolvy.com/main/index.php?s=Hughe%20Knatchbull-Hugessen&item
24 R. O. Hall. (1950). *Servants of the Universal Church. Chinese Christianity Speaks to the West.* London: SCM Press, 11.
25 Bob Molloy. (2011). *Colossus Unsung.* New Zealand: Xlibris Corporation.
26 See www.kerikeri.co.nz/George_Alderton.cfm; and Elder (2012), 133–135, 128–132.
27 'Changsha Notes', *The Chinese Recorder*, February 1941, p. 106.
28 G. F. S Gray. (1996). *Anglicans in China.* Episcopal Mission China History Project, 74.
29 Blog: The Taiwanese. See www.thetaiwanese.blogspot.com/2006/04/dr-james-laidlaw-maxwell.html
30 'The Story of the Canton Villages Mission'. http://www.archives.presbyterian.org.nz/missions/cvmhistory.htm
31 Presbyterian Church of Aotearoa New Zealand, www.presbyterian.org.nz/. Also see Manying Ip. (1990). *Home Away from Home: Life Stories of Chinese women in New Zealand.* New Zealand: New Women's Press.
32 New Zealand Church Missionary Society Archives; John Kinder Theological Library. http://www.kinderlibrary.ac.nz/default.aspx
33 Read (Bernard and Katherine) Papers. Western Medicine in China, 1800–1950. Collections at Yale University. See web.library.yale. edu/divinity/china-papers/Read_BernardandKatherine
34 Garner (2003).
35 'Hans Shippe'. China Through A Lens. See www.china.org.cn/english/features/149194.htm
36 See www.teara.govt.nz/. . ./skinner-henry-dev. . .
37 'Xi'an Incident'. Oxford Reference. See www.oxfordreference.com/view/10.1093/oi/authority.20110803125214733
38 'Edgar Snow'. Encyclopaedia Britannica. See www.britannica.com/biography/Edgar-Parks-Snow
39 'Doubly a Foreigner in Strange Lands: The Experiences of Eva Dykes Spicer'. International Missionary Bulletin. See www.internationalbulletin.org/issues/2015-03/2015-03-146-seton.html
40 'Charlotte Amy Dorothy Bartrum'. See winsomegriffin.com/Cone/Bartrum_Dorothy.html
41 'Our First Delegates'. New Zealand Red Cross. https://www.redcross.org.nz/about-us/centenary/aid-workers/our-first-delegates/
42 Tremewan Family History.
43 *The YWCA Review*, March 1944, p. 17. Also see November 1942, p. 11.
44 See Nessie to mother, 5 May 1940, MS-Papers-7492-06, ATL.

45 'Wang Ching-Wei'. Encyclopaedia Britannica. www.britannica.com/biography/Wang-Ching-wei
46 'Final Farewell to One Who Truly Loved China', 1 June 2009, *China Daily*. http://www.chinadaily.com.cn/cndy/2009-06/01/content_7957399.htm
47 'Robin Hyde'. Te Ara Encyclopaedia of New Zealand. See www.teara.govt.nz/en/biographies/4h41/hyde-robin
48 Transcription of interview with Nessie by Chris Elder and Michael Green, 8 October 1985.
49 'Stephanie Grace Young'. Te Ara Encyclopaedia of New Zealand. See www.teara.govt.nz/en/biographies/4y2/young-stephanie-grace

Index of Places

The following is a select index of significant place names mentioned in Nessie's letters, alongside their contemporary spellings. Where there is no new spelling, the name remains unchanged. References in ***bold*** *refer to illustrations.*

China

Canton	Guangzhou	42, 73–74, 87–89, 92, 137–40, 142, 145, 148, 160–62, 167, 193, 250
Changsha		116–17, 119–24, 144–45, 160–62, 251
Chefoo	Yantai	138–39, 191, 193–97, 199–203, 205, 207
Chengchow	Zengzhou	93–95, 103, 108, 111, **118**, 132, 135, 252
Chengtu	Chengdu	88, 111, 143, 148–54, 193, 199, 219, 221–24, 236, 244, 246–62
Chinkiang	Jinjiang	64, 81, 85, 101
Chuching	Qujing	239
Chuhsiung	Chuxiong	237–38
Chungking	Chongqing	97–101, 107–8, 126, 153–56, 190–91, 193, 221, 224, 244–46, 248–50, 254–56, 258, 260–61
Formosa	Taiwan	110, 179, 199
Haichow	Haizhou	129
Hainan		149–50
Hangchow	Hangzhou	93, 96, 102, 173, **175**
Hanyang		73, 78–79, 81, 87, 126, 144, 157–59, 168
Hankow	Hankou	April–July 1938, 119–42
		January–March 1938, 91–118
		passim, 19, 63, 73, 143–44, 146, 153, 155–61, 168–70, 174, 177, 193, 214
		September–December 1937, 70–90
Hengyang		145, 160, 162, 164, 248
Hoihow	Haikou	149–50
Honan	Henan	36, 111, 138, 145
Ho Pei (Hopeh, Hupeh)	Hobei	43, 157, 171
Hsuchow	Yuzhou	103, 107–8, 122, 129, 132–33

Ichang	Yichang	119, 126–32, 153, 155–57, 224
Jehol	Chengde	31–36
Kalgan	Zhangjiakou	77
Kao Chiao	Gaoqiao	238–39
Kiangsi	Jiangxi	54, 68
Kiukiang	Juijiang	61, 70–72, 85, 134, 140, 144
Kuling (Guling)	Lushan	53, 60–61, 64, 67–68, 70, 78, 139–40, 174
Kweifu	Fengjie	156
Kweilin	Gulin	130, 134, 137–38, 160–61, 179–80, 248, 251
Kweiyang	Guiyang	119, 130, 137–38, 171, 238–39, 241, 251, 254
Lanchow	Lanzhou	144, 254
Lochang	Lechang	145–46, 166
Nanking	Nanjing	25, 42, 61, 64, 70, 79, 81–82, 85–92, 95, 99, 101, 103–4, 106–7, 122, 132, 159
Neichang	Neijang	245
Pakhoi	Beihai	150, 171
Pan Shih	Pingshi	146, 165
Paoshan	Baoshan	233–35
Paoting	Baoding	103
Peking (Peiping)	Beijing	19, 25–51, 53, 61–66, 78, 107–8, 182–83, 193, 195–96, 198–99, 203, 252
Pukow	Pukou	86, 108
Shanghai		March–May 1939, 185–92
		October–December 1938, 169–76
		passim, 21, 53–68, 73–76, 78–79, 81–82, 84–86, 89–90, 139, 184, 193, 196–201, 219–21, 250
		September 1939–July 1940, 205–18
Shanhaikuan	Shanhaiguan	32
Shanshi Province	Shanxi	54
Shantung Province	Shandong	36, 92, 114, 122, 125
Shasi	Shashi	157
Shichiachung	Shijiazhuang	77, 103
Sian	Xi’an	111, 116, 119, 141, 193, 248, 251–52
Siangyun	Xiangyun	236
Sung K’an	Songkan	241–44
Szechuan	Sichuan	99, 115, 129, 146, 152, 157, 221, 239, 241, 259
Taierchuang	Taierzhuang	122
Taiyuan		54, 77–78
Tatung	Datong	76–77
Tientsin	Tianjin	36
Tsinan	Jinan	92, 191, 193, 195–97
Tung Tzu	Tongzi	213, 241
Wanhsien	Wanzian	155–56
Wuchang		26, 68, 70, 73–74, 92, 115, 119, 121–22, 135–37, 141, 144, 160, 168
Wuhu		79, 87, 91, 93

Ya-an		258
Yochow	Yueyang	144, 160–61
Yunnan	Yunan	89, 95, 120, 143, 145, 160, 231, 246
Yunnanfu (Kunming)	Kunming	149–54, 221, 224, 235–41, 244, 252, 257–58, 261
Burma	**Myanmar**	
Hsipaw		228
Kalaw		227–28
Kutkai		229
Laihka		228
Lashio		221, 228–29, 232
Loilem		228
Mandalay		225–27
Maymo	Pyin Oo Lwin	255
Meiktila		226
Mongkung		228
Pegu		225
Pinmana	Pyinmana	225
Rangoon	Yangon	219, 221–36, **242**
Taungyi	Taunggyi	227
Thazi		227
Toungyoo	Toungoo	225
French Indochina	**Vietnam, Cambodia, Laos**	
Haiphong		148–150, 152, 171
Hanoi		149–51
Lao-Kay	Lào Cai	151
Pho moi		151

General Index

*References in **bold** refer to illustrations.*

American Baptist Foreign Mission Society, 99, 223, 257
American Church Mission, 96, 127–28, 142, 179
American–Japanese relations, 96, 178
Austrian refugees, 187–88

birthday, Nessie's, 131, 220, 263, 265
boat, journeys by, 61, 71–72, 127, 129–32, 153–57, 160–61, 195–97, 205–7, 222–23, 244–45, 259, 261, 263
bombings, *see* raids, air
British concession, 142, 195–96, 199–200
British–Chinese relations, 41–42, 65, 85, 87, 125
British–Japanese relations, 74, 87–88, 96, 130, 155, 158–59, 182, 190, 196, 199–203, 209
Burma Road, travels via, 222–46
business secretary (YWCA), Nessie as, 211

Canadian Mission Agency, 154, 244
Canton
  attack on, 88–89, 137–40, 142, 145–46
  road trip to, 162–68
  censorship, 84, 90, 124, 134, 191, 199–200, 202, 210, 218
Changsha, YWCA work in, 119–24
Chengdu
  family in, 150–54
  national office (YWCA), Nessie's role at, 219, 221, 247–58
China Inland Mission, 144, 146, 195, 232, 237, 240, 261
China Travel Service, 61, 63–64, 71, 224, 231, 237, 239–41, 245
Christianity, 17, 21, 26, 28, 50, 170, 172, 255, 258
Christmas celebrations, 25–28, **30**, 173–74, 213
Chungking national office (YWCA), 255, 258, 261
Church Missionary Society, 148, 152, **175**, 238–39, 246
  cinema, 104, 181, 258

city coordinator (YWCA), Nessie as, 119–24, 126–30, 134–42, 193, 248
communism, 92, 101, 106, 108, 171
conventions and conferences (YWCA), 43, **75**, 123–25, 143, 146–48, 221, 247, 257
custody, Nessie in, 203

death, Nessie's, 265

Easter celebrations, 121–22, 189
English secretary (YWCA), Nessie as, 247
Evening Post (newspaper), 53, 77, 220
exchange rates, 194, 196, 209, 213–14, 232, 251, 257, 260

floods, 26, 70–72, 159, 225–26, 261
food shortages, 29, 32, 41, 67–68, 74, 81, 101, 116, 212–14, 250, 265
Foreign Residents Association, 109, 135–36, 139
foreign secretary (YWCA), Nessie as, 19, 21–23, 54–60, **75**, 92, 98–99, 103, **183**
French concession, 57, 63, 89, 98, 109, 139, 157, 159, 186
French Indochina, travels to, 149–50
French-Japanese relations, 139
furlough (YWCA), 21–22, 53, 198, 214–15, 219

general secretary (YWCA of Wellington), Nessie as, 263–65
Germany
  Nazism, 207–9
  refugees from, 187–88, 190, 193–94, 208
Ginling College, 39, 99, 252
godown, Hankow International Red Cross, 82–84, 91–118
Great Wall, 31, 34, 36, 38, **52**

Hankow
  godown, 82–84, 91–118
  during Sino-Japanese war, 78–81, 84–89, 93, 96–104, 107–19, 123, 132–42, 144, 157–60, 169
health, Nessie's, 134, 171–74, 180, 219–20, 263–65
Helping Fund (YWCA), 57–58
Hitler, 209
Holocaust, 187
Hong Kong
  vacation in, 177–84
  work in, 143, 146–48, 168
hospitals, 36, 70, 80–82, 92–93, 108, 127, 132–33, 142, 157–60, 179
Hunan University, 120–21

Ichang, work in, 119, 126–32
inflation, 23, 250–51, 253
Italian–Japanese relations, 89–90

Japanese concession, 63, 74, 80–81, 157, 159–60
Japanese–Chinese relations
  Nessie's observations, 32–34, 42, 63–64, 74, 76, 90–92, 99–103, 106–7, 110, 122, 129–30, 132, 157–59, 174, 179, 191–92, 196, 199–200, 203, 209–10, 251
  war, *see* Sino-Japanese war
Jewish refugees, 187–88, 190, 193, 208

League of Nations, 55, 90–91, 159, 168
London Missionary Society, 28, **35**, 252
Lutheran Mission Home, 73, 87, 89, 97, 120, 135, 138, 143, 169

malaria, 233–35, 238
medical supplies, 70, 80–84, 92–93, 95, 111
Methodist Hospital, 158
military, Chinese, 31–34, 42, 79, 102
missionaries, 21, 28, 142, 189, 223–24, 237
Missionary Fellowship, 116, 120, 170
musical performances, 170–71, 189, 200–201, 216–17

National Christian Council for Religion Education Conference, 172
nationalism, Chinese, 32–34, 42, 81–82, 106
Nazism, 207–9
New Life Movement, 140, 180
New Zealand Girl, The (YWCA publication), 68, 82, 168, 219
New Zealand, return trips to, 53, 205, 214, 219–20, 260–65
northern associations (YWCA), work with, 193–204

Pearl Harbor, 246, 257
plane, journeys by, 152–54, 260–61
prostitution, 55–57, 200

raids, air, 19, 67, 70, 78–79, 93, 96–104, 107–10, 112–15, 120–23, 125–26, 130, 132, 137, 142–43, 145–46, 157–60, 163–67, 179, 190–92, 238–39
rail, journeys by, 119, 121–23, 143–45, 151–52
railway, Canton–Hankow, 74, 122, 254
railway, Peiping–Hankow, 103, 107–8
Red Cross, International
  formation and role of China office, 36, 77, 81, 110, **118**, 137, 220
  godown (Hankow), 82–84, 91–118
  Nessie's role in, 70, 76, 81–84, 91–118, 220, 224
Red Swastika Society, 36
refugees (Jewish), 187–88, 190, 193, 208
refugees (Sino-Japanese war), 36–37, 68, 76, 79–81, 84, 138, 159, 193
ricshas, 33, **48**, 167, 195, 246
road, journeys by
  Burma Road, 222–46

to Canton, 162–68
Rotary speaking events, 220
rural China
Nessie's work in, 43–51
rural economy reform, 42–45, 50
Russian refugees, 193
Russian–Chinese relations, 85, 108
Russian–Japanese relations, 98
Russo–German Anti-Aggression Pact, 208

Scotland Mission, Church of, 129, 224
Second World War
Pearl Harbour, 246, 257
pre-war tension, 207–8
refugees, 187–88, 190, 193, 208
Shanghai
International Branch (YWCA), 54–55, 57–60, 92, 136, 186
Japanese invasion of, 64–65, 67–68, 73–76, 78–79, 85, 170, 209–10
national office (YWCA), 169–71, 185–93, 198, 200, 205–18
Shanghai Municipal Council, 184, 209–10
shipping, 208
Sino–Japanese war
air raids, 19, 67, 70, 78–79, 93, 96–104, 107–10, 112–15, 120–23, 125–26, 130, 132, 137, 142–43, 145–46, 157–60, 163–67, 179, 190–92, 238–39
Canton, attack on, 88–89, 137–40, 142, 145–46
concessions, foreign, 57, 63, 74, 80–81, 89, 98, 109, 139, 142, 157, 159–60, 186, 195–96, 199–200
Hankow during, 78–81, 84–89, 93, 96–104, 107–19, 123, 132–42, 144, 157–60, 169
Japanese, Nessie's observations of, 32–34, 42, 63–64, 74, 76, 90–92, 99–103, 106–7, 110, 122, 129–30, 132, 157–59, 174, 179, 191–92, 196, 199–200, 203, 209–10, 251
Nanking, attack on, 87, 89–92, 99, 101, 104, 132, 159
pre-invasion situation, 31–42, 63–64
refugees, 36–37, 68, 76, 79–81, 84, 138, 159, 193
role of YWCA during, 31, 33–34, 36–37, 84
Shanghai, invasion of, 64–65, 67–68, 73–76, 78–79, 85, 170, 209–10
student activism, 42–45
Student Christian Movement, 17, 19, 43–44, 78, 84, 195

theatre, 46–47, 104–6
trade, 42, 79–81, 208, 212–14
typhoons, 199, 205–7

vacations, 60–64, 177–84, 248, 251, 256–60
Victoria University of Wellington, 18–20, 84
visas, **56**, 116, **118**, **230**, **242**, **256**

war, *see* Sino–Japanese war; World War II
Wellington Girls' College, 19, 84, 91, 220
West China University, 252–53, 258
Women's Organisations, Committee of, 193
World Fellowship Committee (YWCA), 23, 203, 221–22, 247
World Student Christian Federation, 19, 21

Yangtze River (Yang Tzu), 71, 97, 155, 161, 185, 207, 243–44, 261
Yellow River, 93, 114, 139
Young Women's Christian Association (China)
  business secretary, Nessie as, 211
  city coordinator, Nessie as, 119–24, 126–30, 134–42, 193, 248
  conventions and conferences, 43, **75**, 123–25, 143, 146–48, 247, 257
  discontinuation of roles, 253
  English language secretary, Nessie as, 247
  foreign secretary, Nessie as, 19, 21–23, 54–60, **75**, 92, 98–99, 103, **183**
  furlough, Nessie on, 21–22, 53, 198, 214–15, 219
  growth of organisation, 21–22, 28–34, 54–55, 119, 129, 248
  Helping Fund, 57–58
  International Branch (Shanghai), 54–55, 57–60, 92, 136, 186
  national office (Chengtu), Nessie's role at, 219, 221, 247–58
  national office (Chungking), 255, 258, 261
  national office (Shanghai), Nessie's role at, 169–71, 185–93, 198, 200, 205–18
  northern associations, work with, 193–204
  office closures, 251–52
  playground, 29, 31, **40**
  residence (Peiping), **24**–25
  role during Sino–Japanese conflict, 31, 33–34, 36–37, 84
  students' hostel (Peiping), 25–28, **30**, 37–38
Young Women's Christian Association (New Zealand)
  Centennial Exhibition, 187
  committee member, Nessie as, 17
  conventions, 221
  discontinuation of roles in China, 253
  general secretary, Nessie as, 263–65
  growth of organisation, 21–22
  reports to, 18, 25, 31, 34, 77, 168, 212, 214–15, 219–23, 247–58, 263
  World Fellowship Committee, 23, 203, 221–22, 247
  YWCA Review, The (publication), 249, 251, 253, 255, 261